THE WILDERNESS WORLD OF
JOHN MUIR

The Wilderness World of
John Muir

WITH AN INTRODUCTION
AND INTERPRETIVE COMMENTS
by
EDWIN WAY TEALE

ILLUSTRATED BY HENRY B. KANE

HOUGHTON MIFFLIN COMPANY BOSTON
1976

The selections from *Our National Parks* by John Muir, copyright, 1901, by John Muir, are reprinted by permission of the publishers, Houghton Mifflin Company.

The selection from *Stickeen* by John Muir, copyright, 1909, by John Muir, is reprinted by permission of the publishers, Houghton Mifflin Company.

The selections from *The Mountains of California* by John Muir, copyright, 1911, by the Century Company, are reprinted by permission of the publishers, Appleton-Century-Crofts, Inc.

The selections from *My First Summer in the Sierra* by John Muir, copyright, 1911, by John Muir, are reprinted by permission of the publishers, Houghton Mifflin Company.

The selections from *The Yosemite* by John Muir, copyright, 1912, by the Century Company, are reprinted by permission of the publishers, Appleton-Century-Crofts, Inc.

The selections from *The Story of My Boyhood and Youth* by John Muir, copyright, 1913, by John Muir, are reprinted by permission of the publishers, Houghton Mifflin Company.

The selections from *Travels in Alaska* by John Muir, copyright, 1915, by Houghton Mifflin Company, are reprinted by permission of the publishers, Houghton Mifflin Company.

The selections from *A Thousand-Mile Walk to the Gulf* by John Muir, copyright, 1916, by Houghton Mifflin Company, are reprinted by permission of the publishers, Houghton Mifflin Company.

The selections from *The Cruise of the Corwin* by John Muir, copyright, 1917, by Houghton Mifflin Company, are reprinted by permission of the publishers, Houghton Mifflin Company.

The selections from *Steep Trails* by John Muir, copyright, 1918, by Houghton Mifflin Company, are reprinted by permission of the publishers, Houghton Mifflin Company.

The selections from *The Life and Letters of John Muir*, copyright, 1923, 1924, by Houghton Mifflin Company, are reprinted by permission of the publishers, Houghton Mifflin Company.

The selections from *John of the Mountains*, edited by Linnie Marsh Wolfe, copyright, 1938, by Wanda Muir Hanna, are reprinted by permission of the publishers, Houghton Mifflin Company.

ISBN 0-395-08241-2 (cloth)
ISBN 0-395-24083-2 (paper)

Printed in the United States of America

C 20 19 18 17 16 15 14 13 12 11 10 9

Dedicated to

THE SIERRA CLUB

THE WILDERNESS SOCIETY

THE NATIONAL PARKS ASSOCIATION

and all those
who are fighting the good fight
to preserve what John Muir sought to save

Acknowledgments

IN FOLLOWING or crossing John Muir's trail I have visited many of the places associated with his life — the Portage and Madison areas in Wisconsin; Indianapolis, Indiana; Cedar Keys, Florida; Murphy, North Carolina; Savannah, Georgia; the Yosemite Valley; Oakland, Martinez and Daggett in California. On numerous occasions I have had the benefit of recollections or other help from various persons. To them all I wish to express my heartfelt thanks, especially to William E. Colby, Inez M. Haring, Josephine L. Harper, Thomas H. Kearney, Jr., Don Greame Kelley, Charlotte E. Mauk and Marion Randall Parsons. It need hardly be added that none of the selections from Muir's writings has been changed, and where it has been necessary to shorten some to bring the whole within the compass of a single volume every effort has been made to preserve the continuity and flow of Muir's thought and expression.

❀

Contents

Introduction

AMONG THE RARE BOOKS at the Yale University Library there is a rusty-brown volume with penciled notations running along the margins and spilling over onto the flyleaves at the back. The book is Volume I of *The Prose Works of Ralph Waldo Emerson*, published in 1870 by Fields, Osgood & Company, of Boston. It was this book that John Muir carried with him, read and reread, during his mountain days in the high Sierra.

Emerson was one of the great admirations of Muir's life. The Concord philosopher replied in kind for when, in his old age, he set down his list of "My Men," the ones who had influenced him most, he began it with Thomas Carlyle and ended it with John Muir. Thus Muir's reflections on Emerson's words, especially points of divergence, have particular interest in revealing qualities of his mind and outlook.

In *Spiritual Laws*, Emerson declares: "The Vale of Tempe, Tivoli, and Rome are earth and water, rocks and sky. There are as good earth and water in a thousand places, yet how unaffecting." Beside these words, Muir has written, "They are not unaffecting." Again, in *Nature*, Emerson observes: "There is in woods and waters a certain enticement and flattery, together with a failure to yield a present satisfaction. This disappointment is felt in every landscape." Muir dissents: "No — always we find more than we expect."

Always, in truth, he found more than he expected in nature. Never did he get enough of wildness. Of those who have written of nature surpassingly well — Gilbert White, Henry Thoreau, Richard Jefferies, W. H. Hudson — John Muir was the wildest. He was the most active, the most at home in the wilderness, the most daring, the most capable, the most self-reliant.

I remember Julian Burroughs telling me of a time when Muir came to visit his father, John Burroughs, at Slabsides. As they rowed across the Hudson from the New York Central station, Muir waved his hand toward the sunset and the darkening hills and said he could sleep "anywhere there." This was neither an idle nor an empty boast. It was a mere statement of fact. Across glaciers and on the bleak heights of the Sierra he wandered without so much as an overcoat or blanket. When night overtook him he burrowed into the needles beneath some mountain evergreen, warmed only by a small fire which he replenished at half-hour intervals till dawn. C. Hart Merriam, who accompanied Muir on one trip to the mountains, later wrote: "He could choose a sheltered spot for the night, was an adept in building a small fire in a safe place and could make an excellent cup of coffee in his tin cup. But of the art and conveniences of camping as ordinarily understood he was as innocent as a child."

All he needed to do to get ready for an expedition, Muir said, was to "throw some tea and bread in an old sack and jump over the back fence." He preferred bread with a thick crust and always dried it thoroughly to prevent molding. It was his habit occasionally to let his breadsack roll downhill before him, thus producing the fragments which, with a cup of tea, formed his frugal meals. While in the wilderness, he declared, he lived on "essences and crumbs" and his pack was as "unsubstantial as a squirrel's tail." Throughout his life — from his childhood in Scotland, with its brutality and floggings, his years of labor on the pioneer Wisconsin farm and his wanderings alone in the wilds of Canada, the South and among the mountains of the Far West — Muir was stoically indifferent to physical hardship.

He never carried a gun. Traveling alone and far from any other human being for weeks at a time, he never was harmed by bear or rattlesnake, never was seriously injured in an accident. Eliphaz the Temanite might well have addressed to Muir his words: ". . . thou shalt be in league with the stones of the field; and the beasts of the field will be at peace with thee." In this world where men are afraid they will catch cold, afraid they will lose their way, afraid they will be eaten by bears or bitten by

snakes or touch poison ivy or fall over a log, John Muir, faring
forth into the wilderness unarmed and alone, was the man unafraid. He was unafraid of danger, of hardship, of wildness, of
being alone, of facing death. He was unafraid of public opinion. He was unafraid of work and poverty and hunger. He
knew them all and he remained unafraid.

There is, in Muir's published journals, *John of the Mountains*,
a moving photograph of the author as an old man peering up at
the Sierra cliffs he had scaled in his prime. But always, even in
his most daring undertakings, there was a goal of importance.
He was never merely seeking thrills or going afield for trophies.
To understand Muir and the fire that burned in him, it is necessary to realize that for him all outdoors was at once a laboratory
for research and a temple for worship.

Repelled by the harsh fanaticism of his father's religion, John
Muir belonged to no church. He gave freely when solicited by
Protestant and Catholic alike. But he affiliated himself with no
formal creed. Yet he was intensely religious. The forests and
the mountains formed his temple. His approach to all nature
was worshipful. He saw everything evolving yet everything the
direct handiwork of God. There was a spiritual and religious
exaltation in his experiences with nature. And he came down
from the mountains like some bearded prophet to preach of the
beauty and healing he had found in this natural temple where
he worshiped. He spoke with the fire of the old Covenanters.
This religious fervor and spiritual intensity in Muir's response to
nature contributed much to the power of his pleading for the
cause of conservation. He never based his arguments on eco-
nomic considerations alone. He always appealed to men on a
high moral plane. I know of no other writer, with the exception
of Henry Thoreau, who had so pure and lofty a vision of man's
ultimate relationship to nature.

Marion Randall Parsons, the friend who helped John Muir
with his last book, *Travels in Alaska*, told me that one day he
said to her: "To get these glorious works of God into yourself
— that's the thing; not to write about them!" Muir was fifty-six
when his first book appeared. He had written only two by the

time he was seventy. The remarkable thing is not that his books were so slow to appear, so long delayed, but rather that they appeared at all. He was too busy living to stop and write. When urged to set down his observations for publication he always replied that he could not give up field work until he was too old to climb mountains. He told a friend that it would take a second lifetime to do his writing and he died leaving notes for a dozen books that he never completed.

All of his early journals were set down with no thought of publication. He shaped his books from his notes more to entice people to look at nature's loveliness than from the pleasure writing gave him. Muir talked easily, fluently. But he wrote laboriously, rewriting, polishing, complaining that it took him a month to write a chapter that could be read in an hour. While laboring with his pen in San Francisco, he wrote to his sister Sarah: "My life these days is like the life of a glacier, one eternal grind, and the top of my head suffers a weariness at times that you know nothing about." Moreover he disliked the solitary confinement of authorship. He was always delighted to see a friend arrive so he could drop writing for a good talk. He never used a typewriter. In his earlier years he cut his own quill pens, sometimes from eagle feathers he found among the mountains. His handwriting grew progressively worse, until at last it was almost as illegible as Thoreau's. His final work was done in a cluttered upstairs study at the ranch house at Martinez, California, where he lived alone with a taciturn Chinese employee who could speak hardly thirty words of English after three decades in America, and who invariably replied when Muir asked him if he understood directions he had given him, "Too muchee talk!"

Before his first book came from the press John Muir was already famous as a writer. His sequence of "Sierra Studies" in the old *Overland Monthly* and his articles in the *Century Magazine* had had wide influence and had given him a national reputation. In the 1880's and early 1890's, the present tidal wave of printed matter was only a ripple and leading periodicals had a permanence and standing unknown today. Subscribers read them carefully from first page to last. It was among such readers that

Muir was first recognized as a writer of importance. An exactness and depth of firsthand observation characterizes all his pages. He was by turn a scientist, a poet, a mystic, a philosopher, a humorist. Because he saw everything, mountains and streams and landscapes, as evolving, unfinished, in the process of creation, there is a pervading sense of vitality in all he wrote. Even his records of scientific studies read like adventure stories.

There have been those who have complained, with some basis, that Muir's books tended to be "adjectivorous," that all his mountain streams "sang psalms," that he overworked such words as "glorious." No doubt there were, in the early 1900's, sentimental imitators who, without Muir's background of observation, sang unthinkingly of "happy" birds and "glad" brooks and "joyous" wildflowers. Muir himself was aware of his fondness for certain adjectives and wrote to his friend Robert Underwood Johnson of *Century Magazine* that he had been busy slaughtering "gloriouses" in his manuscript. However, his overworking of this adjective was, in itself, a key to his character. For him, always, the world *was* glorious.

Twice Muir had prospects of making a large fortune. Both times he turned aside from the path to wealth to return to these glories of nature. In the library of the Wisconsin Historical Society, at Madison, I once examined charts John Muir had made to increase the efficiency of the wagon-wheel factory at Indianapolis, Indiana, where he worked in 1866 and 1867. Had he continued to devote his inventive and administrative abilities to factory work, there is no doubt he would have become an extremely wealthy man. A sharp pointed file that slipped early in March 1867 and pierced the edge of the cornea of his right eye turned him forever away from machines and back to nature. As he lay in a darkened room during convalescence, shut away from all the beauties of the out-of-doors, he resolved to waste no more of his years in indoor work. Almost as soon as his sight was restored, he set out on his thousand-mile walk to the Gulf.

Again, after his marriage to Louie Wanda Strenzel of Martinez, California, in 1880, Muir rented land from his father-in-law in the alluvial Alhambra valley and concentrated on raising Tokay grapes, Bartlett pears and other fruit. By devising special equipment for setting out orchard trees, by care in packing, by developing new markets for his fruit, by sharp management and Scotch thrift, he cleared $10,000 a year for ten years. It was his habit to visit the Martinez bank carrying his deposits and valuable papers in a white sack conspicuously marked "Laundry." Other ranchers in the region soon discovered they had to get up early in the morning, literally, to keep ahead of Muir. The wooden lug-boxes in which the fruit was shipped to San Francisco were returned empty to a nearby railroad station on a train that arrived around midnight. They were unmarked but each rancher knew the number that belonged to him. Muir used to get up in the middle of the night to be first on hand. He took exactly his number of boxes but he always picked the perfect, undamaged ones. An innovator in everything he did, John Muir was the first to ship grapes from California to Hawaii. At the end of ten years he told his long-time friend William E. Colby that he had cleared $100,000 and had all the wealth he would ever want. He turned his back once more on money-making. During the Harriman Expedition to Alaska in 1899, someone mentioned the great wealth of the sponsor, the railroad magnate, E. H. Harriman. Muir replied, "Why, I am richer than Harriman. I have all the money I want and he hasn't."

During his years in the Yosemite Muir used to view with sadness the distinguished visitors who were so "time-poor" that they could spend only one day among the glories of the mountains. He chose to be time-rich first of all. "I might have become a millionaire," he once said, "but I chose to become a tramp." To his sister Sarah, he wrote: "I have not yet in all my wanderings found a single person so free as myself. When in the woods I sit at times for hours watching birds or squirrels or looking down into the faces of flowers without suffering any feeling of haste." A friend who once accompanied him in the mountains told me they took ten hours to walk ten miles. They would stop to observe a bird or sit down beside a wildflower without regard to the passing of time.

While visiting friends, Muir sometimes would talk four hours at breakfast. Although he early declared, "I have chosen the lonely way," he was never misanthropic. He made friends easily. He prized congenial companions. He delighted in conversation. This, however, was oftentimes one-sided. Muir's conversational endurance is legendary. He disliked being interrupted by questions and tended to take the bit in his teeth and keep going. John Burroughs grumbled that when Muir told the story of the preacher's dog, Stickeen, you got "the whole theory of glaciation thrown in." But if Muir talked at length he was never pointless or boring or loud.

His voice was pleasant, rather low-pitched, a good speaking voice. He had only a slight Scotch burr. Humorous and something of a tease, he also had decided opinions and delighted in argument. Sometimes his assertiveness made people assume he was provoked when he was not. His whole individualistic life, in which he went his way without too much regard for the attitude of others, gave him little training in consideration for the feelings of those around him. He was, at times, brusque and tactless. Once during an argument, John Burroughs complained, "I guess you don't think I know much about geology." "Johnnie," Muir told him, "if all you know about geology were thrown into the ocean it wouldn't make a splash bigger than a raindrop!"

If he was forthright and outspoken, his sense of honor was high and he was a lifelong hater of sham and subterfuge. He disliked politics and rarely discussed current events. Civilization, he declared, drives its victims in flocks. He, himself, showed scant regard for conventions. His clothes were clean but rarely pressed. Although he was under six feet in height, Muir stood out in a crowd. His head was well proportioned, his eyes deep blue and remarkably piercing. He never shaved in his life. His beard and hair, the latter having an especially silky texture, were reddish brown.

Each Christmas it was Muir's custom to obtain five-dollar gold pieces from the bank and give one to each of the neighbor children. To his own two daughters, Helen and Wanda, he was a loving, if at times stern, parent. His study, with pictures of Thoreau and Emerson on the mantel, was inviolate; no one was permitted to dust or clean it. Muir never owned an automobile and he disliked to ride in one. This was to be expected from a naturalist who had complained that it was impossible to see anything worthwhile from a stagecoach traveling forty miles a day.

Henry James once commented that Thoreau was not provincial, he was parochial. Muir, on the other hand, was continental and global. When he started his walk to the Gulf, he inscribed on the flyleaf of his journal: *John Muir, Earth-Planet, Universe.* He needed 1000-mile walks and whole mountain ranges for his studies. In many parts of the country — in Indiana, in the southern Appalachians, on the west coast of Florida, in Wisconsin, in Arizona, in the Sierra, on the Mojave Desert — I have crossed John Muir's trail. The impress of his work and character has been recorded on many maps.

In Alaska there is a Muir Glacier. In Wisconsin there is a Muir Lake and a Muir Knoll. In Washington, at the Mount Rainier National Park, there is a Camp Muir. And in California, as Erwin G. Gudde notes in his *California Place Names*, Muir has been commemorated in the nomenclature of the state more times than any other individual. Marin County has the Muir Woods National Monument, Tulare County has Mount Muir and Lake Muir, Los Angeles County, Muir Peak. There is a Muir Gorge in the Yosemite National Park, a Muir Pass in the Kings Canyon National Park, a Muir Crest and a Muir Grove in the Sequoia National Park. The John Muir Trail runs among the lofty peaks of the Sierra. Pasadena has a John Muir College; the Santa Fe Railroad named one of its stops Muir Station; and, during the First World War, a liberty ship was christened the SS *John Muir.*

In talking to those who knew Muir, I found considerable disagreement as to which phase of natural history held first importance in his mind. One thought it was trees. Another believed it was geology. A third suggested it was plants. A fourth, probably the nearest right of all, thought it was the whole interrelationships of life, the complete, rounded picture of the mountain world. Today Muir probably would be called an ecologist. This breadth of his interests is reflected in the varied categories in which his name appears on the lists of science. One of the rock rabbits, or conies, of the Yosemite bears a scientific name honoring Muir. Asa Gray, the celebrated Harvard botanist, similarly commemorated him in naming an arctic Erigeron that Muir brought back from the *Corwin* expedition of 1880. And one of several butterflies new to science that Muir captured in the Sierra received the name *Thecla muiri*. Not only did Muir discover new species of plants and insects in his wanderings, he contributed in other substantial ways to the progress of science.

He was the first to discover living glaciers in the Sierra. He was the first to explore Glacier Bay in Alaska. He was the first to point out the role glaciers played in forming Yosemite Valley. Unknown and in his early thirties when he advanced this theory, he was opposed by the distinguished and dogmatic California State Geologist, Dr. Josiah Dwight Whitney, formerly of Harvard. Whitney maintained that glaciers had nothing to do with Yosemite, that the floor of the valley had dropped down in some ancient cataclysm. Muir scoffed, "The bottom never fell out of anything God made." Whitney rejoined that the glacial hypothesis was merely the idea of a "sheepherder." So began three summers of exhausting, lone-handed field work in which Muir traced to their sources all the streams of the Tuolumne Divide. Often returning to the valley only long enough to replenish his breadsack, he followed nameless watercourses through wild canyons in which no white man had ever set foot. Fragment by fragment, glacier-scratch by glacier-scratch, he amassed his evidence. By 1873 he was ready to publish his findings in his series of "Sierra Studies." Today no scientist doubts the part glaciers played in the formation of the Yosemite Valley.

Considerable as was John Muir's contribution to science, even greater was his stature in the long fight for conservation. During those critical years around the turn of the century, his was the most eloquent and powerful voice raised in defense of nature. He was the spearhead of the western movement to preserve wild beauty, a prime mover in the national park system so valued today. Beside a campfire at Soda Springs on the Tuolumne Meadows in 1889, he and Robert Underwood Johnson mapped the seventeen-year battle that preserved Yosemite as a national park. Beside other campfires under sequoias, while on a three-day outing with Theodore Roosevelt in 1903, he presented the case for the preservation of numerous wilderness areas with moving effect. Major credit for saving the Grand Canyon and the Petrified Forest, in Arizona, is ascribed to John Muir. He was president of the Sierra Club from the formation of that militant conservation organization in 1892 until the time of his death in 1914. His last long battle to save Hetch Hetchy, the beautiful Yosemite Park valley flooded to form a reservoir for San Francisco water — water that could have been obtained elsewhere — ended only the year before he died. It represents one of the great heroic struggles of conservation, no less heroic because the cause was lost.

Near the end of his life Muir said to a close friend, "I have lived a bully life. I have done what I set out to do." Rich in time, rich in enjoyment, rich in appreciation, rich in enthusiasm, rich in understanding, rich in expression, rich in friends, rich in knowledge, John Muir lived a full and rounded life, a life unique in many ways, admirable in many ways, valuable in many ways. "A man in his books," he once wrote, "may be said to walk the earth long after he had gone." In his writings and in his conservation achievements, Muir seems especially present in a world that is better because he lived here. His finest monument is the wild beauty he called attention to and helped preserve — beauty, however, that is never entirely safe, beauty that needs as vigilant protection today and tomorrow as it needed yesterday.

I

MEMORIES OF YOUTH

Boyhood in Scotland

JOHN MUIR was born on April 21, 1838, in Dunbar, Scotland, the third child and the first boy in the family of Daniel and Ann Muir. Until he was eleven, the family lived above his father's store on High Street, in Dunbar. The surname Muir — meaning in the Scottish tongue a moor or wild stretch of wasteland — is particularly appropriate for one who all his life was deeply in love with the wildness of nature.

Like W. H. Hudson's Far Away and Long Ago, *John Muir's* The Story of My Boyhood and Youth, *from which this first selection is taken, was a product of his last years. It appeared in March 1913, only twenty-one months before his death. The book might never have been written except for E. H. Harriman, the railroad magnate with whom Muir traveled to Alaska in 1899. During the summer of 1908, Harriman invited Muir to visit him at his Pelican Bay lodge, on Klamath Lake in Oregon. There he assigned his expert stenographer to take down Muir's recollections as he walked in the woods or sat by the fire in the evening. The typed record of these shorthand notes ran to more than 1000 pages. Revised, condensed and rewritten, they formed the book which appeared five years later.*

WHEN I was a boy in Scotland I was fond of everything that was wild, and all my life I've been growing fonder and fonder of wild places and wild creatures. Fortunately around my native town of Dunbar, by the stormy North Sea, there was no lack of wildness, though most of the land lay in smooth cultivation.

With red-blooded playmates, wild as myself, I loved to wander in the fields to hear the birds sing, and along the sea-shore to gaze and wonder at the shells and sea-weeds, eels and crabs in the pools among the rocks when the tide was low; and best of all to watch the waves in awful storms thundering on the black headlands and craggy ruins of the old Dunbar Castle when the sea and the sky, the waves and the clouds, were mingled together as one. We never thought of playing truant, but after I was five or six years old I ran away to the sea-shore or the fields almost every Saturday, and every day in the school vacations except Sundays, though solemnly warned that I must play at home in the garden and back yard, lest I should learn to think bad thoughts and say bad words. All in vain. In spite of the sure sore punishments that followed like shadows, the natural inherited wildness in our blood ran true on its glorious course as invincible and unstoppable as stars.

My earliest recollections of the country were gained on short walks with my grandfather when I was perhaps not over three years old. On one of the walks grandfather took me to Lord Lauderdale's gardens, where I saw figs growing against a sunny wall and tasted some of them, and got as many apples to eat as I wished. On another memorable walk in a hayfield, when we sat down to rest on one of the haycocks, I heard a sharp, prickly, stinging cry, and, jumping up eagerly, called grandfather's attention to it. He said he heard only the wind, but I insisted on digging into the hay and turning it over until we discovered the source of the strange exciting sound — a mother field mouse with half a dozen naked young hanging to her teats. This to me was a wonderful discovery. No hunter could have been more excited on discovering a bear and her cubs in a wilderness den.

I was sent to school before I had completed my third year. The first schoolday was doubtless full of wonders, but I am not able to recall any of them. I remember the servant washing my face and getting soap in my eyes, and mother hanging a little green bag with my first book in it around my neck so I would not lose it, and its blowing back in the sea-wind like a flag. But before I was sent to school my grandfather, as I was told, had taught me my letters from shop signs across the street. I can remember distinctly how proud I was when I had spelled my way through the little first book into the second, which seemed large and important, and so on to the third. Going from one book to another formed a grand triumphal advancement, the memories of which still stand out in clear relief.

The third book contained interesting stories as well as plain reading- and spelling-lessons. To me the best story of all was "Llewellyn's Dog," the first animal that comes to mind after the needle-voiced field mouse. It so deeply interested and touched me and some of my classmates that we read it over and over with aching hearts, both in and out of school and shed bitter tears over the brave faithful dog, Gelert, slain by his own master, who imagined that he had devoured his son because he came to him all bloody when the boy was lost, though he had saved the child's life by killing a big wolf. We have to look far back to learn how great may be the capacity of a child's heart for sorrow and sympathy with animals as well as with human friends and neighbors. This auld-lang-syne story stands out in the throng of old schoolday memories as clearly as if I had myself been one of that Welsh hunting-party — heard the bugles blowing, seen Gelert slain, joined in the search for the lost child, discovered it at last happy and smiling among the grass and bushes beside the dead, mangled wolf, and wept with Llewellyn over the sad fate of his noble, faithful dog friend.

Another favorite in this book was Southey's poem "The Inchcape Bell," a story of a priest and a pirate. A good priest in order to warn seamen in dark stormy weather hung a big bell on the dangerous Inchcape Rock. The greater the storm and higher the waves, the louder rang the warning bell, until it was cut off and sunk by wicked Ralph the Rover. One fine day, as the story goes, when the bell was ringing gently, the pirate put out to the rock, saying, "I'll sink that bell and plague the Abbot of Aberbrothok." So he cut the rope, and down went the bell "with a gurgling sound; the bubbles rose and burst around," etc. Then "Ralph the Rover sailed away; he scoured the seas for many a day; and now, grown rich with plundered store, he steers his course for Scotland's shore." Then came a terrible storm with cloud darkness and night darkness and high roaring waves. "Now where we are," cried the pirate, "I cannot tell, but I wish I could hear the Inchcape bell." And the story goes on to tell how the wretched rover "tore his hair," and "curst himself in his despair," when "with a shivering shock" the stout ship struck on the Inchcape Rock, and went down with Ralph and his plunder beside the good priest's bell. The story appealed to our love of kind deeds and of wildness and fair play.

A lot of terrifying experiences connected with these first schooldays grew out of crimes committed by the keeper of a low lodging-house in Edinburgh, who allowed poor homeless wretches to sleep on benches or the floor for a penny or so a night, and, when kind Death came to their relief, sold the bodies for dissection to Dr. Hare of the medical school. None of us children ever heard anything like the original story. The servant girls told us that "Dandy Doctors," clad in long black cloaks and supplied with a store of sticking-plaster of wondrous adhesiveness, prowled at night about the country lanes and even the town streets, watching for children to choke and sell. The Dandy Doctor's business method, as the servants explained it, was with lightning quickness to clap a sticking-plaster on the face of a scholar, covering mouth and nose, preventing breathing or crying for help, then pop us under his long black cloak and carry us to Edinburgh to be sold and sliced into small pieces for folk to learn how we were made. We always mentioned the name "Dandy Doctor" in a fearful whisper, and never dared venture out of doors after dark. In the short winter days it got dark before school closed, and in cloudy weather we sometimes had difficulty in finding our way home unless a servant with a lantern was sent for us; but during the Dandy Doctor period the school was closed earlier, for if detained until the usual hour the teacher could not get us to leave the schoolroom. We would rather stay all night supperless than dare the mysterious doctors supposed to be lying in wait for us. We had to go up a hill called the Davel Brae that lay between the schoolhouse and the main street. One evening just before dark,

as we were running up the hill, one of the boys shouted, "A
Dandy Doctor! A Dandy Doctor!" and we all fled pellmell back
into the schoolhouse to the astonishment of Mungo Siddons,
the teacher. I can remember to this day the amused look on the
good dominie's face as he stared and tried to guess what had got
into us, until one of the older boys breathlessly explained that
there was an awful big Dandy Doctor on the Brae and we
couldna gang hame. Others corroborated the dreadful news.
"Yes! We saw him, plain as onything, with his lang black cloak to
hide us in, and some of us thought we saw a sticken-plaister ready
in his hand." We were in such a state of fear and trembling that
the teacher saw he wasn't going to get rid of us without going
himself as leader. He went only a short distance, however, and
turned us over to the care of the two biggest scholars, who led us
to the top of the Brae and then left us to scurry home and dash
into the door like pursued squirrels diving into their holes.

Just before school skaled (closed), we all arose and sang the
fine hymn "Lord, dismiss us with Thy blessing." In the spring
when the swallows were coming back from their winter homes
we sang —

> *"Welcome, welcome, little stranger,*
> *Welcome from a foreign shore;*
> *Safe escaped from many a danger . . . "*

and while singing we all swayed in rhythm with the music. "The
Cuckoo," that always told his name in the spring of the year, was
another favorite song, and when there was nothing in particular to
call to mind any special bird or animal, the songs we sang were
widely varied, such as

> *"The whale, the whale is the beast for me,*
> *Plunging along through the deep, deep sea."*

But the best of all was "Lord, dismiss us with Thy blessing,"
though at that time the most significant part I fear was the first
three words.

With my school lessons father made me learn hymns and Bible verses. For learning "Rock of Ages" he gave me a penny, and I thus became suddenly rich. Scotch boys are seldom spoiled with money. We thought more of a penny those economical days than the poorest American schoolboy thinks of a dollar. To decide what to do with that first penny was an extravagantly serious affair. I ran in great excitement up and down the street, examining the tempting goodies in the shop windows before venturing on so important an investment. My playmates also became excited when the wonderful news got abroad that Johnnie Muir had a penny, hoping to obtain a taste of the orange, apple, or candy it was likely to bring forth.

At this time infants were baptized and vaccinated a few days after birth. I remember very well a fight with the doctor when my brother David was vaccinated. This happened, I think, before I was sent to school. I couldn't imagine what the doctor, a tall, severe-looking man in black, was doing to my brother, but as mother, who was holding him in her arms, offered no objection, I looked on quietly while he scratched the arm until I saw blood. Then, unable to trust even my mother, I managed to spring up high enough to grab and bite the doctor's arm, yelling that I wasna gan to let him hurt my bonnie brither, while to my utter astonishment mother and the doctor only laughed at me. So far from complete at times is sympathy between parents and children, and so much like wild beasts are baby boys, little fighting, biting, climbing pagans.

Father was proud of his garden and seemed always to be trying to make it as much like Eden as possible, and in a corner of it he gave each of us a little bit of ground for our very own in which we planted what we best liked, wondering how the hard dry seeds could change into soft leaves and flowers and find their way out to the light; and, to see how they were coming on, we used to dig up the larger ones, such as peas and beans, every day. My aunt had a corner assigned to her in our garden which she filled with lilies, and we all looked with the utmost respect and admiration at that precious lily-bed and wondered whether when we grew up we should ever be rich enough to own one anything like so grand. We imagined that each lily was worth an enormous sum of money and never dared to touch a single leaf or petal of them. We really stood in awe of them. Far, far was I then from the wild lily gardens of California that I was destined to see in their glory.

When I was a little boy at Mungo Siddons's school a flower-show was held in Dunbar, and I saw a number of the exhibitors carrying large handfuls of dahlias, the first I had ever seen. I thought them marvelous in size and beauty and, as in the case of my aunt's lilies, wondered if I should ever be rich enough to own some of them.

Although I never dared to touch my aunt's sacred lilies, I have good cause to remember stealing some common flowers from an apothecary, Peter Lawson, who also answered the purpose of a regular physician to most of the poor people of the town and adjacent country. He had a pony which was considered very wild and dangerous, and when he was called out of town he mounted this wonderful beast, which, after standing long in the stable, was frisky and boisterous, and often to our delight reared and jumped and danced about from side to side of the street before he could be persuaded to go ahead. We boys gazed in awful admiration and wondered how the druggist could be so brave and able as to get on and stay on that wild beast's back. This famous Peter loved flowers and had a fine garden surrounded by an iron fence, through the bars of which, when I thought no one saw me, I oftentimes snatched a flower and took to my heels. One day Peter discovered me in this mischief, dashed out into the street and caught me. I screamed that I wouldna steal any more if he would let me go. He didn't say anything but just dragged me along to the stable where he kept the wild pony, pushed me in right back of its heels, and shut the door. I was screaming, of course, but as soon as I was imprisoned the fear of being kicked quenched all noise. I hardly dared breathe. My only hope was in motionless silence. Imagine the agony I endured! I did not steal any more of his flowers. He was a good hard judge of boy nature.

I was in Peter's hands some time before this, when I was about two and a half years old. The servant girl bathed us small folk before putting us to bed. The smarting soapy scrubbings of the Saturday nights in preparation for the Sabbath were particularly severe, and we all dreaded them. My sister Sarah, the next older than I, wanted the long-legged stool I was sitting on awaiting my turn, so she just tipped me off. My chin struck on the edge of the bath-tub, and, as I was talking at the time, my tongue happened to be in the way of my teeth when they were closed by the blow, and a deep gash was cut on the side of it, which bled profusely. Mother came running at the noise I made, wrapped me up, put me in the servant girl's arms and told her to run with me through the garden and out by a back way to Peter Lawson to have something done to stop the bleeding. He simply pushed a wad of cotton into my mouth after soaking it in some brown astringent stuff, and told me to be sure to keep my mouth shut and all would soon be well. Mother put me to bed, calmed my fears, and told me to lie still and sleep like a gude bairn. But just as I was dropping off to sleep I swallowed the bulky wad of medicated cotton and with it, as I imagined, my tongue also. My screams over so great a loss brought mother, and when she anxiously took me in her arms and inquired what was the matter, I told her that I had swallowed my tongue. She only laughed at me, much to my astonishment, when I expected that she would bewail the awful loss her boy had sustained. My sisters, who were older than I, oftentimes said when I happened to be talking too much, "It's a pity you hadn't swallowed at least half of that long tongue of yours when you were little."

It appears natural for children to be fond of water, although the Scotch method of making every duty dismal contrived to make necessary bathing for health terrible to us. I well remember among the awful experiences of childhood being taken by the servant to the sea-shore when I was between two and three years old, stripped at the side of a deep pool in the rocks, plunged into it among crawling crawfish and slippery wriggling snake-like eels, and drawn up gasping and shrieking only to be plunged down again and again. As the time approached for this terrible bathing, I used to hide in the darkest corners of the house, and oftentimes a long search was required to find me. But after we were a few years older, we enjoyed bathing with other boys as we wandered along the shore, careful, however, not to get into a pool that had an invisible boy-devouring monster at the bottom of it. Such pools, miniature maelstroms, were called "sookin-in-goats" and were well known to most of us. Nevertheless we never ventured into any pool on strange parts of the coast before we had thrust a stick into it. If the stick were not pulled out of our hands, we boldly entered and enjoyed plashing and ducking long ere we had learned to swim.

One of our best playgrounds was the famous old Dunbar Castle, to which King Edward fled after his defeat at Bannockburn. It was built more than a thousand years ago, and though we knew little of its history, we had heard many mysterious stories of the battles fought about its walls, and firmly believed that every bone we found in the ruins belonged to an ancient warrior. We tried to see who could climb highest on the crumbling peaks and crags, and took chances that no cautious mountaineer would try. That I did not fall and finish my rock-scrambling in those adventurous boyhood days seems now a reasonable wonder.

Among out best games were running, jumping, wrestling, and scrambling. I was so proud of my skill as a climber that when I first heard of hell from a servant girl who loved to tell its horrors and warn us that if we did anything wrong we would be cast into it, I always insisted that I could climb out of it. I imagined it was only a sooty pit with stone walls like those of the castle, and I felt sure there must be chinks and cracks in the masonry for fingers and toes. Anyhow the terrors of the horrible place seldom lasted long beyond the telling; for natural faith casts out fear.

Most of the Scotch children believe in ghosts, and some under peculiar conditions continue to believe in them all through life. Grave ghosts are deemed particularly dangerous, and many of the most credulous will go far out of their way to avoid passing through or near a graveyard in the dark. After being instructed by the servants in the nature, looks, and habits of the various

black and white ghosts, boowuzzies, and witches we often specu-
lated as to whether they could run fast, and tried to believe that
we had a good chance to get away from most of them. To improve our speed and wind, we often took long runs into the
country. Tam o' Shanter's mare outran a lot of witches — at least
until she reached a place of safety beyond the keystone of the
bridge — and we thought perhaps we also might be able to outrun
them.

Our house formerly belonged to a physician, and a servant
girl told us that the ghost of the dead doctor haunted one of the
unoccupied rooms in the second story that was kept dark on account of a heavy window-tax. Our bedroom was adjacent to the
ghost room, which had in it a lot of chemical apparatus — glass
tubing, glass and brass retorts, test-tubes, flasks, etc. — and we
thought that those strange articles were still used by the old dead
doctor in compounding physic. In the long summer days David
and I were put to bed several hours before sunset. Mother tucked
us in carefully, drew the curtains of the big old-fashioned bed, and
told us to lie still and sleep like gude bairns; but we were usually
out of bed, playing games of daring called "scootchers," about as
soon as our loving mother reached the foot of the stairs, for we
couldn't lie still, however hard we might try. Going into the
ghost room was regarded as a very great scootcher. After venturing in a few steps and rushing back in terror, I used to dare David
to go as far without getting caught.

The roof of our house, as well as the crags and walls of the old
castle, offered fine mountaineering exercise. Our bedroom was
lighted by a dormer window. One night I opened it in search of
good scootchers and hung myself out over the slates, holding on
to the sill, while the wind was making a balloon of my nightgown.
I then dared David to try the adventure, and he did. Then I went
out again and hung by one hand, and David did the same. Then
I hung by one finger, being careful not to slip, and he did that
too. Then I stood on the sill and examined the edge of the left
wall of the window, crept up the slates along its side by slight
finger-holds, got astride of the roof, sat there a few minutes looking at the scenery over the garden wall while the wind was

howling and threatening to blow me off, then managed to slip down, catch hold of the sill, and get safely back into the room. But before attempting this scootcher, recognizing its dangerous character, with commendable caution I warned David that in case I should happen to slip I would grip the rain-trough when I was going over the eaves and hang on, and that he must then run fast downstairs and tell father to get a ladder for me, and tell him to be quick because I would soon be tired hanging dangling in the wind by my hands. After my return from this capital scootcher, David, not to be outdone, crawled up to the top of the window-roof, and got bravely astride of it; but in trying to return he lost courage and began to greet (to cry), "I canna get doon. Oh, I canna get doon." I leaned out of the window and shouted encouragingly, "Dinna greet, Davie, dinna greet, I'll help ye doon. If you greet, fayther will hear, and gee us baith an awfu' skelping." Then, standing on the sill and holding on by one hand to the window-casing, I directed him to slip his feet down within reach, and, after securing a good hold, I jumped inside and dragged him in by his heels. This finished scootcher-scrambling for the night and frightened us into bed.

In the short winter days, when it was dark even at our early bedtime, we usually spent the hours before going to sleep playing voyages around the world under the bed-clothing. After mother had carefully covered us, bade us goodnight and gone downstairs, we set out on our travels. Burrowing likes moles, we visited France, India, America, Australia, New Zealand, and all the places we had ever heard of; our travels never ending until we fell asleep. When mother came to take a last look at us, before she went to bed, to see that we were covered, we were oftentimes covered so well that she had difficulty in finding us, for we were hidden in all sorts of positions where sleep happened to overtake us, but in the morning we always found ourselves in good order, lying straight like gude bairns, as she said.

Some fifty years later, when I visited Scotland, I got one of my Dunbar schoolmates to introduce me to the owners of our old home, from whom I obtained permission to go upstairs to examine our bedroom window and judge what sort of adventure

getting on its roof must have been, and with all my after experience in mountaineering, I found that what I had done in
daring boyhood was now beyond my skill.

Boys are often at once cruel and merciful, thoughtlessly hard-
hearted and tender-hearted, sympathetic, pitiful, and kind in
ever changing contrasts. Love of neighbors, human or animal,
grows up amid savage traits, coarse and fine. When my father
made out to get us securely locked up in the back yard to prevent our shore and field wanderings, we had to play away the
comparatively dull time as best we could. One of our amusements was hunting cats without seriously hurting them. These
sagacious animals knew, however, that, though not very dangerous, boys were not to be trusted. One time in particular I remember, when we began throwing stones at an experienced old Tom,
not wishing to hurt him much, though he was a tempting mark.
He soon saw what we were up to, fled to the stable, and climbed
to the top of the hay manger. He was still within range, however, and we kept the stones flying faster and faster, but he just
blinked and played possum without wincing either at our best
shots or at the noise we made. I happened to strike him pretty
hard with a good-sized pebble, but he still blinked and sat still as
if without feeling. "He must be mortally wounded," I said, "and
now we must kill him to put him out of pain," the savage in us
rapidly growing with indulgence. All took heartily to this sort
of cat mercy and began throwing the heaviest stones we could
manage, but that old fellow knew what characters we were, and
just as we imagined him mercifully dead he evidently thought
the play was becoming too serious and that it was time to retreat; for suddenly with a wild whirr and gurr of energy he
launched himself over our heads, rushed across the yard in a blur
of speed, climbed to the roof of another building and over the
garden-wall, out of pain and bad company, with all his lives
wide-awake and in good working order.

After we had thus learned that Tom had at least nine lives, we
tried to verify the common saying that no matter how far cats
fell they always landed on their feet unhurt. We caught one
in our back yard, not Tom but a smaller one of manageable size,

and somehow got him smuggled up to the top story of the house. I don't know how in the world we managed to let go of him, for as soon as we opened the window and held him over the sill he knew his danger and made violent efforts to scratch and bite his way back into the room; but we determined to carry the thing through, and at last managed to drop him. I can remember to this day how the poor creature in danger of his life strained and balanced as he was falling and managed to alight on his feet. This was a cruel thing for even wild boys to do, and we never tried the experiment again, for we sincerely pitied the poor fellow when we saw him creeping slowly away, stunned and frightened, with a swollen black and blue chin.

Again — showing the natural savagery of boys — we delighted in dog-fights, and even in the horrid red work of slaughter-houses, often running long distances and climbing over walls and roofs to see a pig killed, as soon as we heard the desperately earnest squealing. And if the butcher was good-natured, we begged him to let us get a near view of the mysterious insides and to give us a bladder to blow up for a foot-ball.

But here is an illustration of the better side of boy nature. In our back yard there were three Elm trees and in the one nearest the house a pair of robin-redbreasts had their nest. When the young were almost able to fly, a troop of the celebrated "Scottish Grays" visited Dunbar, and three or four of the fine horses were lodged in our stable. When the soldiers were polishing their swords and helmets, they happened to notice the nest, and just as they were leaving, one of them climbed the tree and robbed it. With sore sympathy we watched the young birds as the hard-hearted robber pushed them one by one beneath his jacket — all but two that jumped out of the nest and tried to fly, but they were easily caught as they fluttered on the ground, and were hidden away with the rest. The distress of the bereaved parents, as they hovered and screamed over the frightened crying children they so long had loved and sheltered and fed, was pitiful to see; but the shining soldier rode grandly away on his big gray horse, caring only for the few pennies the young songbirds would bring and the beer they would buy, while we all, sisters and brothers, were crying and sobbing. I remember, as if it happened this day, how my heart fairly ached and choked me. Mother put us to bed and tried to comfort us, telling us that the little birds would be well fed and grow big, and soon learn to sing in pretty cages; but again and again we rehearsed the sad story of the poor bereaved birds and their frightened children, and could not be comforted. Father came into the room when we were half asleep and still sobbing, and I heard mother telling him that ' a' the bairns' heart were broken over the robbing of the nest in the Elm."

After attaining the manly, belligerent age of five or six years, very few of my schooldays passed without a fist fight, and half a dozen was no uncommon number. When any classmate of our own age questioned our rank and standing as fighters, we always made haste to settle the matter at a quiet place on the Davel Brae. To be a "gude fechter" was our highest ambition, our dearest aim in life or out of school. To be a good scholar was a secondary consideration, though we tried hard to hold high places in our classes and gloried in being Dux. We fairly reveled in the battle stories of glorious William Wallace and Robert the Bruce, with which every breath of Scotch air is saturated, and of course we were all going to be soldiers. On the Davel Brae battle-ground we often managed to bring on something like real war, greatly more exciting than personal combat. Choosing leaders we divided into two armies. In winter damp snow furnished plenty of ammunition to make the thing serious, and in summer sand and grass sods. Cheering and shouting some battle-cry such as "Bannockburn! Bannockburn! Scotland forever! The Last War in India!" we were led bravely on. For heavy battery work we stuffed our Scotch blue bonnets with snow and sand, sometimes mixed with gravel, and fired them at each other as cannon-balls.

Of course we always looked eagerly forward to vacation days and thought them slow in coming. Old Mungo Siddons gave us a lot of gooseberries or currants and wished us a happy time. Some sort of special closing-exercises — singing, recitations, etc. — celebrated the great day, but I remember only the berries, freedom from school work, and opportunities for runaway rambles in the fields and along the wave-beaten sea-shore.

An exciting time came when at the age of seven or eight years I left the auld Davel Brae school for the grammar school. Of course I had a terrible lot of fighting to do, because a new scholar had to meet every one of his age who dared to challenge him, this being the common introduction to a new school. It was very strenuous for the first month or so, establishing my fighting rank, taking up new studies, especially Latin and French, getting acquainted with new classmates and the master and his rules. In the first few Latin and French lessons the new teacher, Mr. Lyon, blandly smiled at our comical blunders, but pedagogical weather of the severest kind quickly set in, when for every mistake, everything short of perfection, the taws was promptly applied. We had to get three lessons every day in Latin, three in French, and as many in English, besides spelling, history, arithmetic, and geography. Word lessons in particular, the wouldst-couldst-shouldst-have-loved kind, were kept up, with much warlike thrashing, until I had committed the whole of the French, Latin, and English grammars to memory, and in connection with reading-lessons we were called on to recite parts of them with the rules over and over again, as if all the regular and irregular incomprehensible verb stuff was poetry. In addition to all this, father made me learn so many Bible verses every day that by the time I was eleven years of age I had about three fourths of the Old Testament and all of the New by heart and by sore flesh. I could recite the New Testament from the beginning of Matthew to the end of Revelation without a single stop. The dangers of cramming and of making scholars study at home instead of letting their little brains rest were never heard of in those days. We carried our school-books home in a strap every night and committed to memory our next day's lessons before we went to bed, and to do that we had to bend our attention as closely on our tasks as lawyers on great million-dollar cases. I can't conceive of anything that would now enable me to concentrate my attention more fully than when I was a mere stripling boy, and it was all done by whipping — thrashing in general. Old-fashioned Scotch teachers spent no time in seeking short roads to knowledge, or in trying any of the new-fangled psychological methods so much in vogue nowadays. There was nothing said about making the seats easy or the lessons easy. We were simply driven pointblank against our books like soldiers against the enemy, and sternly ordered, "Up and at 'em. Commit your lessons to memory!" If we failed in any part, however slight, we were whipped; for the grand, simple, all-sufficing Scotch discovery had been made that there was a close connection between the skin and the memory, and that irritating the skin excited the memory to any required degree.

Fighting was carried on still more vigorously in the high school than in the common school. Whenever anyone was challenged, either the challenge was allowed or it was decided by a battle on the sea-shore, where with stubborn enthusiasm we battered each other as if we had not been sufficiently battered by the teacher. When we were so fortunate as to finish a fight without getting a black eye, we usually escaped a thrashing at home and another next morning at school, for other traces of the fray could be easily washed off at a well on the church brae, or concealed, or passed as results of playground accidents; but a black eye could never be explained away from downright fighting. A good double thrashing was the inevitable penalty, but all without avail; fighting went on without the slightest abatement, like natural storms; for no punishment less than death could quench the ancient inherited belligerence burning in our pagan blood. Nor could we be made to believe it was fair that father and teacher should thrash us so industriously for our good, while begrudging us the pleasure of thrashing each other for our good. All these various thrashings, however, were admirably influential in developing not only memory but fortitude as well. For if we did not endure our school punishments and fighting pains without flinching and making faces, we were mocked on the playground, and public opinion on a Scotch playground was a powerful agent in controlling behavior; therefore we at length managed to keep our features in smooth repose while enduring pain that would try anybody but an American Indian. Far from feeling that we were called on to endure too much pain, one of

our playground games was thrashing each other with whips
about two feet long made from the tough, wiry stems of a species
of polygonum fastened together in a stiff, firm braid. One of us
handing two of these whips to a companion to take his choice,
we stood up close together and thrashed each other on the legs
until one succumbed to the intolerable pain and thus lost the
game. Nearly all of our playground games were strenuous —
shin-battering shinny, wrestling, prisoners' base, and dogs and
hares — all augmenting in no slight degree our lessons in fortitude. Moreover, we regarded our punishments and pains of every
sort as training for war, since we were all going to be soldiers.
Besides single combats we sometimes assembled on Saturdays to
meet the scholars of another school, and very little was required
for the growth of strained relations, and war. The immediate
cause might be nothing more than a saucy stare. Perhaps the
scholar stared at would insolently inquire, "What are ye glow-
erin' at, Bob?" Bob would reply, "I'll look where I hae a mind
and hinder me if ye daur." "Weel, Bob," the outraged stared-at
scholar would reply, "I'll soon let ye see whether I daur or no!"
and give Bob a blow on the face. This opened the battle, and
every good scholar belonging to either school was drawn into it.
After both sides were sore and weary, a strong-lunged warrior
would be heard above the din of battle shouting, "I'll tell ye what
we'll dae wi' ye. If ye let us alane we'll let ye alane!" and the
school war ended as most wars between nations do; and some of
them begin in much the same way.

Notwithstanding the great number of harshly enforced rules,
not very good order was kept in school in my time. There were
two schools within a few rods of each other, one for mathematics,
navigation, etc., the other, called the grammar school, that I attended. The masters lived in a big freestone house within eight
or ten yards of the schools, so that they could easily step out for
anything they wanted or send one of the scholars. The moment
our master disappeared, perhaps for a book or a drink, every
scholar left his seat and his lessons, jumped on top of the benches
and desks or crawled beneath them, tugging, rolling, wrestling,
accomplishing in a minute a depth of disorder and din unbelievable

save by a Scottish scholar. We even carried on war, class against class, in those wild, precious minutes. A watcher gave the alarm when the master opened his house-door to return, and it was a great feat to get into our places before he entered, adorned in awful majestic authority, shouting "Silence!" and striking resounding blows with his cane on a desk or on some unfortunate scholar's back.

Forty-seven years after leaving this fighting school, I returned on a visit to Scotland, and a cousin in Dunbar introduced me to a minister who was acquainted with the history of the school, and obtained for me an invitation to dine with the new master. Of course I gladly accepted, for I wanted to see the old place of fun and pain, and the battle-ground on the sands. Mr. Lyon, our able teacher and thrasher, I learned, had held his place as master of the school for twenty or thirty years after I left it, and had recently died in London, after preparing many young men for the English Universities. At the dinner-table, while I was recalling the amusements and fights of my old schooldays, the minister remarked to the new master, "Now, don't you wish that you had been teacher in those days, and and gained the honor of walloping John Muir?" This pleasure so merrily suggested showed that the minister also had been a fighter in his youth. The old freestone school-building was still perfectly sound, but the carved, ink-stained desks were almost whittled away.

The highest part of our playground back of the school commanded a view of the sea, and we loved to watch the passing ships and, judging by their rigging, make guesses as to the ports they had sailed from, those to which they were bound, what they were loaded with, their tonnage, etc. In stormy weather they were all smothered in clouds and spray, and showers of salt scud torn from the tops of the waves came flying over the playground wall. In those tremendous storms many a brave ship foundered or was tossed and smashed on the rocky shore. When a wreck occurred within a mile or two of the town, we often managed by running fast to reach it and pick up some of the spoils. In particular I remember visiting the battered fragments of an unfortunate brig or schooner that had been loaded with apples, and finding fine unpitiful sport in rushing into the spent waves and picking up the red-cheeked fruit from the frothy seething foam.

All our school-books were extravagantly illustrated with drawings of every kind of sailing-vessel, and every boy owned some sort of craft whittled from a block of wood and trimmed with infinite pains — sloops, schooners, brigs, and full-rigged ships, with their sails and string ropes properly adjusted and named for us by some old sailor. These precious toy craft with lead keels we learned to sail on a pond near the town. With the sails set at the proper angle to the wind, they made fast straight voyages across the pond to boys on the other side, who readjusted the sails and started them back on the return voyages. Oftentimes fleets of half a dozen or more were started together in exciting races.

Our most exciting sport, however, was playing with gunpowder. We made guns out of gas-pipe, mounted them on sticks of any shape, clubbed our pennies together for powder, gleaned pieces of lead here and there and cut them into slugs, and, while one aimed, another applied a match to the touch-hole. With these awful weapons we wandered along the beach and fired at the gulls and solan-geese as they passed us. Fortunately we never hurt any of them that we knew of. We also dug holes in the ground, put in a handful or two of powder, tamped it well around a fuse made of a wheat-stalk, and, reaching cautiously forward, touched a match to the straw. This we called making earthquakes. Oftentimes we went home with singed hair and faces well peppered with powder-grains that could not be washed out. Then, of course, came a correspondingly severe punishment from both father and teacher.

Another favorite sport was climbing trees and scaling garden-walls. Boys eight or ten years of age could get over almost any wall by standing on each other's shoulders, thus making living ladders. To make walls secure against marauders, many of them were finished on top with broken bottles imbedded in lime, leaving the cutting edges sticking up; but with bunches of grass and weeds we could sit or stand in comfort on top of the jaggedest of them.

Like squirrels that begin to eat nuts before they are ripe, we began to eat apples about as soon as they were formed, causing, of course, desperate gastric disturbances to be cured by castor oil. Serious were the risks we ran in climbing and squeezing through hedges, and, of course, among the country folk we were far from welcome. Farmers passing us on the roads often shouted by way of greeting: "Oh, you vagabonds! Back to the toon wi' ye. Gang back where ye belang. You 're up to mischief, Ise warrant. I can see it. The gamekeeper'll catch ye, and maist like ye'll a' be hanged some day."

Breakfast in those auld-lang-syne days was simple oatmeal porridge, usually with a little milk or treacle, served in wooden dishes called "luggies," formed of staves hooped together like miniature tubs about four or five inches in diameter. One of the staves, the lug or ear, a few inches longer than the others, served as a handle, while the number of luggies ranged in a row on a dresser indicated the size of the family. We never dreamed of anything to come after the porridge, or of asking for more. Our portions were consumed in about a couple of minutes; then off to school. At noon we came racing home ravenously hungry. The midday meal, called dinner, was usually vegetable broth, a small piece of boiled mutton, and barley-meal scone. None of us liked the barley scone bread, therefore we got all we wanted of it, and in desperation had to eat it, for we were always hungry, about as hungry after as before meals. The evening meal was called "tea" and was served on our return from school. It consisted, as far as we children were concerned, of half a slice of white bread without butter, barley scone, and warm water with a little milk and sugar in it, a beverage called "content," which warmed but neither cheered nor inebriated. Immediately after tea we ran across the street with our books to Grandfather Gilrye, who took pleasure in seeing us and hearing us recite our next day's lessons. Then back home to supper, usually a boiled potato and piece of barley scone. Then family worship, and to bed.

Our amusement on Saturday afternoons and vacations depended mostly on getting away from home into the country, especially in the spring when the birds were calling loudest.

Father sternly forbade David and me from playing truant in the fields with plundering wanderers like ourselves, fearing we might go on from bad to worse, get hurt in climbing over walls, caught by gamekeepers, or lost by falling over a cliff into the sea. "Play as much as you like in the back yard and garden," he said, "and mind what you'll get when you forget and disobey." Thus he warned us with an awfully stern countenance, looking very hard-hearted, while naturally his heart was far from hard, though he devoutly believed in eternal punishment for bad boys both here and hereafter. Nevertheless, like devout martyrs of wildness, we stole away to the sea-shore or the green, sunny fields with almost religious regularity, taking advantage of opportunities when father was very busy, to join our companions, oftenest to hear the birds sing and hunt their nests, glorying in the number we had discovered and called our own. A sample of our nest chatter was something like this: Willie Chisholm would proudly exclaim — "I ken (know) seventeen nests, and you, Johnnie, ken only fifteen."

"But I wouldna gie my fifteen for your seventeen, for five of mine are larks and mavises. You ken only three o' the best singers."

"Yes, Johnnie, but I ken six goldies and you ken only one. Maist of yours are only sparrows and linties and robin-redbreasts."

Then perhaps Bob Richardson would loudly declare that he "kenned mair nests than onybody," for he kenned "twenty-three, with about fifty eggs in them and mair than fifty young birds — maybe a hundred. Some of them naething but raw gorblings but lots of them as big as their mithers and ready to flee. And aboot fifty craw's nests and three fox dens."

"Oh, yes, Bob, but that's no fair, for naebody counts craws' nests and fox holes, and then you live in the country at Bellehaven where ye have the best chance."

"Yes, but I ken a lot of bumbees' nests, baith the red-legged and the yellow-legged kind."

"Oh, wha cares for bumbees' nests!"

"Weel, but here's something! Ma father let me gang to a fox hunt, and man, it was grand to see the hounds and the lang-legged horses lowpin the dykes and burns and hedges!"

The nests, I fear, with the beautiful eggs and young birds, were prized quite as highly as the songs of the glad parents, but no Scotch boy that I know of ever failed to listen with enthusiasm to the songs of the skylarks. Oftentimes on a broad meadow near Dunbar we stood for hours enjoying their marvelous singing and soaring. From the grass where the nest was hidden the male would suddenly rise, as straight as if shot up, to a height of perhaps thirty or forty feet, and, sustaining himself with rapid wing-beats, pour down the most delicious melody, sweet and clear and strong, overflowing all bounds, then suddenly he would soar higher again and again, ever higher and higher, soaring and singing until lost to sight even on perfectly clear days, and oftentimes in cloudy weather "far in the downy cloud," as the poet says.

To test our eyes we often watched a lark until he seemed a faint speck in the sky and finally passed beyond the keenest-sighted of us all. "I see him yet!" we would cry, "I see him yet!" "I see him yet!" "I see him yet!" as he soared. And finally only one of us would be left to claim that he still saw him. At last he, too, would have to admit that the singer had soared beyond his sight, and still the music came pouring down to us in glorious profusion, from a height far above our vision, requiring marvelous power of wing and marvelous power of voice, for that rich, delicious, soft, and yet clear music was distinctly heard after the bird was out of sight. Then, suddenly ceasing, the glorious singer would appear, falling like a bolt straight down to his nest, where his mate was sitting on the eggs.

It was far too common a practice among us to carry off a young lark just before it could fly, place it in a cage, and fondly, laboriously feed it. Sometimes we succeeded in keeping one alive for a year or two, and when awakened by the spring weather it was pitiful to see the quivering imprisoned soarer of the heavens rapidly beating its wings and singing as though it were flying and hovering in the air like its parents. To keep it in health we were taught that we must supply it with a sod of grass the size of the bottom of the cage, to make the poor bird feel as though it were at home on its native meadow — a meadow perhaps a foot or at most two feet square. Again and again it would try to hover over that miniature meadow from its miniature sky just underneath the top of the cage. At last, conscience-stricken, we carried the beloved prisoner to the meadow west of Dunbar where it was born, and, blessing its sweet heart, bravely set it free, and our exceeding great reward was to see it fly and sing in the sky.

In the winter, when there was but little doing in the fields, we organized running-matches. A dozen or so of us would start out on races that were simply tests of endurance, running on and on along a public road over the breezy hills like hounds, without stopping or getting tired. The only serious trouble we ever felt in these long races was an occasional stitch in our sides. One of the boys started the story that sucking raw eggs was a sure cure for the stitches. We had hens in our back yard, and on the next Saturday we managed to swallow a couple of eggs apiece, a disgusting job, but we would do almost anything to mend our speed, and as soon as we could get away after taking the cure we set out on a ten- or twenty-mile run to prove its worth. We thought nothing of running right ahead ten or a dozen miles before turning back; for we knew nothing about taking time by the sun, and none of us had a watch in those days. Indeed, we never cared about time until it began to get dark. Then we thought of home and the thrashing that awaited us. Late or early, the thrashing was sure, unless father happened to be away. If he was expected to return soon, mother made haste to get us to bed before his arrival. We escaped the thrashing the next morning, for father never felt like thrashing us in cold blood on the calm holy Sabbath. But no punishment, however sure and severe, was of any avail against the attraction of the fields and woods. It had other uses, developing memory, etc., but in keeping us at home it was of no use at all. Wildness was ever sounding in our ears, and Nature saw to it that besides school lessons and church lessons some of her own lessons should be learned, perhaps with a view to the time when we should be called to wander in wildness to our heart's content. Oh, the blessed enchantment of those Saturday runaways in the prime of the spring! How our young wondering eyes reveled in the sunny, breezy glory of the hills and the sky, every particle of us thrilling and tingling with the bees and glad birds and glad streams! Kings may be blessed; we were glorious, we were free — school cares and scoldings, heart thrashings and flesh thrashings alike, were forgotten in the fullness of Nature's glad wildness. These were my first excursions — the beginning of life-long wanderings.

(The Story of My Boyhood and Youth)

The New World

ON FEBRUARY 19, 1849, John Muir sailed from Glasgow for the New World with his father, his brother David and his sister Sarah. Although this was the year of the Forty-niners and the California gold rush, the elder Muir had not left home in search of wealth. He was a religious zealot who eventually joined and parted company with almost every sect in America. His reason for leaving Scotland was to seek more congenial religious surroundings. The rough passage of the Atlantic lasted more than six weeks. It was the fifth of April when the sailing vessel dropped anchor in New York harbor. Up the Hudson, through the Erie Canal and across the Great Lakes, the emigrants traveled by water to reach Milwaukee, the gateway to the "oak openings" region of central Wisconsin. In the fall of the year, after a home had been established on the Fox River northeast of Portage, the rest of the family crossed the Atlantic. It was forty-four years before John Muir saw Dunbar again. He visited it and renewed old friendships on a trip to Europe in 1893.

ONE NIGHT, when David and I were at grandfather's fireside solemnly learning our lessons as usual, my father came in with news, the most wonderful, most glorious, that wild boys ever heard. "Bairns," he said, "you needna learn your lessons the nicht, for we're gan to America the morn!" No more grammar, but boundless woods full of mysterious good things; trees full of sugar, growing in ground full of gold; hawks, eagles, pigeons, filling the sky; millions of birds' nests, and no gamekeepers to stop us in all the wild, happy land. We were utterly, blindly glorious. After father left the room, grandfather gave David and me a gold coin apiece for a keepsake, and looked very serious, for he was about to be deserted in his lonely old age. And when we in fullness of young joy spoke of what we were going to do, of the wonderful birds and their nests that we should find, the sugar and gold, etc., and promised to send him a big box full of that tree sugar packed in gold from the glorious paradise over the sea, poor lonely grandfather, about to be forsaken, looked with downcast eyes on the floor and said in a low, trembling, troubled voice, "Ah, poor laddies, poor laddies, you'll find something else ower the sea forbye gold and sugar, birds' nests and freedom fra lessons and schools. You'll find plenty hard, hard work." And so we did. But nothing he could say could cloud our joy or abate the fire of youthful, hopeful, fearless adventure. Nor could we in the midst of such measureless excitement see or feel the shadows and sorrows of his darkening old age. To my schoolmates, met that night on the street, I shouted the glorious news, "I'm gan to Amaraka the morn!" None could believe it. I said, "Weel, just you see if I am at the skule the morn!"

Next morning we went by rail to Glasgow and thence joyfully sailed away from beloved Scotland, flying to our fortunes on the wings of the winds, carefree as thistle seeds. We could not then know what we were leaving, what we were to encounter in the New World, nor what our gains were likely to be. We were too young and full of hope for fear or regret, but not too young to look forward with eager enthusiasm to the wonderful schoolless bookless American wilderness. Even the natural heart-pain of parting from Grandfather and Grandmother Gilrye, who loved us so well, and from mother and sisters and brother was quickly quenched in young joy. Father took with him only my sister Sarah (thirteen years of age), myself (eleven), and brother David (nine), leaving my eldest sister Margaret, and the three youngest of the family, Daniel, Mary, and Anna, with mother, to join us after a farm had been found in the wilderness and a comfortable house made to receive them.

In crossing the Atlantic before the days of steamships, or even the American clippers, the voyages made in old-fashioned sailing-vessels were very long. Ours was six weeks and three days. But because we had no lessons to get, that long voyage had not a dull moment for us boys. Father and sister Sarah, with most of the old folk, stayed below in rough weather, groaning in the miseries of seasickness, many of the passengers wishing they had never ventured in "the auld rockin' creel," as they called our bluff-bowed, wave-beating ship, and, when the weather was moderately calm, singing songs in the evenings — "The Youthful Sailor Frank and Bold," "Oh, why left I my hame, why did I cross the deep," etc. But no matter how much the old tub tossed about and battered the waves, we were on deck every day, not in the least seasick, watching the sailors at their rope-hauling and climbing work; joining in their songs, learning the names of the ropes and sails, and helping them as far as they would let us; playing games with other boys in calm weather when the deck was dry, and in stormy weather rejoicing in sympathy with the big curly-topped waves.

The captain occasionally called David and me into his cabin and asked us about our schools, handed us books to read, and seemed surprised to find that Scotch boys could read and pronounce English with perfect accent and knew so much Latin and French. In Scotch schools only pure English was taught, although not a word of English was spoken out of school. All through life, however well educated, the Scotch spoke Scotch among their own folk, except at times when unduly excited on the only two subjects on which Scotchmen get much excited, namely religion and politics. So long as the controversy went on with fairly level temper, only gude braid Scots was used, but if one became angry, as was likely to happen, then he immediately began speaking severely correct English, while his antagonist, drawing himself up, would say: "Weel, there's na use pursuing this subject ony further, for I see ye hae gotten to your English."

As we neared the shore of the great new land, with what eager wonder we watched the whales and dolphins and porpoises and sea-birds, and made the good-natured sailors teach us their names and tell us stories about them!

There were quite a large number of emigrants aboard, many
of them newly married couples, and the advantages of the different parts of the New World they expected to settle in were often
discussed. My father started with the intention of going to the
backwoods of Upper Canada. Before the end of the voyage,
however, he was persuaded that the States offered superior advantages, especially Wisconsin and Michigan, where the land was
said to be as good as in Canada and far more easily brought under
cultivation; for in Canada the woods were so close and heavy
that a man might wear out his life in getting a few acres cleared
of trees and stumps. So he changed his mind and concluded to
go to one of the Western States.

On our wavering westward way a grain-dealer in Buffalo told
father that most of the wheat he handled came from Wisconsin;
and this influential information finally determined my father's
choice. At Milwaukee a farmer who had come in from the
country near Fort Winnebago with a load of wheat agreed to
haul us and our formidable load of stuff to a little town called
Kingston for thirty dollars. On that hundred-mile journey, just
after the spring thaw, the roads over the prairies were heavy and
miry, causing no end of lamentation, for we often got stuck in
the mud, and the poor farmer sadly declared that never, never
again would he be tempted to try to haul such a cruel, heart-
breaking, wagon-breaking, horse-killing load, no, not for a
hundred dollars. In leaving Scotland, father, like many other
homeseekers, burdened himself with far too much luggage, as if
all America were still a wilderness in which little or nothing
could be bought. One of his big iron-bound boxes must have
weighed about four hundred pounds, for it contained an old-
fashioned beam-scales with a complete set of cast iron counter-
weights, two of them fifty-six pounds each, a twenty-eight, and
so on down to a single pound. Also a lot of iron wedges, carpenter's tools, and so forth, and at Buffalo, as if on the very edge
of the wilderness, he gladly added to his burden a big cast-iron
stove with pots and pans, provisions enough for a long siege, and
a scythe and cumbersome cradle for cutting wheat, all of which
he succeeded in landing in the primeval Wisconsin woods.

A land-agent at Kingston gave father a note to a farmer by the name of Alexander Gray, who lived on the border of the settled part of the country, knew the section-lines, and would probably help him to find a good place for a farm. So father went away to spy out the land, and in the mean time left us children in Kingston in a rented room. It took us less than an hour to get acquainted with some of the boys in the village; we challenged them to wrestle, run races, climb trees, etc., and in a day or two we felt at home, carefree and happy, notwithstanding our family was so widely divided. When father returned he told us that he had found fine land for a farm in sunny open woods on the side of a lake, and that a team of three yoke of oxen with a big wagon was coming to haul us to Mr. Gray's place.

We enjoyed the strange ten-mile ride through the woods very much, wondering how the great oxen could be so strong and wise and tame as to pull so heavy a load with no other harness than a chain and a crooked piece of wood on their necks, and how they could sway so obediently to right and left past roadside trees and stumps when the driver said *haw* and *gee*. At Mr. Gray's house, father again left us for a few days to build a shanty on the quarter-section he had selected four or five miles to the westward. In the mean while we enjoyed our freedom as usual, wandering in the fields and meadows, looking at the trees and flowers, snakes and birds and squirrels. With the help of the nearest neighbors the little shanty was built in less than a day after the rough Bur Oak logs for the walls and the White Oak boards for the floor and roof were got together.

To this charming hut, in the sunny woods, overlooking a flowery glacier meadow and a lake rimmed with white water-lilies, we were hauled by an ox-team across trackless carex swamps and low rolling hills sparsely dotted with round-headed Oaks. Just as we arrived at the shanty, before we had time to look at it or the scenery about it, David and I jumped down in a hurry off the load of household goods, for we had discovered a bluejay's nest, and in a minute or so we were up in the tree beside it, feasting our eyes on the beautiful green eggs and beautiful birds — our first memorable discovery. The handsome birds had not seen Scotch boys before and made a desperate screaming as if we were robbers like themselves; though we left the eggs untouched, feeling that we were already beginning to get rich, and wondering how many more nests we should find in the grand sunny woods. Then we ran along the brow of the hill that the shanty stood on, and down to the meadow, searching the trees and grass tufts and bushes, and soon discovered a bluebird's and a woodpecker's nest, and began an acquaintance with the frogs and snakes and turtles in the creeks and springs.

This sudden plash into pure wildness — baptism in Nature's warm heart — how utterly happy it made us! Nature streaming into us, wooingly teaching her wonderful glowing lessons, so unlike the dismal grammar ashes and cinders so long thrashed into us. Here without knowing it we still were at school; every wild lesson a love lesson, not whipped but charmed into us. Oh, that glorious Wisconsin wilderness! Everything new and pure in the very prime of the spring when Nature's pulses were beating highest and mysteriously keeping time with our own! Young hearts, young leaves, flowers, animals, the winds and the streams and the sparkling lake, all wildly, gladly rejoicing together!

The old Scotch fashion of whipping for every act of disobedience or of simple, playful forgetfulness was still kept up in the wilderness, and of course many of those whippings fell upon me. Most of them were outrageously severe, and utterly barren of fun. But here is one that was nearly all fun.

Father was busy hauling lumber for the frame house that was to be got ready for the arrival of my mother, sisters, and brother, left behind in Scotland. One morning, when he was ready to start for another load, his ox-whip was not to be found. He asked me if I knew anything about it. I told him I didn't know where it was, but Scotch conscience compelled me to confess that when I was playing with it I had tied it to Watch's tail, and that he ran away, dragging it through the grass, and came back without it. "It must have slipped off his tail," I said, and so I didn't know where it was. This honest, straightforward little story made father so angry that he exclaimed with heavy, foreboding emphasis: "The very deevil's in that boy!" David, who had been playing with me and was perhaps about as responsible for the loss of the whip as I was, said never a word, for he was always prudent enough to hold his tongue when the parental weather was stormy, and so escaped nearly all punishment. And, strange to say, this time I also escaped, all except a terrible scolding, though the thrashing weather seemed darker than ever. As if unwilling to let the sun see the shameful job, father took me into the cabin where the storm was to fall, and sent David to the woods for a switch. While he was out selecting the switch, father put in the spare time sketching my play-wickedness in awful colors, and of course referred again and again to the place prepared for bad boys. In the midst of this terrible word-storm, dreading most the impending thrashing, I whimpered that I was only playing because I couldn't help it; didn't know I was doing wrong; wouldn't do it again, and so forth. After this miserable dialogue was about exhausted, father became impatient at my brother for taking so long to find the switch; and so was I, for I wanted to have the thing over and done with. At last, in came David, a picture of open-hearted innocence, solemnly dragging a young Bur Oak sapling, and handed the end of it to father, saying it was the best switch he could find. It was an awfully heavy one, about two and a half inches thick at the butt and ten feet long, almost big enough for a fence-pole. There wasn't room enough in the cabin to swing it, and the moment I saw it I burst out laughing in the midst of my fears. But father failed to see the fun and was very angry at David, heaved the Bur Oak outside and passionately demanded his reason for fetching "sic a muckle rail like that instead o' a switch? Do ye ca' that a switch? I have a gude mind to thrash you instead o' John." David, with demure, downcast eyes, looked preternaturally righteous, but as usual prudently answered never a word.

It was a hard job in those days to bring up Scotch boys in the way they should go; and poor overworked father was determined to do it if enough of the right kind of switches could be found. But this time, as the sun was getting high, he hitched up old Tom and Jerry and made haste to the Kingston lumber-yard, leaving me unscathed and as innocently wicked as ever; for hardly had father got fairly out of sight among the Oaks and Hickories, ere all our troubles, hell-threatenings, and exhortations were forgotten in the fun we had lassoing a stubborn old sow and laboriously trying to teach her to go reasonably steady in rope harness. She was the first hog that father bought to stock the farm, and we boys regarded her as a very wonderful beast. In a few weeks she had a lot of pigs, and of all the queer, funny, animal children we had yet seen, none amused us more. They were so comic in size and shape, in their gait and gestures, their merry sham fights, and the false alarms they got up for the fun of scampering back to their mother and begging her in most persuasive little squeals to lie down and give them a drink.

After her darling short-snouted babies were about a month old, she took them out to the woods and gradually roamed farther and farther from the shanty in search of acorns and roots. One afternoon we heard a rifle-shot, a very noticeable thing, as we had no near neighbors, as yet. We thought it must have been fired by an Indian on the trail that followed the right bank of the Fox River between Portage and Packwaukee Lake and passed our shanty at a distance of about three quarters of a mile. Just a few minutes after that shot was heard, along came the poor mother rushing up to the shanty for protection, with her pigs, all out of breath and terror-stricken. One of them was missing, and we supposed of course that an Indian had shot it for food. Next day, I discovered a blood-puddle where the Indian trail crossed the outlet of our lake. One of father's hired men told us that the Indians thought nothing of levying this sort of blackmail whenever they were hungry. The solemn awe and fear in the eyes of that old mother and those little pigs I can never forget; it was as unmistakable and deadly a fear as I ever saw expressed by any human eye, and corroborates in no uncertain way the oneness of all of us.

(*The Story of My Boyhood and Youth*)

A Paradise of Birds

THE PASSENGER PIGEON became extinct the very year John Muir died. Of all the hordes that crossed the skies in his youth, but a single bird remained in 1914. Caged at the Cincinnati zoo, it died on September 1. On the instant of its passing, a species that had numbered uncounted millions hardly more than half a century before, disappeared from the earth. In innumerable other, though less dramatic, ways the wildlife of America suffered during the decades that elapsed between Muir's boyhood at boggy Fountain Lake Farm and the time he set his memories down on paper. Early in life, when his funds were slender, Muir tried unsuccessfully to buy a part of the Wisconsin homestead to be set aside untouched as a natural sanctuary to show future generations the plants and wildflowers familiar to the pioneers. Today one of the major goals of conservationists is the preserving of just such typical "specimen" habitat areas. Thus John Muir was a pioneer not only in the great conservation battles to save Yosemite and the Grand Canyon but also in the effort to preserve, in sanctuary form, small typical areas of natural beauty.

THE WISCONSIN OAK openings were a summer paradise for songbirds, and a fine place to get acquainted with them; for the trees stood wide apart, allowing one to see the happy home-seekers as they arrived in the spring, their mating, nest-building, the brooding and feeding of the young, and, after they were full-fledged and strong, to see all the families of the neighborhood gathering and getting ready to leave in the fall. Excepting the geese and ducks and pigeons nearly all our summer birds arrived singly or in small draggled flocks, but when frost and falling leaves brought their winter homes to mind they assembled in large flocks on dead or leafless trees by the side of a meadow or field, perhaps to get acquainted and talk the thing over. Some species held regular daily meetings for several weeks before finally setting forth on their long southern journeys. Strange to say, we never saw them start. Some morning we would find them gone. Doubtless they migrated in the night time. Comparatively few species remained all winter, the nuthatch, chickadee, owl, prairie chicken, quail, and a few stragglers from the main flocks of ducks, jays, hawks, and bluebirds. Only after the country was settled did either jays or bluebirds winter with us.

The brave, frost-defying chickadees and nuthatches stayed all the year wholly independent of farms and man's food and affairs.

With the first hints of spring came the brave little bluebirds, darling singers as blue as the best sky, and of course we all loved them. Their rich, crispy warbling is perfectly delightful, soothing and cheering, sweet and whisperingly low, Nature's fine love touches, every note going straight home into one's heart. And withal they are hardy and brave, fearless fighters in defense of home. When we boys approached their knot-hole nests, the bold little fellows kept scolding and diving at us and tried to strike us in the face, and oftentimes we were afraid they would prick our eyes. But the boldness of the little housekeepers only made us love them the more.

None of the bird people of Wisconsin welcomed us more heartily than the common robin. Far from showing alarm at the coming of settlers into their native woods, they reared their young around our gardens as if they liked us, and how heartily we admired the beauty and fine manners of these graceful birds and their loud cheery song of *Fear not, fear not, cheer up, cheer up*. It was easy to love them for they reminded us of the robin-redbreast of Scotland. Like the bluebirds they dared every danger in defense of home, and we often wondered that birds so gentle could be so bold and that sweet-voiced singers could so fiercely fight and scold.

Of all the great singers that sweeten Wisconsin one of the best known and best loved is the brown thrush or thrasher, strong and able without being familiar, and easily seen and heard. Rosy-purple evenings after thunder-showers are the favorite song-times, when the winds have died away and the steaming ground and the leaves and flowers fill the air with fragrance. Then the male makes haste to the topmost spray of an Oak tree and sings loud and clear with delightful enthusiasm until sundown, mostly I suppose for his mate sitting on the precious eggs in a brush heap. And how faithful and watchful and daring he is! Woe to the snake or squirrel that ventured to go nigh the nest! We often saw him diving on them, pecking them about the head and driving them away as bravely as the kingbird drives away hawks. Their rich and varied strains make the air fairly quiver. We boys often tried to interpret the wild ringing melody and put it into words.

After the arrival of the thrushes came the bobolinks, gushing, gurgling, inexhaustible fountains of song, pouring forth floods of sweet notes over the broad Fox River meadows in wonderful variety and volume, crowded and mixed beyond description, as they hovered on quivering wings above their hidden nests in the grass. It seemed marvelous to us that birds so moderate in size could hold so much of this wonderful song stuff. Each one of them poured forth music enough for a whole flock, singing as if its whole body, feathers and all, were made up of music, flowing, glowing, bubbling melody interpenetrated here and there with small scintillating prickles and spicules. We never became so intimately acquainted with the bobolinks as with the thrushes, for they lived far out on the broad Fox River meadows, while the thrushes sang on the tree-tops around every home. The bobolinks were among the first of our great singers to leave us in the fall, going apparently direct to the rice-fields of the Southern States, where they grew fat and were slaughtered in countless numbers for food. Sad fate for singers so purely divine.

One of the gayest of the singers is the red-wing blackbird. In the spring, when his scarlet epaulets shine brightest, and his little modest gray wife is sitting on the nest, built on rushes in a swamp, he sits on a near-by Oak and devotedly sings almost all day. His rich simple strain is *baumpalee, baumpalee,* or *bobalee* as interpreted by some. In summer, after nesting cares are over, they assemble in flocks of hundreds and thousands to feast on Indian corn when it is in the milk. Scattering over a field, each selects an ear, strips the husk down far enough to lay bare an inch or two of the end of it, enjoys an exhilarating feast, and after all are full they rise simultaneously with a quick birr of wings like an old-fashioned church congregation fluttering to their feet when the minister after giving out the hymn says, "Let the congregation arise and sing." Alighting on near-by trees, they sing with a hearty vengeance, bursting out without any puttering prelude in gloriously glad concert, hundreds or thousands of exulting voices with sweet gurgling *baumpalees* mingled with chippy vibrant and exploding globules of musical notes, making a most enthusiastic, indescribable joy-song, a combination unlike anything to be heard elsewhere in the bird kingdom; something like bagpipes, flutes, violins, pianos, and human-like voices all bursting and bubbling at once. Then suddenly some one of the joyful congregation shouts *Chirr! Chirr!* and all stop as if shot.

The sweet-voiced meadowlark with its placid, simple song of *peery-eery-ódical* was another favorite, and we soon learned to admire the Baltimore oriole and its wonderful hanging nests, and the scarlet tanager glowing like fire amid the green leaves.

But no singer of them all got farther into our hearts than the little speckle-breasted song sparrow, one of the first to arrive and begin nest-building and singing. The richness, sweetness, and pathos of this small darling's song as he sat on a low bush often brought tears to our eyes.

The little cheery, modest chickadee midget, loved by every innocent boy and girl, man and woman, and by many not altogether innocent, was one of the first of the birds to attract our attention, drawing nearer and nearer to us as the winter advanced, bravely singing his faint silvery, lisping tinkling notes ending with a bright *dee, dee, dee!* however frosty the weather.

The nuthatches, who also stayed all winter with us, were favorites with us boys. We loved to watch them as they traced the bark-furrows of the Oaks and Hickories head downward, deftly flicking off loose scales and splinters in search of insects, and braving the coldest weather as if their little sparks of life were as safely warm in winter as in summer, unquenchable by the severest frost. With the help of the chickadees they made a delightful stir in the solemn winter days, and when we were out chopping we never ceased to wonder how their slender naked toes could be kept warm when our own were so painfully frosted though clad in thick socks and boots. And we wondered and admired the more when we thought of the little midgets sleeping in knot-holes when the temperature was far below zero, sometimes thirty-five degrees below, and in the morning, after a minute breakfast of a few dozen insects and hoarfrost crystals, playing and chatting in cheery tones as if food, weather, and everything was according to their own warm hearts. Our Yankee told us that the name of this darling was Devil-downhead.

Their big neighbors the owls also made good winter music, singing out loud in wild, gallant strains bespeaking brave comfort, let the frost bite as it might. The solemn hooting of the species with the widest throat seemed to us the very wildest of all the winter sounds.

Prairie chickens came strolling in family flocks about the shanty, picking seeds and grasshoppers like domestic fowls, and they became still more abundant as wheat- and corn-fields were multiplied, but also wilder, of course, when every shotgun in the country was aimed at them. The booming of the males during the mating season was one of the loudest and strangest of the early spring sounds, being easily heard on calm mornings at a distance of a half or three fourths of a mile. As soon as the snow was off the ground, they assembled in flocks of a dozen or two on an open spot, usually on the side of a ploughed field, ruffled up their feathers, inflated the curious colored sacks on the sides of their necks, and strutted about with queer gestures something like turkey gobblers, uttering strange loud, rounded, drumming calls — *boom! boom! boom!* interrupted by choking sounds. My brother Daniel caught one while she was sitting on her nest in our corn-field. The young are just like domestic chicks, run with the mother as soon as hatched, and stay with her until autumn, feeding on the ground, never taking wing unless disturbed. In winter, when full-grown, they assemble in large flocks, fly about sundown to selected roosting-places on tall trees, and to feeding-places in the morning — unhusked corn-fields, if any are to be found in the neighborhood, or thickets of dwarf Birch and Willows, the buds of which furnish a considerable part of their food when snow covers the ground.

The wild rice-marshes along the Fox River and around Puca-way Lake were the summer homes of millions of ducks, and in the Indian summer, when the rice was ripe, they grew very fat. The magnificent mallards in particular afforded our Yankee neighbors royal feasts almost without price, for often as many as a half-dozen were killed at a shot, but we seldom were allowed a single hour for hunting and so got very few. The autumn duck season was a glad time for the Indians also, for they feasted and grew fat not only on the ducks but on the wild rice, large quantities of which they gathered as they glided through the midst of the generous crops in canoes, bending down handfuls over the sides, and beating out the grain with small paddles.

The warmth of the deep spring fountains of the creek in our meadow kept it open all the year, and a few pairs of wood ducks, the most beautiful, we thought, of all the ducks, wintered in it. I well remember the first specimen I ever saw. Father shot it in the creek during a snowstorm, brought it into the house, and called us around him saying: "Come, bairns, and admire the work of God displayed in this bonnie bird. Naebody but God could paint feathers like these. Juist look at the colors, hoo they shine, and hoo fine they overlap and blend thegether like the colors o' the rainbow." And we all agreed that never, never before had we seen so awfu' bonnie a bird. A pair nested every year in the hollow top of an Oak stump about fifteen feet high that stood on the side of the meadow, and we used to wonder how they got the fluffy young ones down from the nest and across the meadow to the lake when they were only helpless, featherless midgets; whether the mother carried them to the water on her back or in her mouth. I never saw the thing done or found anybody who had until this summer, when Mr. Holabird, a keen observer, told me that he once saw the mother carry them from the nest tree in her mouth, quickly coming and going to a near-by stream, and in a few minutes get them all together and proudly sail away.

Sometimes a flock of swans were seen passing over at a great height on their long journeys, and we admired their clear bugle notes, but they seldom visited any of the lakes in our neighborhood, so seldom that when they did it was talked of for years. One was shot by a blacksmith on a millpond with a long-range Sharps rifle, and many of the neighbors went far to see it.

The common gray goose, Canada honker, flying in regular harrow-shaped flocks, was one of the wildest and wariest of all the large birds that enlivened the spring and autumn. They seldom ventured to alight in our small lake, fearing, I suppose, that hunters might be concealed in the rushes, but on account of their fondness for the young leaves of winter wheat when they were a few inches high, they often alighted on our fields when passing on their way south, and occasionally even in our cornfields when a snowstorm was blowing and they were hungry and wing-weary, with nearly an inch of snow on their backs. In such times of distress we used to pity them, even while trying to get a shot at them. They were exceedingly cautious and circumspect; usually flew several times round the adjacent thickets and fences to make sure that no enemy was near before settling down, and one always stood on guard, relieved from time to time, while the flock was feeding. Therefore there was no chance to creep up on them unobserved; you had to be well hidden before the flock arrived. It was the ambition of boys to be able to shoot these wary birds. I never got but two, both of them at one so-called lucky shot. When I ran to pick them up, one of them flew away, but as the poor fellow was sorely wounded he didn't fly far. When I caught him after a short chase, he uttered a piercing cry of terror and despair, which the leader of the flock heard at a distance of about a hundred rods. They had flown off in frightened disorder, of course, but had got into the regular harrow-shaped order when the leader heard the cry, and I shall never forget how bravely he left his place at the head of the flock and hurried back screaming and struck at me in trying to save his companion. I dodged down and held my hands over my head, and thus escaped a blow of his elbows. Fortunately I had left my gun at the fence, and the life of this noble bird was spared after he had risked it in trying to save his wounded friend or neighbor or family relation. For so shy a bird boldly to attack a hunter showed wonderful sympathy and courage. This is one of my strangest hunting experiences. Never before had I regarded wild geese as dangerous, or capable of such noble self-sacrificing devotion.

The loud clear call of the handsome bobwhites was one of the pleasantest and most characteristic of our spring sounds, and we soon learned to imitate it so well that a bold cock often accepted our challenge and came flying to fight. The young run as soon as they are hatched and follow their parents until spring, roosting on the ground in a close bunch, heads out ready to scatter and fly. These fine birds were seldom seen when we first arrived in the wilderness, but when wheat-fields supplied abundance of food they multiplied very fast, although oftentimes sore pressed during hard winters when the snow reached a depth of two or three feet, covering their food, while the mercury fell to twenty or thirty degrees below zero. Occasionally, although shy on account of being persistently hunted, under pressure of extreme hunger in the very coldest weather when the snow was deepest they ventured into barnyards and even approached the doorsteps of houses, searching for any sort of scraps and crumbs, as if piteously begging for food. One of our neighbors saw a flock come creeping up through the snow, unable to fly, hardly able to walk, and while approaching the door several of them actually fell down and died; showing that birds, usually so vigorous and apparently independent of fortune, suffer and lose their lives in extreme weather like the rest of us, frozen to death like settlers caught in blizzards. None of our neighbors perished in storms, though many had feet, ears, and fingers frost-nipped or solidly frozen.

As soon as the lake ice melted, we heard the lonely cry of the loon, one of the wildest and most striking of all the wilderness sounds, a strange, sad, mournful, unearthly cry, half laughing, half wailing. Nevertheless the great northern diver, as our species is called, is a brave, hardy, beautiful bird, able to fly under water as well as above it, and to spear and capture the swiftest fishes for food. Those that haunted our lake were so wary none was shot for years, though every boy hunter in the neighborhood was ambitious to get one to prove his skill. On one of our bitter cold New Year holidays I was surprised to see a loon in the small open part of the lake at the mouth of the inlet that was kept from freezing by the warm spring water. I knew that it could not fly out of so small a place, for these heavy birds have to beat the water for half a mile or so before they can get fairly on the wing. Their narrow, fin-like wings are very small as compared with the weight of the body and are evidently made for flying through water as well as through the air, and it is by means of their swift flight through the water and the swiftness of the blow they strike with their long, spear-like bills that they are able to capture the fishes on which they feed. I ran down the meadow with the gun, got into my boat, and pursued that poor winter-bound straggler. Of course he dived again and again, but had to come up to breathe, and I at length got a quick shot at his head and slightly wounded or stunned him, caught him, and ran proudly back to the house with my prize. I carried him in my arms; he didn't struggle to get away or offer to strike me, and when I put him on the floor in front of the kitchen stove, he just rested quietly on his belly as noiseless and motionless as if he were a stuffed specimen on a shelf, held his neck erect, gave no sign of suffering from any wound, and though he was motionless, his small black eyes seemed to be ever keenly watchful. His formidable bill, very sharp, three or three and a half inches long, and shaped like a pickaxe, was held perfectly level. But the wonder was that he did not struggle or make the slightest movement. We had a tortoise-shell cat, an old Tom of great experience, who was so fond of lying under the stove in frosty weather that it was difficult even to poke him out with a broom; but when he saw and smelled that strange big fishy, black and white, speckledy bird, the like of which he had never before seen, he rushed wildly to the farther corner of the kitchen, looked back cautiously and suspiciously, and began to make a careful study of the handsome but dangerous-looking stranger. Becoming more and more curious and interested, he at length advanced a step or two for a nearer view and nearer smell; and as the wonderful bird kept absolutely motionless, he was encouraged to venture gradually nearer and nearer until within perhaps five or six feet of its breast. Then the wary loon, not liking Tom's looks in so near a view, which perhaps recalled to his mind the plundering minks and muskrats he had to fight when they approached his nest, prepared to defend himself by slowly, almost imperceptibly drawing back his long pickaxe bill, and without the slightest fuss or stir held it level and ready just over his tail. With that dangerous bill drawn so far back out of the way, Tom's confidence in the stranger's peaceful intentions seemed almost complete, and, thus encouraged, he at last ventured forward with wondering, questioning eyes and quivering nostrils until he was only eighteen or twenty inches from the loon's smooth white breast. When the beautiful bird, apparently as peaceful and inoffensive as a flower, saw that his hairy yellow enemy had arrived at the right distance, the loon, who evidently was a fine judge of the reach of his spear, shot it forward quick as a lightning-flash, in marvelous contrast to the wonderful slowness of the preparatory poising, backward motion. The aim was true to a hair-breadth. Tom was struck right in the centre of his forehead, between the eyes. I thought his skull was cracked. Perhaps it was. The sudden astonishment of that outraged cat, the virtuous indignation and wrath, terror, and pain, are far beyond description. His eyes and screams and desperate retreat told all that. When the blow was received, he made a noise that I never heard a cat make before or since; an awfully deep, condensed, screechy, explosive *Wuck!* as he bounced straight up in the air like a bucking bronco; and when he alighted after his spring, he rushed madly across the room and made frantic efforts to climb up the hard-finished plaster wall. Not satisfied to get the width of the kitchen away from his mysterious enemy, for the first time that cold winter he tried to get out of the house, anyhow, anywhere out of that loon-infested room. When he finally ventured to look back and saw that the barbarous bird was still there, tranquil and motionless in front of the stove, he regained command of some of his shattered senses and carefully commenced to examine his wound. Backed against the wall in the farthest corner, and keeping his eye on the outrageous bird, he tenderly touched and washed the sore spot, wetting his paw with his tongue, pausing now and then as his courage increased to glare and stare and growl at his enemy with looks and tones wonderfully human, as if saying: "You confounded fishy, unfair rascal! What did you do that for? What had I done to you? Faithless, legless, long-nosed wretch!" Intense experiences like the above bring out the humanity that is in all animals. One touch of nature, even a cat-and-loon touch, makes all the world kin.

It was a great memorable day when the first flock of passenger pigeons came to our farm, calling to mind the story we had read about them when we were at school in Scotland. Of all God's feathered people that sailed the Wisconsin sky, no other bird seemed to us so wonderful. The beautiful wanderers flew like the winds in flocks of millions from climate to climate in accord with the weather, finding their food — acorns, beechnuts, pine-nuts, cranberries, strawberries, huckleberries, juniper berries, hack-berries, buckwheat, rice, wheat, oats, corn — in fields and forests thousands of miles apart. I have seen flocks streaming south in the fall so large that they were flowing over from horizon to horizon in an almost continuous stream all day long, at the rate of forty or fifty miles an hour, like a mighty river in the sky, widening, contracting, descending like falls and cataracts, and rising suddenly here and there in huge ragged masses like high-plashing spray. How wonderful the distances they flew in a day — in a year — in a lifetime! They arrived in Wisconsin in the spring just after the sun had cleared away the snow, and alighted in the woods to feed on the fallen acorns that they had missed the previous autumn. A comparatively small flock swept thousands of acres perfectly clean of acorns in a few minutes, by moving straight ahead with a broad front. All got their share, for the rear constantly became the van by flying over the flock and alighting in front, the entire flock constantly changing from rear to front, revolving something like a wheel with a low buzzing wing roar that could be heard a long way off. In summer they feasted on wheat and oats and were easily approached as they rested on the trees along the sides of the field after a good full meal, displaying beautiful iridescent colors as they moved their necks backward and forward when we went very near them. Every shotgun was aimed at them and everybody feasted on pigeon pies, and not a few of the settlers feasted also on the beauty of the wonderful birds. The breast of the male is a fine rosy red, the lower part of the neck behind and along the sides changing from the red of the breast to gold, emerald-green, and rich crimson. The general color of the upper parts is grayish blue, the under parts white. The extreme length of the bird is about seventeen inches; the finely modeled slender tail about eight inches, and extent of wings twenty-four inches. The females are scarcely less beautiful. "Oh, what bonnie, bonnie birds!" we exclaimed over the first that fell into our hands. "Oh, what colors! Look at their breasts, bonnie as roses, and at their necks aglow wi' every color juist like the wonderfu' wood ducks. Oh, the bonnie, bonnie creatures, they beat a'! Where did they a' come fra, and where are they a' gan? It's awfu' like a sin to kill them!" To this some smug, practical old sinner would remark: "Aye, it's a peety, as ye say, to kill the bonnie things, but they were made to be killed, and sent for us to eat as the quails were sent to God's chosen people, the Israelites, when they were starving in the desert ayont the Red Sea." And I must confess that meat was never put up in neater, handsomer-painted packages.

In the New England and Canada woods beechnuts were their best and most abundant food, farther north, cranberries and huckleberries. After everything was cleaned up in the north and winter was coming on, they went south for rice, corn, acorns, haws, wild grapes, crab-apples, sparkle-berries, etc. They seemed to require more than half of the continent for feeding-grounds, moving from one table to another, field to field, forest to forest, finding something ripe and wholesome all the year round. In going south in the fine Indian-summer weather they flew high and followed one another, though the head of the flock might be hundreds of miles in advance. But against head winds they took advantage of the inequalities of the ground, flying comparatively low. All followed the leader's ups and downs over hill and dale though far out of sight, never hesitating at any turn of the way, vertical or horizontal, that the leaders had taken, though the largest flocks stretched across several States, and belts of different kinds of weather.

(The Story of My Boyhood and Youth)

The Well

BY THE TIME Muir was seventeen the thin soil of the original homestead had given out and the family moved to a half-section of virgin land six miles to the southeast. This place was given the name of Hickory Hill Farm. Here the labor of clearing land began all over again with John, the eldest son, bearing the brunt of the work. His father, soon after moving to the new place, gave up farming to devote himself to reading the Bible, sitting at a window where he could keep a commanding eye on his boys doing the heavy labor of the fields. Thomas H. Kearney, Jr., one of the scientists with the 1899 Harriman Expedition to Alaska, told me of hearing Muir tell how his father used to thrash him soundly every evening in his boyhood. Sometimes he would say, "I dinna ken any wrong ye have done this day but I'll thrash ye the same for I hae no doot ye deserve it!" As long as he lived Muir never forgot or forgave his father's harsh treatment during his youth.

In the fall of 1952, when I visited Hickory Hill Farm, where Muir so laboriously chipped his way downward through nearly ninety feet of hard sandstone to provide the homestead with a well, I found the same source of water still in use. A windmill rises above the well and heavy planks now cover the opening through which Muir was lowered on his near-fatal descent. After the passing of nearly a century, the underground springs still supply an abundant flow of cool pure water.

WE CALLED our second farm Hickory Hill, from its many fine Hickory trees and the long gentle slope leading up to it. Compared with Fountain Lake farm it lay high and dry. The land was better, but it had no living water, no spring or stream or meadow or lake. A well ninety feet deep had to be dug, all except the first ten feet or so in fine-grained sandstone. When the sandstone was struck,' my father, on the advice of a man who had worked in mines, tried to blast the rock; but from lack of skill the blasting went on very slowly, and father decided to have me do all the work with mason's chisels, a long, hard job, with a good deal of danger in it. I had to sit cramped in a space about three feet in diameter, and wearily chip, chip, with heavy hammer and chisels from early morning until dark, day after day, for weeks and months. In the morning, father and David lowered me in a wooden bucket by a windlass, hauled up what chips were left from the night before, then went away to the farm work and left me until noon, when they hoisted me out for dinner. After dinner I was promptly lowered again, the forenoon's accumulation of chips hoisted out of the way, and I was left until night.

One morning, after the dreary bore was about eighty feet deep, my life was all but lost in deadly choke-damp — carbonic acid gas that had settled at the bottom during the night. Instead of clearing away the chips as usual when I was lowered to the bottom, I swayed back and forth and began to sink under the poison. Father, alarmed that I did not make any noise, shouted, "What's keeping you so still?" to which he got no reply. Just as I was settling down against the side of the wall, I happened to catch a glimpse of a branch of a Bur Oak tree which leaned out over the mouth of the shaft. This suddenly awakened me, and to father's excited shouting I feebly murmured, "Take me out." But when he began to hoist he found I was not in the bucket and in wild alarm shouted, "Get in! Get in the bucket and hold on! Hold on!" Somehow I managed to get into the bucket, and that is all

I remembered until I was dragged out, violently gasping for breath.

One of our near neighbors, a stone mason and miner by the name of William Duncan, came to see me, and after hearing the particulars of the accident he solemnly said: "Weel, Johnnie, it's God's mercy that you're alive. Many a companion of mine have I seen dead with choke-damp, but none that I ever saw or heard of was so near to death in it as you were and escaped without help." Mr. Duncan taught father to throw water down the shaft to absorb the gas, and also to drop a bundle of brush or hay attached to a light rope, dropping it again and again to carry down pure air and stir up the poison. When, after a day or two, I had recovered from the shock, father lowered me again to my work, after taking the precaution to test the air with a candle and stir it up well with a brush-and-hay bundle. The weary hammer-and-chisel-chipping went on as before, only more slowly, until ninety feet down, when at last I struck a fine, hearty gush of water. Constant dropping wears away stone. So does constant chipping, while at the same time wearing away the chipper. Father never spent an hour in that well. He trusted me to sink it straight and plumb, and I did, and built a fine covered top over it, and swung two iron-bound buckets in it from which we all drank for many a day.

(The Story of My Boyhood and Youth)

Knowledge and Inventions

UNTIL LATE in his twenties, John Muir was torn between his love of inventing and his love of the out-of-doors. His skill with his hands seems to have been inherited from his father who, as a small boy in Scotland, had made himself a violin when he had no money to buy one. Muir's inventions on the farm, whittled from scraps of wood and assembled with various odds and ends, often ran to the extravagant but many had real practical value. His self-setting rotary saw, run by the waterpower of a dammed-up brook, was unlike any other saw in the region. At the time he left the farm, the year after he was twenty-one, he intended to seek work in a machine shop where he could make his living as a professional inventor.

I REMEMBER as a great and sudden discovery that the poetry of the Bible, Shakespeare, and Milton was a source of inspiring, exhilarating, uplifting pleasure; and I became anxious to know all the poets, and saved up small sums to buy as many of their books as possible. Within three or four years I was the proud possessor of parts of Shakespeare's, Milton's, Cowper's, Henry Kirke White's, Campbell's, and Akenside's works, and quite a number of others seldom read nowadays. I think it was in my fifteenth year that I began to relish good literature with enthusiasm, and smack my lips over favorite lines, but there was desperately little time for reading, even in the winter evenings — only a few stolen minutes now and then. Father's strict rule was, straight to bed immediately after family worship, which in winter was usually over by eight o'clock. I was in the habit of lingering in the kitchen with a book and candle after the rest of the family had retired, and considered myself fortunate if I got five minutes' reading before father noticed the light and ordered me to bed; an order that of course I immediately obeyed. But night after night I tried to steal minutes in the same lingering way, and how keenly precious those minutes were, few nowadays can know. Father failed perhaps two or three times in a whole winter to notice my light for nearly ten minutes, magnificent golden blocks of time, long to be remembered like holidays or geological periods. One evening when I was reading Church history father was particularly irritable, and called out with hope-killing emphasis, *"John, go to bed!* Must I give you a separate order every night to get you to go to bed? Now, I will have no irregularity in the family; you *must* go, when the rest go, and without my having to tell you." Then, as an afterthought, as if judging that his words and tone of voice were too severe for so pardonable an offense as reading a religious book he unwarily added: "If you *will* read, get up in the morning and read. You may get up in the morning as early as you like."

That night I went to bed wishing with all my heart and soul that somebody or something might call me out of sleep to avail myself of this wonderful indulgence; and next morning to my joyful surprise I awoke before father called me. A boy sleeps soundly after working all day in the snowy woods, but that frosty morning I sprang out of bed as if called by a trumpet blast, rushed downstairs, scarce feeling my chilblains, enormously eager to see how much time I had won; and when I held up my candle to a little clock that stood on a bracket in the kitchen I found that it was only one o'clock. I had gained five hours, almost half a day! "Five hours to myself!" I said, "five huge, solid hours!" I can hardly think of any other event in my life, any discovery I ever made that gave birth to joy so transportingly glorious as the possession of these five frosty hours.

In the glad, tumultuous excitement of so much suddenly acquired time-wealth, I hardly knew what to do with it. I first thought of going on with my reading, but the zero weather would make a fire necessary, and it occurred to me that father might object to the cost of firewood that took time to chop. Therefore, I prudently decided to go down cellar, and begin work on a model of a self-setting sawmill I had invented. Next morning I managed to get up at the same gloriously early hour, and though the temperature of the cellar was a little below the freezing point, and my light was only a tallow candle the mill work went joyfully on. There were a few tools in a corner of the cellar — a vise, files, a hammer, chisels, etc., that father had brought from Scotland, but no saw excepting a coarse crooked one that was unfit for sawing dry Hickory or Oak. So I made a fine-tooth saw suitable for my work out of a strip of steel that had formed part of an old-fashioned corset, that cut the hardest wood smoothly. I also made my own bradawls, punches, and a pair of compasses, out of wire and old files.

My workshop was immediately under father's bed, and the filing and tapping in making cogwheels, journals, cams, etc., must, no doubt, have annoyed him, but with the permission he had granted in his mind, and doubtless hoping that I would soon tire of getting up at one o'clock, he impatiently waited about two weeks before saying a word. I did not vary more than five minutes from one o'clock all winter, nor did I feel any bad effects whatever, nor did I think at all about the subject as to whether so little sleep might be in any way injurious; it was a grand triumph of will-power over cold and common comfort and work-weariness in abruptly cutting down my ten hours' allowance of sleep to five. I simply felt that I was rich beyond anything I could have dreamed of or hoped for. I was far more than happy. Like Tam o' Shanter I was glorious, "O'er a' the ills o' life victorious."

Father, as was customary in Scotland, gave thanks and asked a blessing before meals, not merely as a matter of form and decent Christian manners, for he regarded food as a gift derived directly from the hands of the Father in Heaven. Therefore every meal to him was a sacrament requiring conduct and attitude of mind not unlike that befitting the Lord's Supper. No idle word was allowed to be spoken at our table, much less any laughing or fun or story-telling. When we were at the breakfast-table, about two weeks after the great golden time-discovery, father cleared his throat preliminary, as we all knew, to saying something considered important. I feared that it was to be on the subject of my early rising, and dreaded the withdrawal of the permission he had granted on account of the noise I made, but still hoping that, as he had given his word that I might get up as early as I wished, he would as a Scotchman stand to it, even though it was given in an unguarded moment and taken in a sense unreasonably far-reaching. The solemn sacramental silence was broken by the dreaded question: —

"John, what time is it when you get up in the morning?"

"About one o'clock," I replied in a low, meek, guilty tone of voice.

"And what kind of a time is that, getting up in the middle of the night and disturbing the whole family?"

I simply reminded him of the permission he had freely granted me to get up as early as I wished.

"I *know* it," he said, in an almost agonized tone of voice, "I *know* I gave you that miserable permission, but I never imagined that you would get up in the middle of the night."

To this I cautiously made no reply, but continued to listen for the heavenly one-o'clock call, and it never failed.

After completing my self-setting sawmill I dammed one of the streams in the meadow and put the mill in operation. This invention was speedily followed by a lot of others — water-wheels, curious doorlocks and latches, thermometers, hygrometers, pyrometers, clocks, a barometer, an automatic contrivance for feeding the horses at any required hour, a lamp-lighter and fire-lighter, an early-or-late-rising machine, and so forth.

After the sawmill was proved and discharged from my mind, I happened to think it would be a fine thing to make a timekeeper which would tell the day of the week and the day of the month, as well as strike like a common clock and point out the hours; also to have an attachment whereby it could be connected with a bedstead to set me on my feet at any hour in the morning: also to start fires, light lamps, etc. I had learned the time laws of the pendulum from a book, but with this exception I knew nothing of time-keepers, for I had never seen the inside of any sort of clock or watch. After long brooding, the novel clock was at length completed in my mind, and was tried and found to be durable and to work well and look well before I had begun to build it in wood. I carried small parts of it in my pocket to whittle at when I was out at work on the farm, using every spare or stolen moment within reach without father's knowing anything about it. In the middle of summer, when harvesting was in progress, the novel time-machine was nearly completed. It was hidden upstairs in a spare bedroom where some tools were kept. I did the making and mending on the farm, but one day at noon, when I happened to be away, father went upstairs for a hammer or something and discovered the mysterious machine back of the bedstead. My sister Margaret saw him on his knees examining it, and at the first opportunity whispered in my ear, "John, fayther saw that thing you're making upstairs." None of the family knew what I was doing, but they knew very well that all such work was frowned on by father, and kindly warned me of any danger that threatened my plans. The fine invention seemed doomed to destruction before its time-ticking commenced, though I thought it handsome, had so long carried it in my mind, and like the nest of Burns's wee mousie it had cost me mony a weary whittling nibble. When we were at dinner several days after the sad discovery, father began to clear his throat to speak, and I feared the doom of martyrdom was about to be pronounced on my grand clock.

"John," he inquired, "what is that thing you are making upstairs?"

I replied in desperation that I didn't know what to call it.

"What! You mean to say you don't know what you are trying to do?"

"Oh, yes," I said, "I know very well what I am doing."

"What, then, is the thing for?"

"It's for a lot of things," I replied, "but getting people up early in the morning is one of the main things it is intended for; therefore it might perhaps be called an early-rising machine."

Getting up so extravagantly early all the last memorable winter to make a machine for getting up perhaps still earlier seemed so ridiculous that he very nearly laughed. But after controlling himself and getting command of a sufficiently solemn face and voice he said severely, "Do you not think it is very wrong to waste your time on such nonsense?"

"No," I said meekly, "I don't think I'm doing any wrong."

"Well," he replied, "I assure you I do; and if you were only half as zealous in the study of religion as you are in contriving and whittling these useless, nonsensical things, it would be infinitely better for you. I want you to be like Paul, who said that he desired to know nothing among men but Christ and Him crucified."

To this I made no reply, gloomily believing my fine machine was to be burned, but still taking what comfort I could in realizing that anyhow I had enjoyed inventing and making it.

After a few days, finding that nothing more was to be said, and that father after all had not had the heart to destroy it, all necessity for secrecy being ended, I finished it in the half-hours that we had at noon and set it in the parlor between two chairs, hung moraine boulders that had come from the direction of Lake Superior on it for weights, and set it running. We were then hauling grain into the barn. Father at this period devoted himself entirely to the Bible and did no farm work whatever. The clock had a good loud tick, and when he heard it strike, one of my sisters told me that he left his study, went to the parlor, got down on his knees and carefully examined the machinery, which was all in plain sight, not being enclosed in a case. This he did repeatedly, and evidently seemed a little proud of my ability to invent and whittle such a thing, though careful to give no encouragement for anything more of the kind in future.

But somehow it seemed impossible to stop. Inventing and whittling faster than ever, I made another Hickory clock, shaped like a scythe to symbolize the scythe of Father Time. The pendulum is a bunch of arrows symbolizing the flight of time. It hangs on a leafless mossy Oak snag showing the effect of time, and on the snath is written, "All flesh is grass." This, especially the inscription, rather pleased father, and, of course, mother and all my sisters and brothers admired it. Like the first it indicates the days of the week and month, starts fires and beds at any given hour and minute, and, though made more than fifty years ago, is still a good timekeeper.

My mind still running on clocks, I invented a big one like a town clock with four dials, with the time-figures so large they could be read by all our immediate neighbors as well as ourselves when at work in the fields, and on the side next the house the days of the week and month were indicated. It was to be placed on the peak of the barn roof. But just as it was all but finished, father stopped me, saying that it would bring too many people around the barn. I then asked permission to put it on the top of a Black Oak tree near the house. Studying the larger main branches, I thought I could secure a sufficiently rigid foundation for it, while the trimmed sprays and leaves would conceal the angles of the cabin required to shelter the works from the weather, and the two-second pendulum, fourteen feet long, could be snugly encased on the side of the trunk. Nothing about the grand, useful time-keeper, I argued, would disfigure the tree, for it would look something like a big hawk's nest. "But that," he objected, "would draw still bigger bothersome trampling crowds about the place, for who ever heard of anything so queer as a big clock on the top of a tree?" So I had to lay aside its big wheels and cams and rest content with the pleasure of inventing it, and looking at it in my mind and listening to the deep solemn throbbing of its long two-second pendulum with its two old axes back to back for the bob.

One of my inventions was a large thermometer made of an iron rod, about three feet long and five eighths of an inch in diameter, that had formed part of a wagon-box. The expansion and con-traction of this rod was multiplied by a series of levers made of strips of hoop iron. The pressure of the rod against the levers was kept constant by a small counterweight, so that the slightest change in the length of the rod was instantly shown on a dial about three feet wide multiplied about thirty-two thousand times. The zero-point was gained by packing the rod in wet snow. The scale was so large that the big black hand on the white-painted dial could be seen distinctly and the temperature read while we were ploughing in the field below the house. The extremes of heat and cold caused the hand to make several revolutions. The number of these revolutions was indicated on a small dial marked on the larger one. This thermometer was fastened on the side of the house, and was so sensitive that when any one approached it within four or five feet the heat radiated from the observer's body caused the hand of the dial to move so fast that the motion was plainly visible, and when he stepped back, the hand moved slowly back to its normal position. It was regarded as a great wonder by the neighbors and even by my own all-Bible father.

Boys are fond of the books of travelers, and I remember that one day, after I had been reading Mungo Park's travels in Africa, mother said: "Weel, John, maybe you will travel like Park and Humboldt some day." Father overheard her and cried out in solemn deprecation, "Oh, Anne! dinna put sic notions in the laddie's heed." But at this time there was precious little need of such prayers. My brothers left the farm when they came of age, but I stayed a year longer, loath to leave home. Mother hoped I might be a minister some day; my sisters that I would be a great inventor. I often thought I should like to be a physician, but I saw no way of making money and getting the necessary education, excepting as an inventor. So, as a beginning, I decided to try to get into a big shop or factory and live a while among machines. But I was naturally extremely shy and had been taught to have a poor opinion of myself, as of no account, though all our neighbors encouragingly called me a genius, sure to rise in the world. When I was talking over plans one day with a friendly neighbor, he said: "Now, John, if you wish to get into a machine-shop, just take some of your inventions to the State Fair, and you may be sure that as soon as they are seen they will open the door of any shop in the country for you. You will be welcomed everywhere." And when I doubtingly asked if people would care to look at things made of wood, he said, "Made of wood! Made of wood! What does it matter what they're made of when they are so out-

and-out original. There's nothing else like them in the world. That is what will attract attention, and besides they're mighty handsome things anyway to come from the backwoods." So I was encouraged to leave home and go at his direction to the State Fair when it was being held in Madison.

(The Story of My Boyhood and Youth)

The World and the University

ABRAHAM LINCOLN *had been nominated for the presidency and the Civil War was drawing near when, in September 1860, John Muir broke home ties and started out into the world. He carried his whittled-out inventions and in his pocket was all the money he had, about fifteen dollars. At the University of Wisconsin he sustained himself on such cheap foods as graham mush, baked potatoes and bread and molasses. So frugally did he manage that often his expenses were only fifty cents a week. Once during this period his father sent him ten dollars with a note admonishing him to be temperate and not to forget the poor destitute heathen. With his rough homemade clothes and untrimmed beard, he no doubt seemed an odd genius in university days. A fellow student once told him, "If I had a beard like yours I'd set fire to it!" The celebrated desk that Muir whittled from bits of wood and that allowed him fifteen minutes of study before it automatically pushed a new book before him, is still on exhibit at the museum of the Wisconsin State Historical Society. When I examined it nearly a century after it was made, I found the pencil marks, with which Muir drew the rough outline of the parts, still visible on the wood. At the University Muir took the studies he was most interested in and did not receive a degree. Thirty-four years after he left, in 1897, Wisconsin awarded him an honorary LL.D. degree. Other honorary degrees were bestowed upon him by Harvard, Yale and the University of California.*

WHEN I told father that I was about to leave home, and inquired whether, if I should happen to be in need of money, he would send me a little, he said, "No; depend entirely on yourself." Good advice, I suppose, but surely needlessly severe for a bashful, home-loving boy who had worked so hard. I had the gold sovereign that my grandfather had given me when I left Scotland, and a few dollars, perhaps ten, that I had made by raising a few bushels of grain on a little patch of sandy abandoned ground. So when I left home to try the world I had only about fifteen dollars in my pocket.

Strange to say, father carefully taught us to consider ourselves very poor worms of the dust, conceived in sin, etc., and devoutly believed that quenching every spark of pride and self-confidence was a sacred duty, without realizing that in so doing he might at the same time be quenching everything else. Praise he considered most venomous, and tried to assure me that when I was fairly out in the wicked world making my own way I would soon learn that although I might have thought him a hard taskmaster at times, strangers were far harder. On the contrary, I found no lack of kindness and sympathy. All the baggage I carried was a package made up of the two clocks and a small thermometer made of a piece of old washboard, all three tied together, with no covering or case of any sort, the whole looking like one very complicated machine.

The aching parting from mother and my sisters was, of course, hard to bear. Father let David drive me down to Pardeeville, a place I had never before seen, though it was only nine miles south of the Hickory Hill home. When we arrived at the village tavern, it seemed deserted. Not a single person was in sight. I set my clock baggage on the rickety platform. David said good-by and started for home, leaving me alone in the world. The grinding noise made by the wagon in turning short brought out the landlord, and the first thing that caught his eye was my strange bundle. Then he looked at me and said, "Hello, young man, what's this?"

"Machines," I said, "for keeping time and getting up in the morning, and so forth."

"Well! Well! That's a mighty queer get-up. You must be a Down-East Yankee. Where did you get the pattern for such a thing?"

"In my head," I said.

Some one down the street happened to notice the landlord looking intently at something and came up to see what it was. Three or four people in that little village formed an attractive crowd, and in fifteen or twenty minutes the greater part of the population of Pardeeville stood gazing in a circle around my strange Hickory belongings. I kept outside of the circle to avoid being seen, and had the advantage of hearing the remarks without being embarrassed. Almost every one as he came up would say, "What's that? What's it for? Who made it?" The landlord would answer them all alike, "Why, a young man that lives out in the country somewhere made it, and he says it's a thing for keeping time, getting up in the morning, and something that I didn't understand. I don't know what he meant." "Oh, no!" one of the crowd would say, "that can't be. It's for something else — something mysterious. Mark my words, you'll see all about it in the newspapers some of these days." A curious little fellow came running up the street, joined the crowd, stood on tiptoe to get sight of the wonder, quickly made up his mind, and shouted in crisp, confident, cock-crowing style, "I know what that contraption's for. It's a machine for taking the bones out of fish."

This was in the time of the great popular phrenology craze, when the fences and barns along the roads throughout the country were plastered with big skull-bump posters, headed, "Know Thyself," and advising everybody to attend schoolhouse lectures to have their heads explained and be told what they were good for and whom they ought to marry. My mechanical bundle seemed to bring a good deal of this phrenology to mind, for many of the onlookers would say, "I wish I could see that boy's head — he must have a tremendous bump of invention." Others complimented me by saying, "I wish I had that fellow's head. I'd rather have it than the best farm in the State."

I stayed overnight at this little tavern, waiting for a train. In the morning I went to the station, and set my bundle on the platform. Along came the thundering train, a glorious sight, the first train I had ever waited for. When the conductor saw my queer baggage, he cried, "Hello! What have we here?"

"Inventions for keeping time, early rising, and so forth. May I take them into the car with me?"

"You can take them where you like," he replied, "but you had better give them to the baggage-master. If you take them into the car they will draw a crowd and might get broken."

So I gave them to the baggage-master and made haste to ask the conductor whether I might ride on the engine. He good-naturedly said: "Yes, it's the right place for you. Run ahead, and tell the engineer what I say." But the engineer bluntly refused to let me on, saying: "It don't matter what the conductor told you. *I* say you can't ride on my engine."

By this time the conductor, standing ready to start his train, was watching to see what luck I had, and when he saw me returning came ahead to meet me.

"The engineer won't let me on," I reported.

"Won't he?" said the kind conductor. "Oh! I guess he will. You come down with me." And so he actually took the time and patience to walk the length of that long train to get me on to the engine.

"Charlie," said he, addressing the engineer, "don't you ever take a passenger?"

"Very seldom," he replied.

"Anyhow, I wish you would take this young man on. He has the strangest machines in the baggage-car I ever saw in my life. I believe he could make a locomotive. He wants to see the engine running. Let him on." Then in a low whisper he told me to jump on, which I did gladly, the engineer offering neither encouragement nor objection.

As soon as the train was started, the engineer asked what the "strange thing" the conductor spoke of really was.

"Only inventions for keeping time, getting folk up in the morning, and so forth," I hastily replied, and before he could ask any more questions I asked permission to go outside of the cab to see the machinery. This he kindly granted, adding, "Be careful not to fall off, and when you hear me whistling for a station you come back, because if it is reported against me to the superintendent that I allow boys to run all over my engine I might lose my job."

Assuring him that I would come back promptly, I went out and walked along the foot-board on the side of the boiler, watching the magnificent machine rushing through the landscapes as if glorying in its strength like a living creature. While seated on the cow-catcher platform, I seemed to be fairly flying, and the wonderful display of power and motion was enchanting. This was the first time I had ever been on a train, much less a locomotive, since I had left Scotland. When I got to Madison, I thanked the kind conductor and engineer for my glorious ride, inquired the way to the Fair, shouldered my inventions, and walked to the Fair Ground.

When I applied for an admission ticket at a window by the gate I told the agent that I had something to exhibit.

"What is it?" he inquired.

"Well, here it is. Look at it."

When he craned his neck through the window and got a glimpse of my bundle, he cried excitedly, "Oh! *you* don't need a ticket — come right in."

When I inquired of the agent where such things as mine should be exhibited, he said, "You see that building up on the hill with a big flag on it? That's the Fine Arts Hall, and it's just the place for your wonderful invention."

So I went up to the Fine Arts Hall and looked in, wondering if they would allow wooden things in so fine a place.

I was met at the door by a dignified gentleman, who greeted me kindly and said, "Young man, what have we got here?"

"Two clocks and a thermometer," I replied.

"Did you make these? They look wonderfully beautiful and

novel and must, I think, prove the most interesting feature of the fair."

"Where shall I place them?" I inquired.

"Just look around, young man, and choose the place you like best, whether it is occupied or not. You can have your pick of all the building, and a carpenter to make the necessary shelving and assist you every way possible!"

So I quickly had a shelf made large enough for all of them, went out on the hill and picked up some glacial boulders of the right size for weights, and in fifteen or twenty minutes the clocks were running. They seemed to attract more attention than anything else in the hall. I got lots of praise from the crowd and the newspaper-reporters. The local press reports were copied into the Eastern papers. It was considered wonderful that a boy on a farm had been able to invent and make such things, and almost every spectator foretold good fortune. But I had been so lectured by my father above all things to avoid praise that I was afraid to read those kind newspaper notices, and never clipped out or preserved any of them, just glanced at them and turned away my eyes from beholding vanity. They gave me a prize of ten or fifteen dollars and a diploma for wonderful things not down in the list of exhibits.

Many years later, after I had written articles and books, I received a letter from the gentleman who had charge of the Fine Arts Hall. He proved to be the Professor of English Literature in the University of Wisconsin at this Fair time, and long afterward he sent me clippings of reports of his lectures. He had a lecture on me, discussing style, etcetera, and telling how well he remembered my arrival at the Hall in my shirt-sleeves with those mechanical wonders on my shoulder, and so forth, and so forth. These inventions, though of little importance, opened all doors for me and made marks that have lasted many years, simply, I suppose, because they were original and promising.

I was looking around in the mean time to find out where I should go to seek my fortune. An inventor at the Fair, by the name of Wiard, was exhibiting an iceboat he had invented to run on the upper Mississippi from Prairie du Chien to St. Paul during the winter months, explaining how useful it would be thus to make a highway of the river while it was closed to ordinary navigation by ice. After he saw my inventions he offered me a place in his foundry and machine-shop in Prairie du Chien and promised to assist me all he could. So I made up my mind to accept his offer and rode with him to Prairie du Chien in his ice-boat, which was mounted on a flat car. I soon found, however, that he was seldom at home and that I was not likely to learn much at his small shop. I found a place where I could work for my board and devote my spare hours to mechanical drawing, geometry, and physics, making but little headway, however, although the Pelton family, for whom I worked, were very kind. I made up my mind after a few months' stay in Prairie du Chien to return to Madison, hoping that in some way I might be able to gain an education.

At Madison I raised a few dollars by making and selling a few of those bedsteads that set the sleepers on their feet in the morning — inserting in the footboard the works of an ordinary clock that could be bought for a dollar. I also made a few dollars addressing circulars in an insurance office, while at the same time I was paying my board by taking care of a pair of horses and going errands. This is of no great interest except that I was thus winning my bread while hoping that something would turn up that might enable me to make money enough to enter the State University. This was my ambition, and it never wavered no matter what I was doing. No University, it seemed to me, could be more admirably situated, and as I sauntered about it, charmed with its fine lawns and trees and beautiful lakes, and saw the students going and coming with their books, and occasionally practising with a theodolite in measuring distances, I thought that if I could only join them it would be the greatest joy of life. I was desperately hungry and thirsty for knowledge and willing to endure anything to get it.

One day I chanced to meet a student who had noticed my inventions at the Fair and now recognized me. And when I said, "You are fortunate fellows to be allowed to study in this beautiful place. I wish I could join you," "Well, why don't you?" he asked. "I haven't money enough," I said. "Oh, as to money," he reassuringly explained, "very little is required. I presume you're able to enter the Freshman class, and you can board yourself as quite a number of us do at a cost of about a dollar a week. The baker and milkman come every day. You can live on bread and milk." Well, I thought, maybe I have money enough for at least one beginning term. Anyhow I couldn't help trying.

With fear and trembling, overladen with ignorance, I called on Professor Stirling, the Dean of the Faculty, who was then Acting President, presented my case, and told him how far I had got on with my studies at home, and that I hadn't been to school since leaving Scotland at the age of eleven years, excepting one short term of a couple of months at a district school, because I could not be spared from the farm work. After hearing my story, the kind professor welcomed me to the glorious University — next, it seemed to me, to the Kingdom of Heaven. After a few weeks in the preparatory department I entered the Freshman class. In Latin I found that one of the books in use I had already studied in Scotland. So, after an interruption of a dozen years, I began my Latin over again where I had left off; and, strange to say, most of it came back to me, especially the grammar which I had committed to memory at the Dunbar Grammar School.

During the four years that I was in the University, I earned enough in the harvest-fields during the long summer vacations to carry me through the balance of each year, working very hard, cutting with a cradle four acres of wheat a day, and helping to put it in the shock. But, having to buy books and paying, I think, thirty-two dollars a year for instruction, and occasionally buying acids and retorts, glass tubing, bell-glasses, flasks, etc., I had to cut down expenses for board now and then to half a dollar a week.

One winter I taught school ten miles south of Madison, earning much-needed money at the rate of twenty dollars a month, "boarding round," and keeping up my University work by studying at night. As I was not then well enough off to own a watch, I used one of my Hickory clocks, not only for keeping time, but for starting the school fire in the cold mornings, and regulating class-times. I carried it out on my shoulder to the old log school-house, and set it to work on a little shelf nailed to one of the knotty, bulging logs. The winter was very cold, and I had to go to the schoolhouse and start the fire about eight o'clock to warm it before the arrival of the scholars. This was a rather trying job, and one that my clock might easily be made to do. Therefore, after supper one evening I told the head of the family with whom I was boarding that if he would give me a candle I would go back to the schoolhouse and make arrangements for lighting the fire at eight o'clock, without my having to be present until time to open the school at nine. He said, "Oh! young man, you have some curious things in the school-room, but I don't think you can do that." I said, "Oh, yes! It's easy," and in hardly more than an hour the simple job was completed. I had only to place a teaspoon-ful of powdered chlorate of potash and sugar on the stove-hearth near a few shavings and kindling, and at the required time make the clock, through a simple arrangement, touch the inflammable mixture with a drop of sulphuric acid. Every evening after school was dismissed, I shoveled out what was left of the fire into the snow, put in a little kindling, filled up the big box-stove with heavy Oak wood, placed the lighting arrangement on the hearth, and set the clock to drop the acid at the hour of eight; all this requiring only a few minutes.

The first morning after I had made this simple arrangement I invited the doubting farmer to watch the old squat schoolhouse from a window that overlooked it, to see if a good smoke did not rise from the stovepipe. Sure enough, on the minute, he saw a tall column curling gracefully up through the frosty air, but instead of congratulating me on my success he solemnly shook his head and said in a hollow, lugubrious voice, "Young man, you will be setting fire to the schoolhouse." All winter long that faithful clock fire never failed, and by the time I got to the schoolhouse the stove was usually red-hot.

At the beginning of the long summer vacations I returned to the Hickory Hill farm to earn the means in the harvest-fields to continue my University course, walking all the way to save rail-road fares. And although I cradled four acres of wheat a day, I made the long, hard, sweaty day's work still longer and harder by keeping up my study of plants. At the noon hour I collected a large handful, put them in water to keep them fresh, and after supper got to work on them and sat up till after midnight, analyzing and classifying, thus leaving only four hours for sleep; and by the end of the first year, after taking up botany, I knew the principal flowering plants of the region.

I received my first lesson in botany from a student by the name of Griswold, who is now County Judge of the County of Waukesha, Wisconsin. In the University he was often laughed at on account of his anxiety to instruct others, and his frequently saying with fine emphasis, "Imparting instruction is my greatest enjoyment." One memorable day in June, when I was standing on the stone steps of the north dormitory, Mr. Griswold joined me and at once began to teach. He reached up, plucked a flower from an overspreading branch of a Locust tree, and, handing it to me, said, "Muir, do you know what family this tree belongs to?"

"No," I said, "I don't know anything about botany."

"Well, no matter," said he, "what is it like?"

"It's like a pea flower," I replied.

"That's right. You're right," he said, "it belongs to the Pea Family."

"But how can that be," I objected, "when the pea is a weak, clinging, straggling herb, and the Locust a big, thorny hardwood tree?"

"Yes, that is true," he replied, "as to the difference in size, but it is also true that in all their essential characters they are alike, and therefore they must belong to one and the same family. Just look at the peculiar form of the locust flower; you see that the upper petal, called the banner, is broad and erect, and so is the upper petal of the pea flower; the two lower petals, called the wings, are outspread and wing-shaped; so are those of the pea; and the two petals below the wings are united on their edges, curve upward, and form what is called the keel, and so you see are the corresponding petals of the pea flower. And now look at the stamens and pistils. You see that nine of the ten stamens have their filaments united into a sheath around the pistil, but the tenth stamen has its filament free. These are very marked characters, are they not? And, strange to say, you will find them the same in the tree and in the vine. Now look at the ovules or seeds of the Locust, and you will see that they are arranged in a pod or legume like those of the pea. And look at the leaves. You see the leaf of the locust is made up of several leaflets, and so also is the leaf of the pea. Now taste the Locust leaf."

I did so and found that it tasted like the leaf of the pea. Nature has used the same seasoning for both, though one is a straggling vine, the other a big tree.

"Now, surely you cannot imagine that all these similar characters are mere coincidences. Do they not rather go to show that the Creator in making the pea vine and Locust tree had the same idea in mind, and that plants are not classified arbitrarily? Man has nothing to do with their classification. Nature has attended to all that, giving essential unity with boundless variety, so that the botanist has only to examine plants to learn the harmony of their relations."

This fine lesson charmed me and sent me flying to the woods and meadows in wild enthusiasm. Like everybody else I was always fond of flowers, attracted by their external beauty and purity. Now my eyes were opened to their inner beauty, all alike revealing glorious traces of the thoughts of God, and leading on and on into the infinite cosmos. I wandered away at every opportunity, making long excursions round the lakes, gathering specimens and keeping them fresh in a bucket in my room to study at night after my regular class tasks were learned; for my eyes never closed on the plant glory I had seen.

Nevertheless, I still indulged my love of mechanical inventions. I invented a desk in which the books I had to study were arranged in order at the beginning of each term. I also made a bed which set me on my feet every morning at the hour determined on, and in dark winter mornings just as the bed set me on the floor it lighted a lamp. Then, after the minutes allowed for dressing had elapsed, a click was heard and the first book to be studied was pushed up from a rack below the top of the desk, thrown open, and allowed to remain there the number of minutes required. Then the machinery closed the book and allowed it to drop back into its stall, then moved the rack forward and threw up the next in order, and so on, all the day being divided according to the times of recitation, and time required and allotted to each study. Besides this, I thought it would be a fine thing in the summer-time when the sun rose early, to dispense with the clock-controlled bed machinery, and make use of sunbeams instead. This I did simply by taking a lens out of my small spy-glass, fixing it on a frame on the sill of my bedroom window, and pointing it to the sunrise; the sunbeams focused on a thread burned it through, allowing the bed machinery to put me on my feet. When I wished to arise at any given time after sunrise, I had only to turn the pivoted frame that held the lens the requisite number of degrees or minutes. Thus I took Emerson's advice and hitched my dumping-wagon bed to a star.

I also invented a machine to make visible the growth of plants and the action of the sunlight, a very delicate contrivance, enclosed in glass. Besides this I invented a barometer and a lot of novel scientific apparatus. My room was regarded as a sort of show place by the professors, who oftentimes brought visitors to it on Saturdays and holidays. And when, some eighteen years after I had left the University, I was sauntering over the campus in time of vacation, and spoke to a man who seemed to be taking some charge of the grounds, he informed me that he was the janitor; and when I inquired what had become of Pat, the janitor in my time, and a favorite with the students, he replied that Pat was still alive and well, but now too old to do much work. And when I pointed to the dormitory room that I long ago occupied, he said: "Oh! then I know who you are," and mentioned my name. "How comes it that you know my name?" I inquired. He explained that "Pat always pointed out that room to newcomers and told long stories about the wonders that used to be in it." So long had the memory of my little inventions survived.

Although I was four years at the University, I did not take the regular course of studies, but instead picked out what I thought would be most useful to me, particularly chemistry, which opened a new world, and mathematics and physics, a little Greek and Latin, botany and geology. I was far from satisfied with what I had learned, and should have stayed longer. Anyhow I wandered away on a glorious botanical and geological excursion, which has lasted nearly fifty years and is not yet completed, always happy and free, poor and rich, without thought of a diploma or of making a name, urged on and on through endless, inspiring, Godful beauty.

From the top of a hill on the north side of Lake Mendota I gained a last wistful, lingering view of the beautiful University grounds and buildings where I had spent so many hungry and happy and hopeful days. There with streaming eyes I bade my blessed Alma Mater farewell. But I was only leaving one University for another, the Wisconsin University for the University of the Wilderness.

(The Story of My Boyhood and Youth)

II

UNIVERSITY OF THE WILDERNESS

Start of the 1000-Mile Walk

A PERIOD of indecision followed Madison days for John Muir. When he left the University in June 1863, he intended to enter the medical school at Ann Arbor, Michigan, the following autumn. Instead, when his number was not called in the war draft, he wandered north into Canada, botanizing and working at odd jobs. Near Meaford he turned again to inventing, devising machines that increased the output of a factory making handles for brooms and rakes.

On March 1, 1866, this factory burned to the ground during a night blizzard. Soon afterwards Muir started for Indianapolis. He chose this city because of its numerous factories and also because it was situated amid some of the finest deciduous woodland in America. Finding work at Osgood, Smith & Company, the nation's largest manufacturer of carriage parts, he won such quick recognition through his inventive and administrative skill that the following year he was virtually offered a partnership. But it was in that spring of 1867 that an accident nearly blinded him. This turned him away forever from factories and machines. He dreamed of being another Humboldt and planned to explore the Amazon jungles. Returning home, he bade farewell to his family and friends and, back in Indianapolis once more, started on his long walk to the Gulf.

Muir's earliest notebooks, covering his wanderings in Canada, were destroyed in the fire. The first of his journals to survive is the four-by-six-and-a-half-inch notebook he carried tied to his belt during his travels from Louisville to Florida. It was not until after his death that A Thousand-Mile Walk to the Gulf *appeared in book form. Edited from the original journal by William Frederic Badè, it was published in 1916.*

SEPTEMBER 2. Crossing the Ohio at Louisville, I steered through the big city by compass without speaking a word to any one. Beyond the city I found a road running southward, and after passing a scatterment of suburban cabins and cottages I reached the green woods and spread out my pocket map to rough-hew a plan for my journey.

My plan was simply to push on in a general southward direction by the wildest, leafiest, and least trodden way I could find, promising the greatest extent of virgin forest. Folding my map, I shouldered my little bag and plant press and strode away among the old Kentucky Oaks, rejoicing in splendid visions of Pines and Palms and tropic flowers in glorious array, not, however, without a few cold shadows of loneliness, although the great Oaks seemed to spread their arms in welcome.

(A Thousand-Mile Walk to the Gulf)

People by the Way

THROUGHOUT MUIR'S writings there are scattered vivid little vignettes of people encountered in his travels. Some of the most memorable of these sketches appear in his record of the thousand-mile walk to the Gulf. While the details were fresh in his mind, he set them down in the notebook he carried at his belt. Traveling as he did, on foot, in old clothes, carrying his possessions in a bundle, he was able to meet people on a common footing, to see them with none of the aloofness of the conventional traveler.

I THE ROBBER

SEPTEMBER 10. After a few miles of level ground in luxuriant tangles of brooding vines, I began the ascent of the Cumberland Mountains, the first real mountains that my foot ever touched or eyes beheld.

I had climbed but a short distance when I was overtaken by a young man on horseback, who soon showed that he intended to rob me if he should find the job worth while. After he had inquired where I came from, and where I was going, he offered to carry my bag. I told him that it was so light that I did not feel it at all as a burden; but he insisted and coaxed until I allowed him to carry it. As soon as he had gained possession I noticed that he gradually increased his speed, evidently trying to get far enough ahead of me to examine the contents without being observed. But I was too good a walker and runner for him to get far. At a turn of the road, after trotting his horse for about half an hour, and when he thought he was out of sight, I caught him rummaging my poor bag. Finding there only a comb, brush, towel, soap, a change of underclothing, a copy of Burns's poems, Milton's Paradise Lost, and a small New Testament, he waited for me, handed back my bag, and returned down the hill, saying that he had forgotten something.

II THE BLACKSMITH

Toward the top of the Cumberland grade, about two hours before sundown I came to a log house, and as I had been warned that all the broad plateau of the range for forty or fifty miles was desolate, I began thus early to seek a lodging for the night. Knocking at the door, a motherly old lady replied to my request for supper and bed and breakfast, that I was welcome to the best she had, provided that I had the necessary change to pay my bill. When I told her that unfortunately I had nothing smaller than a five-dollar greenback she said, "Well, I'm sorry, but cannot afford to keep you. Not long ago ten soldiers came across from North Carolina, and in the morning they offered a greenback that I couldn't change, and so I got nothing for keeping them, which I was ill able to afford." "Very well," I said, "I'm glad you spoke of this beforehand, for I would rather go hungry than impose upon your hospitality."

As I turned to leave, after bidding her good-by, she, evidently pitying me for my tired looks, called me back and asked me if I would like a drink of milk. This I gladly accepted, thinking that perhaps I might not be successful in getting any other nourishment for a day or two. Then I inquired whether there were any more houses on the road, nearer than North Carolina, forty or fifty miles away. "Yes," she said, "it's only two miles to the next house, but beyond that there are no houses that I know of except empty ones whose owners have been killed or driven away during the war."

Arriving at the last house, my knock at the door was answered by a bright, good-natured, good-looking little woman, who in reply to my request for a night's lodging and food, said, "Oh, I guess so. I think you can stay. Come in and I'll call my husband." "But I must first warn you," I said, "that I have nothing smaller to offer you than a five-dollar bill for my entertainment. I don't want you to think that I am trying to impose on your hospitality."

She then called her husband, a blacksmith, who was at work at his forge. He came out, hammer in hand, bare-breasted, sweaty, begrimed, and covered with shaggy black hair. In reply to his wife's statement, that this young man wished to stop overnight, he quickly replied, "That's all right; tell him to go into the house." He was turning to go back to his shop, when his wife added, "But he says he hasn't any change to pay. He has nothing smaller than a five-dollar bill." Hesitating only a moment, he turned on his heel and said, "Tell him to go into the house. A man that comes right out like that beforehand is welcome to eat my bread."

When he came in after his hard day's work and sat down to dinner, he solemnly asked a blessing on the frugal meal, consisting solely of corn bread and bacon. Then, looking across the table at me, he said, "Young man, what are you doing down here?" I replied that I was looking for plants. "Plants? What kind of plants?" I said, "Oh, all kinds; grass, weeds, flowers, trees, mosses, ferns — almost everything that grows is interesting to me."

"Well, young man," he queried, "you mean to say that you are not employed by the government on some private business?" "No," I said, "I am not employed by any one except just myself. I love all kinds of plants, and I came down here to these Southern States to get acquainted with as many of them as possible."

"You look like a strong-minded man," he replied, "and surely you are able to do something better than wander over the country and look at weeds and blossoms. These are hard times, and real work is required of every man that is able. Picking up blossoms doesn't seem to be a man's work at all in any kind of times."

To this I replied, "You are a believer in the Bible, are you not?" "Oh, yes." "Well, you know Solomon was a strong-minded man, and he is generally believed to have been the very wisest man the world ever saw, and yet he considered it was worth while to study plants; not only to go and pick them up as I am doing, but to study them; and you know we are told that he wrote a book about plants, not only of the great Cedars of Lebanon, but of little bits of things growing in the cracks of the walls.

"Therefore, you see that Solomon differed very much more from you than from me in this matter. I'll warrant you he had many a long ramble in the mountains of Judea, and had he been a Yankee he would likely have visited every weed in the land. And again, do you not remember that Christ told his disciples to 'consider the lilies how they grow,' and compared their beauty with Solomon in all his glory? Now, whose advice am I to take, yours or Christ's? Christ says, 'Consider the lilies,' You say, 'Don't consider them. It isn't worth while for any strong-minded man.' "

This evidently satisfied him, and he acknowledged that he had never thought of blossoms in that way before. He repeated again and again that I must be a very strong-minded man, and admitted that no doubt I was fully justified in picking up blossoms. He then told me that although the war was over, walking across the Cumberland Mountains still was far from safe on account of small bands of guerrillas who were in hiding along the roads, and earnestly entreated me to turn back and not think of walking so far as the Gulf of Mexico until the country became quiet and orderly once more.

I replied that I had no fear, that I had but very little to lose, and that nobody was likely to think it worth while to rob me; that, anyhow, I always had good luck. In the morning he repeated the warning and entreated me to turn back, which never for a moment interfered with my resolution to pursue my glorious walk.

III THE GUERRILLAS

September 11. About noon my road became dim and at last vanished among desolate fields. Lost and hungry, I knew my direction but could not keep it on account of the briers. My path was indeed strewn with flowers, but as thorny, also, as mortal ever trod. In trying to force my way through these cat-plants one is not simply clawed and pricked through all one's clothing, but caught and held fast. The toothed arching branches come down over and above you like cruel living arms, and the more you struggle the more desperately you are entangled, and your wounds deepened and multiplied. The South has plant fly-catchers. It also has plant man-catchers.

After a great deal of defensive fighting and struggling I escaped to a road and a house, but failed to find food or shelter. Toward sundown, as I was walking along a straight stretch in the road, I suddenly came in sight of ten mounted men riding abreast. They undoubtedly had seen me before I discovered them, for they had stopped their horses and were evidently watching me. I saw at once that it was useless to attempt to avoid them, for the ground thereabout was quite open. I knew that there was nothing for it but to face them fearlessly, without showing the slightest suspicion of foul play. Therefore, without halting even for a moment, I advanced rapidly with long strides as though I intended to walk through the midst of them. When I got within a rod or so I looked up in their faces and smilingly bade them "Howdy." Stopping never an instant, I turned to one side and walked around them to get on the road again, and kept on without venturing to look back or betray the slightest fear of being robbed.

After I had gone about one hundred or one hundred and fifty yards, I ventured a quick glance back, without stopping, and saw in this flash of an eye that all the ten had turned their horses toward me and were evidently talking about me; supposedly, with reference to what my object was, where I was going, and whether it would be worth while to rob me. They all were mounted on rather scrawny horses, and all wore long hair hanging down on their shoulders. Evidently they belonged to the most irreclaimable of the guerrilla bands who, long accustomed to plunder, deplored the coming of peace. I was not followed, however, probably because the plants projecting from my plant-press made them believe that I was a poor herb doctor, a common occupation in these mountain regions.

About dark I discovered, a little off the road, another house, inhabited by negroes, where I succeeded in obtaining a much needed meal of string beans, buttermilk, and corn bread. At the table I was seated in a bottomless chair, and as I became sore and heavy, I sank deeper and deeper, pressing my knees against my breast, and my mouth settled to the level of my plate. But wild hunger cares for none of these things, and my curiously compressed position prevented the too free indulgence of boisterous appetite. Of course, I was compelled to sleep with the trees in the one great bedroom of the open night.

IV THE SHERIFF

September 19. In Murphy [North Carolina] I was hailed by the sheriff who could not determine by my colors and rigging to what country or craft I belonged. Since the war, every other stranger in these lonely parts is supposed to be a criminal, and all are objects of curiosity or apprehensive concern. After a few minutes' conversation with this chief man of Murphy I was pronounced harmless, and invited to his house, where for the first time since leaving home I found a house decked with flowers and vines, clean within and without, and stamped with the comforts of culture and refinement in all its arrangements.

V THE MOUNTAINEERS

September 22. About noon I reached the last mountain summit on my way to the sea. It is called the Blue Ridge, and before it lies a prospect very different from any I had passed, namely, a vast uniform expanse of dark Pine woods, extending to the sea; an impressive view at any time and under any circumstances, but particularly so to one emerging from the mountains.

Traveled in the wake of three poor but merry mountaineers — an old woman, a young woman, and a young man — who sat, leaned, and lay in the box of a shackly wagon that seemed to be held together by spiritualism, and was kept in agitation by a very large and a very small mule. In going down hill the looseness of the harness and the joints of the wagon allowed the mules to back nearly out of sight beneath the box, and the three who occupied it were slid against the front boards in a heap over the mules' ears. Before they could unravel their limbs from this unmannerly and impolite disorder, a new ridge in the road frequently tilted them with a swish and a bump against the back boards in a mixing that was still more grotesque.

I expected to see man, women, and mules mingled in a piebald ruin at the bottom of some rocky hollow, but they seemed to have full confidence in the back board and the front board of the wagon-box. So they continued to slide comfortably up and down, from end to end, in slippery obedience to the law of gravitation, as the grades demanded. Where the jolting was moderate, they engaged in conversation on love, marriage, and camp-meeting, according to the custom of the country. The old lady, through all the vicissitudes of the transportation, held a bouquet of French marigolds.

VI The Prophet

October 3. Toward evening I arrived at the home of Mr. Cameron, a wealthy planter, who had large bands of slaves at work in his cotton-fields. They still call him "Massa." He tells me that labor costs him less now than it did before the emancipation of the negroes. When I arrived I found him busily engaged in scouring the rust off some cotton-gin saws which had been lying for months at the bottom of his mill-pond to prevent Sherman's "bummers" from destroying them. The most valuable parts of the grist-mill and cotton-press were hidden in the same way. "If Bill Sherman," he said, "should come down now without his army, he would never go back."

When I asked him if he could give me food and lodging for the night he said, "No, no, we have no accommodations for travelers." I said, "But I am traveling as a botanist and either have to find lodgings when night overtakes me or lie outdoors, which I often have had to do in my long walk from Indiana. But you see that the country here is very swampy; if you will at least sell me a piece of bread, and give me a drink at your well, I shall have to look around for a dry spot to lie down on."

Then, asking me a few questions, and narrowly examining me, he said, "Well, it is barely possible that we may find a place for you, and if you will come to the house I will ask my wife." Evidently he was cautious to get his wife's opinion of the kind of creature I was before committing himself to hospitality. He halted me at the door and called out his wife, a fine-looking woman, who also questioned me narrowly as to my object in coming so far down through the South, so soon after the war. She said to her husband that she thought they could, perhaps, give me a place to sleep.

After supper, as we sat by the fire talking on my favorite subject of botany, I described the country I had passed through, its botanical character, etc. Then, evidently, all doubt as to my being a decent man vanished, and they both said they wouldn't for anything have turned me away; but I must excuse their caution, for perhaps fewer than one in a hundred, who passed through this unfrequented part of the country, were to be relied upon. "Only a short time ago we entertained a man who was well spoken and well dressed, and he vanished some time during the night with some valuable silverware."

Mr. Cameron told me that when I arrived he tried me for a Mason, and finding that I was not a Mason he wondered still more that I would venture into the country without being able to gain the assistance of brother Masons in these troublous times.

"Young man," he said, after hearing my talks on botany, "I see that your hobby is botany. My hobby is e-lec-tricity. I believe that the time is coming, though we may not live to see it, when that mysterious power or force, used now only for telegraphy, will eventually supply the power for running railroad trains and steamships, for lighting, and, in a word, electricity will do all the work of the world."

Many times since then I have thought of the wonderfully correct vision of this Georgia planter, so far in advance of almost everybody else in the world. Already nearly all that he foresaw has been accomplished, and the use of electricity is being extended more and more every year.

VII THE NEGRO

October 18. Am walking on land that is almost dry. The dead levels are interrupted here and there by sandy waves a few feet in height. It is said that not a point in all Florida is more than three hundred feet above sea-level — a country where but little grading is required for roads, but much bridging, and boring of many tunnels through forests.

Before reaching this open ground, in a lonely, swampy place in the woods, I met a large, muscular, brawny young negro, who eyed me with a glaring, wistful curiosity. I was very thirsty at the time, and inquired of the man if there were any houses or springs near by where I could get a drink. "Oh, yes," he replied, still eagerly searching me with his wild eyes. Then he inquired where I came from, where I was going, and what brought me to such a wild country, where I was liable to be robbed, and perhaps killed.

"Oh, I am not afraid of any one robbing me," I said, "for I don't carry anything worth stealing." "Yes," said he, "but you can't travel without money." I started to walk on, but he blocked my way. Then I noticed that he was trembling, and it flashed upon me all at once that he was thinking of knocking me down in order to rob me. After glaring at my pockets as if searching for weapons, he stammered in a quavering voice, "Do you carry shooting-irons?" His motives, which I ought to have noted sooner, now were apparent to me. Though I had no pistol, I instinctively threw my hand back to my pistol pocket and, with my eyes fixed on him, I marched up close to him and said, "I allow people to find out if I am armed or not." Then he quailed, stepped aside, and allowed me to pass, for fear of being shot. This was evidently a narrow escape.

(A Thousand-Mile Walk to the Gulf)

A Tennessee Memory

FROM TIME to time, in later journals, John Muir set down additional recollections of his long walk to the Gulf. The following memory of a lonely stretch in the wilderness of Tennessee was recorded, probably in 1870, while Muir was living in Yosemite Valley, California. It first appeared in print in John of the Mountains, *Linnie Marsh Wolfe's selections from Muir's journals, published in 1938.*

ONCE I WAS very hungry and lonely in Tennessee. I had been walking most of the day in the Cumberland Mountains without coming to a single house, but in crossing a dark-shaded stream whose border trees closed over it like a leafy sky I found the frail Dicksonia that I had looked for so long, and the first Magnolia, too, that I had ever seen. I sat down and reveled in the glory of my discoveries. A mysterious breathing of wind moved in the trees, and the stream sang cheerily at every ripple. There is no place so impressively solitary as a dense forest with a stream passing over a rocky bed at a moderate inclination.

Feelings of isolation soon caught me again among these hushed sounds, but one of the Lord's smallest birds came out to me from some bushes at the side of a moss-clad rock. It had a wonderfully expressive eye, and in one moment that cheerful, confiding bird preached me the most effectual sermon on heavenly trust that I had ever heard through all the measured hours of Sabbath, and I went on not half so heart-sick, nor half so weary.

(John of the Mountains)

Camping Among the Tombs

UNDOUBTEDLY on many occasions during his wanderings John Muir saved himself from injury and death by his ability to observe and think clearly. An instance of the kind was his choosing, at Savannah, the one place where he could sleep safest from dangerous bands of maurauding Negroes — a cemetery. From Savannah Muir went by boat to northern Florida and then, on foot, followed the railroad that angled across the peninsula to Cedar Keys. Here, soon after finding work at the Hodgson sawmill, he fell ill of malaria. Sleeping in the open, bitten by mosquitoes, he had become infected at Bonaventure Cemetery or elsewhere in his southern travels. During the weeks of convalescence, he was cared for by the Hodgson family. Thirty years later, while traveling in the South with Charles S. Sargent, the Harvard botanist, Muir returned to renew his friendship with the kindly woman who had nursed him through his illness.

O CTOBER 8. Reached Savannah, but find no word from home, and the money that I had ordered to be sent by express from Portage [Wisconsin] by my brother had not yet arrived. Feel dreadfully lonesome and poor. Went to the meanest looking lodging-house that I could find, on account of its cheapness.

October 9. After going again to the express office and post office, and wandering about the streets, I found a road which led me to the Bonaventure graveyard. If that burying-ground across the Sea of Galilee, mentioned in the Scripture, was half as beautiful as Bonaventure, I do not wonder that a man should dwell among the tombs. It is only three or four miles from Savannah, and is reached by a smooth white shell road.

There is but little to be seen on the way in land, water, or sky, that would lead one to hope for the glories of Bonaventure. The ragged desolate fields, on both sides of the road, are overrun with coarse rank weeds, and show scarce a trace of cultivation. But soon all is changed. Rickety log huts, broken fences, and the last patch of weedy rice-stubble are left behind. You come to beds of purple liatris and living wild-wood trees. You hear the song of birds, cross a small stream, and are with Nature in the grand old forest graveyard, so beautiful that almost any sensible person would choose to dwell here with the dead, rather than with the lazy, disorderly living.

Part of the grounds was cultivated and planted with Live-oak, about a hundred years ago, by a wealthy gentleman who had his country residence here. But much the greater part is undisturbed. Even those spots which are disordered by art, Nature is ever at work to reclaim, and to make them look as if the foot of man had never known them. Only a small plot of ground is occupied with graves and the old mansion is in ruins.

The most conspicuous glory of Bonaventure is its noble avenue of Live-oaks. They are the most magnificent planted trees I have ever seen, about fifty feet high and perhaps three or four feet in diameter, with broad spreading leafy heads. The main branches reach out horizontally until they come together over the drive-way, embowering it throughout its entire length, while each branch is adorned like a garden with ferns, flowers, grasses, and Dwarf Palmettos.

But of all the plants of these curious tree-gardens the most striking and characteristic is the so-called Long Moss (*Tillandsia usneoides*). It drapes all the branches from top to bottom, hanging in long silvery-gray skeins, reaching a length of not less than eight or ten feet, and when slowly waving in the wind they produce a solemn funeral effect singularly impressive.

There are also thousands of smaller trees and clustered bushes, covered almost from sight in the glorious brightness of their own light. The place is half surrounded by the salt marshes and islands of the river, their reeds and sedges making a delightful fringe. Many bald eagles roost among the trees along the side of the marsh. Their screams are heard every morning, joined with the noise of crows, and the songs of countless warblers, hidden deep in their dwellings of leafy bowers. Large flocks of butterflies, all kinds of happy insects, seem to be in a perfect fever of joy and sportive gladness. The whole place seems like a center of life. The dead do not reign there alone.

Bonaventure to me is one of the most impressive assemblages of animal and plant creatures I ever met. I was fresh from the Western prairies, the garden-like openings of Wisconsin, the Beech and Maple and Oak woods of Indiana and Kentucky, the dark mysterious Savannah Cypress forests; but never since I was allowed to walk the woods have I found so impressive a company of trees as the tillandsia-draped Oaks of Bonaventure.

I gazed awe-stricken as one new-arrived from another world. Bonaventure is called a graveyard, a town of the dead, but the few graves are powerless in such a depth of life. The rippling of living waters, the song of birds, the joyous confidence of flowers, the calm, undisturbable grandeur of the Oaks, mark this place of graves as one of the Lord's most favored abodes of life and light.

On no subject are our ideas more warped and pitiable than on death. Instead of the sympathy, the friendly union, of life and death so apparent in Nature, we are taught that death is an accident, a deplorable punishment for the oldest sin, the arch-enemy of life, etc. Town children, especially, are steeped in this death-orthodoxy, for the natural beauties of death are seldom seen or taught in towns.

Of death among our own species, to say nothing of the thousand styles and modes of murder, our best memories, even among happy deaths, yield groans and tears, mingled with morbid exultation; burial companies, black in cloth and countenance; and, last of all, a black box burial in an ill-omened place, haunted by imaginary glooms and ghosts of every degree. Thus death becomes fearful, and the most notable and incredible thing heard around a death-bed is, "I fear not to die."

But let children walk with Nature, let them see the beautiful blendings and communions of death and life, their joyous inseparable unity, as taught in woods and meadows, plains and mountains and streams of our blessed star, and they will learn that death is stingless indeed, and as beautiful as life, and that the grave has no victory, for it never fights. All is divine harmony.

Most of the few graves of Bonaventure are planted with flowers. There is generally a Magnolia at the head, near the strictly erect marble, a rose-bush or two at the foot, and some violets and showy exotics along the sides or on the tops. All is enclosed by a black iron railing, composed of rigid bars that might have been spears or bludgeons from a battlefield in Pandemonium.

It is interesting to observe how assiduously Nature seeks to remedy these labored art blunders. She corrodes the iron and marble, and gradually levels the hill which is always heaped up, as if a sufficiently heavy quantity of clods could not be laid on the dead. Arching grasses come one by one; seeds come flying on downy wings, silent as fate, to give life's dearest beauty for the ashes of art; and strong evergreen arms laden with ferns and tillandsia drapery are spread over all — "Life at work everywhere, obliterating all memory of the confusion of man."

In Georgia many graves are covered with a common shingle roof, supported on four posts as the cover of a well, as if rain and sunshine were not regarded as blessings. Perhaps, in this hot and insalubrious climate, moisture and sun-heat are considered necessary evils to which they do not wish to expose their dead.

The money package that I was expecting did not arrive until the following week. After stopping the first night at the cheap, disreputable-looking hotel, I had only about a dollar and a half left in my purse, and so was compelled to camp out to make it last in buying only bread. I went out of the noisy town to seek a sleeping place that was not marshy. After gaining the outskirts of the town toward the sea, I found some low dunes, yellow with flowering solidagoes.

I wandered wearily from dune to dune sinking ankle-deep in the sand, searching for a place to sleep beneath the tall flowers, free from insects and snakes, and above all from my fellow man. But idle negroes were prowling about everywhere, and I was afraid. The wind had strange sounds, waving the heavy panicles over my head, and I feared sickness from malaria so prevalent here, when I suddenly thought of the graveyard.

"There," thought I, "is an ideal place for a penniless wanderer. There no superstitious prowling mischief-maker dares venture for fear of haunting ghosts, while for me there will be God's rest and peace. And then, if I am to be exposed to unhealthy vapors, I shall have capital compensation in seeing those grand Oaks in the moonlight, with all the impressive and nameless influences of this lonely beautiful place."

By this time it was near sunset, and I hastened across the common to the road and set off for Bonaventure, delighted with my choice, and almost glad to find that necessity had furnished me with so good an excuse for doing what I knew my mother would censure; for she made me promise I would not lie out of doors if I could possibly avoid it. The sun was set ere I was past the negroes' huts and rice-fields, and I arrived near the graves in the silent hour of the gloaming.

I was very thirsty after walking so long in the muggy heat, a distance of three or four miles from the city, to get to this grave-yard. A dull, sluggish, coffee-colored stream flows under the road just outside the graveyard garden park, from which I managed to get a drink after breaking a way down to the water through a dense fringe of bushes, daring the snakes and alligators in the dark. Thus refreshed I entered the weird and beautiful abode of the dead.

All the avenue where I walked was in shadow, but an exposed tombstone frequently shone out in startling whiteness on either hand, and thickets of sparkleberry bushes gleamed like heaps of crystals. Not a breath of air moved the gray moss, and the great black arms of the trees met overhead and covered the avenue. But the canopy was fissured by many a netted seam and leafy-edged opening, through which the moonlight sifted in auroral rays, broidering the blackness in silvery light. Though tired, I sauntered a while enchanted, then lay down under one of the great Oaks. I found a little mound that served for a pillow, placed my plant-press and bag beside me and rested fairly well, though somewhat disturbed by large prickly-footed beetles creeping across my hands and face, and by a lot of hungry stinging mosquitoes.

When I awoke, the sun was up and all Nature was rejoicing. Some birds had discovered me as an intruder, and were making a great ado in interesting language and gestures. I heard the screaming of the bald eagles, and of some strange waders in the rushes. I heard the hum of Savannah with the long jarring hallos of negroes far away. On rising I found that my head had been resting on a grave, and though my sleep had not been quite so sound as that of the person below, I awoke refreshed, and looking about me, the morning sunbeams pouring through the Oaks and gardens dripping with dew, the beauty displayed was so glorious and exhilarating that hunger and care seemed only a dream.

Eating a breakfast cracker or two and watching for a few hours the beautiful light, birds, squirrels, and insects, I returned to Savannah, to find that my money package had not yet arrived. I then decided to go early to the graveyard and make a nest with a roof to keep off the dew, as there was no way of finding out how long I might have to stay. I chose a hidden spot in a dense thicket of sparkleberry bushes, near the right bank of the Savannah River, where the bald eagles and a multitude of singing birds roosted. It was so well hidden that I had to carefully fix its compass bearing in my mind from a mark I made on the side of the main avenue, that I might be able to find it at bedtime.

I used four of the bushes as corner posts for my little hut, which was about four or five feet long by about three or four in width, tied little branches across from forks in the bushes to support a roof of rushes, and spread a thick mattress of Long Moss over the floor for a bed. My whole establishment was on so small a scale that I could have taken up not only my bed, but my whole house, and walked. There I lay that night, eating a few crackers.

Next day I returned to the town and was disappointed as usual in obtaining money. So after spending the day looking at the plants in the gardens of the fine residences and town squares, I returned to my graveyard home. That I might not be observed and suspected of hiding, as if I had committed a crime, I always went home after dark, and one night as I lay down in my moss nest, I felt some cold-blooded creature in it; whether a snake or simply a frog or toad I do not know, but instinctively, instead of drawing back my hand, I grasped the poor creature and threw it over the tops of the bushes. That was the only significant disturbance or fright that I got.

In the morning everything seemed divine. Only squirrels, sunbeams, and birds came about me. I was awakened every morning by these little singers after they discovered my nest. Instead of serenely singing their morning songs they at first came within two or three feet of the hut, and, looking in at me through the leaves, chattered and scolded in half-angry, half-wondering tones. The crowd constantly increased, attracted by the disturbance. Thus I began to get acquainted with my bird-neighbors in this blessed wilderness, and after they learned that I meant them no ill they scolded less and sang more.

After five days of this graveyard life I saw that even with living on three or four cents a day my last twenty-five cents would soon be spent, and after trying again and again unsuccessfully to find some employment, began to think that I must strike farther out into the country, but still within reach of town, until I came to some grain- or rice-field that had not yet been harvested, trusting that I could live indefinitely on toasted or raw corn, or rice.

By this time I was becoming faint, and in making the journey to the town was alarmed to find myself growing staggery and giddy. The ground ahead seemed to be rising up in front of me, and the little streams in the ditches on the sides of the road seemed to be flowing up hill. Then I realized that I was becoming dangerously hungry and became more than ever anxious to receive the money package.

To my delight this fifth or sixth morning when I inquired if the money package had come the clerk replied that it had, but that he could not deliver it without my being identified. I said, "Well, here! read my brother's letter," handing it to him. "It states the amount in the package, where it came from, the day it was put into the office at Portage City, and I should think that would be enough." He said, "No, that is not enough. How do I know that this letter is yours? You may have stolen it. How do I know that you are John Muir?"

I said, "Well, don't you see that this letter indicates that I am a botanist? For in it my brother says, 'I hope you are having a good time and finding many new plants.' Now, you say that I might have stolen this letter from John Muir, and in that way have become aware of there being a money package to arrive from Portage for him. But the letter proves that John Muir must be a botanist, and though, as you say, his letter might have been stolen, it would hardly be likely that the robber would be able to steal John Muir's knowledge of botany. Now I suppose, of course, that you have been to school and know something of botany. Examine me and see if I know anything about it."

At this he laughed good-naturedly, evidently feeling the force of my argument, and, perhaps, pitying me on account of looking pale and hungry, he turned and rapped at the door of a private office — probably the Manager's — called out and said, "Mr. So and So, here is a man who has inquired every day for the last week or so for a money package from Portage, Wisconsin. He is a stranger in the city with no one to identify him. He states correctly the amount and the name of the sender. He has shown me a letter which indicates that Mr. Muir is a botanist, and that although a traveling companion may have stolen Mr. Muir's letter, he could not have stolen his botany, and requests us to examine him."

The head official smiled, took a good stare at my face, waved his hand, and said, "Let him have it." Gladly I pocketed my money, and had not gone along the street more than a few rods before I met a very large negro woman with a tray of gingerbread, in which I immediately invested some of my new wealth, and walked rejoicingly, munching along the street, making no attempt to conceal the pleasure I had in eating. Then, still hunting for more food, I found a sort of eating-place in a market and had a regular meal on top of the gingerbread! Thus my "marching through Georgia" terminated handsomely in a jubilee of bread.

(A Thousand-Mile Walk to the Gulf)

The Cuban Shore

STILL DREAMING of exploring the Amazon, Muir, although weak from malaria, sailed from Cedar Keys for Cuba in January 1868 on the schooner Island Belle. *For several weeks the ship lay at anchor at Havana. Muir slept on board nights and wandered days along the shore studying plants such as the tideline wildflower noted in the short selection below. Unable, fortunately, to find a vessel going to Brazil, he remained with the* Island Belle *as it plowed north through winter storms carrying a cargo of oranges to New York.*

ONE DAY, when walking along the coral shores of Cuba gathering shells, I found a tiny fragile purple flower with its circlet of petals confidingly open to the bright tropic sun. It lived in coral rocks that were washed by the heavy whitecapped waves of every storm from the north. In these "northers," the dread of seamen, wave after wave rolled over it — tons in weight — sufficient to crush a ship, but the little purple plant, tended by its Maker, closed its petals, crouched low in its crevice of a home, and enjoyed the storm in safety.

(John of the Mountains)

New York

"I CAN MAKE my exhilarated way over an unknown ice-field or sure-footedly up a titanic gorge," Muir wrote in later life, "but in these terrible canyons of New York, I am a pitiful, unrelated atom that loses itself at once." A quarter of a century passed after the events recorded in this selection before Muir, in company with Robert Underwood Johnson, visited Central Park. The thing he saw there that interested him most were glacial scratchings on out-croppings of granite.

ON OUR ARRIVAL the Captain, knowing something of the lightness of my purse, told me that I could continue to occupy my bed on the ship until I sailed for California, getting my meals at a near-by restaurant. "This is the way we are all doing," he said. Consulting the newspapers, I found that the first ship, the *Nebraska*, sailed for Aspinwall in about ten days, and that the steerage passage to San Francisco by way of the Isthmus was only forty dollars.

In the mean time I wandered about the city without knowing a single person in it. My walks extended but little beyond sight of my little schooner home. I saw the name Central Park on some of the street-cars and thought I would like to visit it, but, fearing that I might not be able to find my way back, I dared not make the adventure. I felt completely lost in the vast throngs of people, the noise of the streets, and the immense size of the buildings. Often I thought I would like to explore the city if, like a lot of wild hills and valleys, it was clear of inhabitants.

(A Thousand-Mile Walk to the Gulf)

III

THE RANGE OF LIGHT

First Glimpse of the Sierra

MUIR LEFT New York early in March 1868, traveling steerage in a ship jammed with emigrants bound for California. He reached San Francisco on March 28. The man he stopped to ask the quickest way out of town was a carpenter carrying his tools up Market Street. Accompanied by a globe-trotting Cockney named Chilwell whom he had met on shipboard, Muir walked south to Gilroy and then east over the Pacheco Pass. At the top of this eminence he had his first, never-to-be-forgotten sight of the great flower-filled Central Valley of California with the snow-clad Sierra Nevada mountains beyond.

WHEN I SET OUT on the long excursion that finally led to California, I wandered, afoot and alone, from Indiana to the Gulf of Mexico, with a plant-press on my back, holding a generally southward course, like the birds when they are going from summer to winter. From the west coast of Florida I crossed the Gulf to Cuba, enjoyed the rich tropical flora there for a few months, intending to go thence to the north end of South America, make my way through the woods to the head waters of the Amazon, and float down that grand river to the ocean. But I was unable to find a ship bound for South America — fortunately, perhaps, for I had incredibly little money for so long a trip and had not yet fully recovered from a fever caught in the Florida swamps. Therefore I decided to visit California for a year or two to see its wonderful flora and the famous Yosemite Valley. All the world was before me and every day was a holiday, so it did not seem important to which one of the world's wildernesses I first should wander.

Arriving by the Panama steamer, I stopped one day in San Francisco and then inquired for the nearest way out of town. "But where do you want to go?" asked the man to whom I had applied for this important information. "To any place that is wild," I said. This reply startled him. He seemed to fear I might be crazy, and therefore the sooner I was out of town the better, so he directed me to the Oakland ferry.

So on the 1st of April, 1868, I set out afoot for Yosemite. It was the bloom-time of the year over the lowlands and coast ranges; the landscapes of the Santa Clara Valley were fairly drenched with sunshine, all the air was quivering with the songs of the meadow-larks, and the hills were so covered with flowers that they seemed to be painted. Slow, indeed, was my progress through these glorious gardens, the first of the California flora I had seen. Cattle and cultivation were making few scars as yet, and I wandered enchanted in long, wavering curves, knowing by my pocket map that Yosemite Valley lay to the east and that I should surely find it.

Looking eastward from the summit of the Pacheco Pass one shining morning, a landscape was displayed that after all my wanderings still appears as the most beautiful I have ever beheld. At my feet lay the Great Central Valley of California, level and flowery, like a lake of pure sunshine, forty or fifty miles wide, five hundred miles long, one rich furred garden of yellow compositæ. And from the eastern boundary of this vast golden flower-bed rose the mighty Sierra, miles in height, and so gloriously colored and so radiant, it seemed not clothed with light, but wholly composed of it, like the wall of some celestial city. Along the top and extending a good way down, was a rich pearl-gray belt of snow; below it a belt of blue and dark purple, marking the extension of the forests; and stretching along the base of the range a broad belt of rose-purple; all these colors, from the blue sky to the yellow valley smoothly blending as they do in a rainbow, making a wall of light ineffably fine. Then it seemed to me that the Sierra should be called, not the Nevada or Snowy Range, but the Range of Light. And after ten years of wandering and wondering in the heart of it, rejoicing in its glorious floods of light, the white beams of the morning streaming through the passes, the noonday radiance on the crystal rocks, the flush of the alpenglow, and the irised spray of countless waterfalls, it still seems above all others the Range of Light.

(The Yosemite)

Bee Pastures

THE FLOWER FIELDS of the great Central Valley were in their April glory when Muir and his companion descended from Pacheco Pass. Traveling by compass, they crossed to the Merced River and followed it to their destination, Yosemite Valley. Those miles on miles of wildflowers, as he first enjoyed them, remained undimmed in Muir's memory through the rest of his life. He reached California early enough to observe the dramatic and tragic suddenness of change which the blighting decades of lumbering and ranching brought. Watching wildflowers turned into mutton and flower fields into dusty ground, he was stimulated into his great fight for conservation.

WHEN CALIFORNIA was wild, it was one sweet bee garden throughout its entire length, north and south, and all the way across from the snowy Sierra to the ocean.

Wherever a bee might fly within the bounds of this virgin wilderness — through the Redwood forests, along the banks of the rivers, along the bluffs and headlands fronting the sea, over valley and plain, park and grove, and deep, leafy glen, or far up the piny slopes of the mountains — throughout every belt and section of climate up to the timber-line, bee flowers bloomed in lavish abundance. Here they grew more or less apart in special sheets and patches of no great size, there in broad, flowing folds hundreds of miles in length — zones of polleny forests, zones of flowery chaparral, stream tangles of rubus and wild rose, sheets of golden compositæ, beds of violets, beds of mint, beds of bryanthus and clover, and so on, certain species blooming somewhere all the year round.

But of late years plows and sheep have made sad havoc in these glorious pastures, destroying tens of thousands of the flowery acres like a fire, and banishing many species of the best honey plants to rocky cliffs and fence corners, while, on the other hand, cultivation thus far has given no adequate compensation, at least in kind; only acres of alfalfa for miles of the richest wild pasture, ornamental roses and honeysuckles around cottage doors for cascades of wild roses in the dells, and small, square orchards and orange groves for broad mountain belts of chaparral.

The Great Central Plain of California, during the months of March, April, and May, was one smooth, continuous bed of honey bloom, so marvelously rich that, in walking from one end of it to the other, a distance of more than four hundred miles, your foot would press about a hundred flowers at every step. Mints, gilias, nemophilas, castilleias, and innumerable compositæ were so crowded together that, had ninety-nine per cent of them been taken away, the plain would still have seemed to any but Californians extravagantly flowery. The radiant, honeyful corollas, touching and overlapping, and rising above one another, glowed in the living light like a sunset sky — one sheet of purple and gold, with the bright Sacramento pouring through the midst of it from the north, the San Joaquin from the south and their many tributaries sweeping in at right angles from the mountains, dividing the plain into sections fringed with trees.

Along the rivers there is a strip of bottom-land, countersunk beneath the general level, and wider toward the foot-hills, where magnificent Oaks, from three to eight feet in diameter, cast grateful masses of shade over the open, prairie-like levels. And close along the water's edge there was a fine jungle of tropical luxuriance, composed of wild rose and bramble bushes and a great variety of climbing vines, wreathing and interlacing the branches and trunks of Willows and Alders, and swinging across from summit to summit in heavy festoons. Here the wild bees reveled in fresh bloom long after the flowers of the drier plain had withered and gone to seed. And in midsummer, when the "blackberries" were ripe, the Indians came from the mountains to feast — men, women, and babies in long, noisy trains, often joined by the farmers of the neighborhood, who gathered this wild fruit with commendable appreciation of its superior flavor, while their home orchards were full of ripe peaches, apricots, nectarines, and figs, and their vineyards were laden with grapes. But, though these luxuriant, shaggy river-beds were thus distinct from the smooth, treeless plain, they made no heavy dividing lines in general views. The whole appeared as one continuous sheet of bloom bounded only by the mountains.

When I first saw this central garden, the most extensive and regular of all the bee pastures of the State, it seemed all one sheet of plant gold, hazy and vanishing in the distance, distinct as a new map along the foot-hills at my feet.

Descending the eastern slopes of the Coast Range through beds of gilias and lupines, and around many a breezy hillock and bush-crowned headland, I at length waded out into the midst of it. All the ground was covered, not with grass and green leaves, but with radiant corollas, about ankle-deep next the foot-hills, knee-deep or more five or six miles out. Here were bahia, madia, madaria, burrielia, chrysopsis, corethrogyne, grindelia, etc., growing in close social congregations of various shades of yellow, blending finely with the purples of clarkia, orthocarpus, and œnothera, whose delicate petals were drinking the vital sunbeams without giving back any sparkling glow.

Because so long a period of extreme drought succeeds the rainy season, most of the vegetation is composed of annuals, which spring up simultaneously, and bloom together at about the same height above the ground, the general surface being but slightly ruffled by the taller phacelias, pentstemons, and groups of *Salvia carduacea,* the king of the mints.

Sauntering in any direction, hundreds of these happy sun-plants brushed against my feet at every step, and closed over them as if I were wading in liquid gold. The air was sweet with fragrance, the larks sang their blessed songs, rising on the wing as I advanced, then sinking out of sight in the polleny sod, while myriads of wild bees stirred the lower air with their monotonous hum — monotonous, yet forever fresh and sweet as everyday sunshine. Hares and spermophiles showed themselves in considerable numbers in shallow places, and small bands of antelopes were almost constantly in sight, gazing curiously from some slight elevation, and then bounding swiftly away with unrivaled grace of motion. Yet I could discover no crushed flowers to mark their track, nor, indeed, any destructive action of any wild foot or tooth whatever.

The great yellow days circled by uncounted, while I drifted toward the north, observing the countless forms of life thronging about me, lying down almost anywhere on the approach of night. And what glorious botanical beds I had! Oftentimes on awaking I would find several new species leaning over me and looking me full in the face, so that my studies would begin before rising.

(The Mountains of California)

Start for the High Sierra

JOHN MUIR'S first visit to Yosemite Valley, with his companion, Chilwell, lasted about a week and a half. The two then descended to the lowland and for a time worked on a ranch owned by Thomas Eagleson. Chilwell soon drifted on but Muir remained, harvesting, breaking wild horses, shearing sheep. In the fall of 1868, he was hired by Pat Delaney, a man who had been trained for the priesthood, joined the Forty-niners, mined for a time and then turned to ranching. Delaney became his friend as well as his employer. The following spring he proposed that Muir accompany his sheep to the high pastures of the Sierra. A shepherd would do most of the work and Muir would supervise. Thus he would be left free to roam and study at will.

At the time Muir was thirty-one years old. The journal he kept during those mountain months appeared, four decades later, as My First Summer in the Sierra. *Like* Walden, *it is a young man's book, filled with the strength and courage of youth. I have read it many times but the sense of vitality, of health, of delight in new experiences is never lost.*

I N THE GREAT Central Valley of California there are only two seasons — spring and summer. The spring begins with the first rainstorm, which usually falls in November. In a few months the wonderful flowery vegetation is in full bloom, and by the end of May it is dead and dry and crisp, as if every plant had been roasted in an oven.

Then the lolling, panting flocks and herds are driven to the high, cool, green pastures of the Sierra. I was longing for the mountains about this time, but money was scarce and I couldn't see how a bread supply was to be kept up. While I was anxiously brooding on the bread problem, so troublesome to wanderers, and trying to believe that I might learn to live like the wild animals, gleaning nourishment here and there from seeds, berries, etc., sauntering and climbing in joyful independence of money or baggage, Mr. Delaney, a sheep-owner, for whom I had worked a few weeks, called on me, and offered to engage me to go with his shepherd and flock to the head-waters of the Merced and Tuolumne Rivers — the very region I had most in mind. I was in the mood to accept work of any kind that would take me into the mountains whose treasures I had tasted last summer in the Yosemite region. The flock, he explained, would be moved gradually higher through the successive forest belts as the snow melted, stopping for a few weeks at the best places we came to. These I thought would be good centres of observation from which I might be able to make many telling excursions within a radius of eight or ten miles of the camps to learn something of the plants, animals, and rocks; for he assured me that I should be left perfectly free to follow my studies. I judged, however, that I was in no way the right man for the place, and freely explained my shortcomings, confessing that I was wholly unacquainted with the topography of the upper mountains, the streams that would have to be crossed, and the wild sheep-eating animals, etc.; in short that, what with bears, coyotes, rivers, cañons, and thorny, bewildering chaparral, I feared that half or more of his flock would be lost. Fortunately these shortcomings seemed insignificant to Mr. Delaney. The main thing, he said, was to have a man about the camp whom he could trust to see that the shepherd did his duty, and he assured me that the difficulties that seemed so formidable at a distance would vanish as we went on; encouraging me further by saying that the shepherd would do all the herding, that I could study plants and rocks and scenery as much as I liked, and that he would himself accompany us to the first main camp and make occasional visits to our higher ones to replenish our store of provisions and see how we prospered. Therefore I

concluded to go, though still fearing, when I saw the silly sheep
bouncing one by one through the narrow gate of the home corral
to be counted, that of the two thousand and fifty many would
never return.

I was fortunate in getting a fine St. Bernard dog for a companion. His master, a hunter with whom I was slightly acquainted,
came to me as soon as he heard that I was going to spend the
summer in the Sierra and begged me to take his favorite dog,
Carlo, with me, for he feared that if he were compelled to stay
all summer on the plains the fierce heat might be the death of
him. "I think I can trust you to be kind to him," he said, "and
I am sure he will be good to you. He knows all about the mountain animals, will guard the camp, assist in managing the sheep,
and in every way he found able and faithful." Carlo knew we
were talking about him, watched our faces, and listened so attentively that I fancied he understood us. Calling him by name,
I asked him if he was willing to go with me. He looked me in
the face with eyes expressing wonderful intelligence, then turned
to his master, and after permission was given by a wave of the
hand toward me and a farewell patting caress, he quietly followed
me as if he perfectly understood all that had been said and had
known me always.

June 3, 1869. — This morning provisions, camp-kettles, blankets, plant-press, etc., were packed on two horses, the flock headed
for the tawny foot-hills, and away we sauntered in a cloud of
dust: Mr. Delaney, bony and tall, with sharply hacked profile like
Don Quixote, leading the pack-horses, Billy, the proud shepherd,
a Chinaman and a Digger Indian to assist in driving for the first
few days in the brushy foot-hills, and myself with note-book tied
to my belt.

June 8. — The sheep, now grassy and good natured, slowly
nibbled their way down into the valley of the North Fork of
the Merced at the foot of Pilot Peak Ridge to the place selected
by the Don for our first central camp, a picturesque hopper-
shaped hollow formed by converging hill-slopes at a bend of the
river. Here racks for dishes and provisions were made in the
shade of the river-bank trees, and beds of fern fronds, Cedar

plumes, and various flowers, each to the taste of its owner, and a corral back on the open flat for the wool.

June 9. — How deep our sleep last night in the mountain's heart, beneath the trees and stars, hushed by solemn-sounding waterfalls and many small soothing voices in sweet accord whispering peace! And our first pure mountain day, warm, calm, cloudless — how immeasurable it seems, how serenely wild! I can scarcely remember its beginning. Along the river, over the hills, in the ground, in the sky, spring work is going on with joyful enthusiasm, new life, new beauty, unfolding, unrolling in glorious exuberant extravagance — new birds in their nests, new winged creatures in the air, and new leaves, new flowers, spreading, shining, rejoicing everywhere.

(*My First Summer in the Sierra*)

Billy the Shepherd
The Amorous Dog

AS THERE WERE many sides to Muir's character, there were also many sides to his writing. It ranges from the heights of poetry to the humorous portrayal of the foibles of man and beast, as in this delightful description of Billy the Shepherd and his stratified clothing and the succeeding account of his amorous dog, Jack. Muir was a genuine humorist, a fact that contributed to his fame as a teller of campfire tales. These two selections from the account of his first summer in the Sierra represent the sort of human, humorous descriptions that often enliven his books.

BILLY THE SHEPHERD

OUR SHEPHERD is a queer character and hard to place in this wilderness. His bed is a hollow made in red dry-rot punky dust beside a log which forms a portion of the south wall of the corral. Here he lies with his wonderful everlasting clothing on, wrapped in a red blanket, breathing not only the dust of the decayed wood but also that of the corral, as if determined to take ammoniacal snuff all night after chewing tobacco all day. Following the sheep he carries a heavy six-shooter swung from his belt on one side and his luncheon on the other. The ancient cloth in which the meat, fresh from the frying-pan, is tied serves as a filter through which the clear fat and gravy juices drip down on his right hip and leg in clustering stalactites. This oleaginous formation is soon broken up, however, and diffused and rubbed evenly into his scanty apparel, by sitting down, rolling over, crossing his legs while resting on logs, etc., making shirt and trousers water-tight and shiny. His trousers, in particular, have become so ad-hesive with the mixed fat and resin that pine-needles, thin flakes and fibers of bark, hair, mica scales and minute grains of quartz, hornblende, etc., feathers, seed-wings, moth and butterfly wings, legs and antennæ of innumerable insects, or even whole insects such as the small beetles, moths and mosquitoes, with flower petals, pollen dust and indeed bits of all plants, animals, and min-erals of the region adhere to them and are safely imbedded, so that though far from being a naturalist he collects fragmentary specimens of everything and becomes richer than he knows. His specimens are kept passably fresh, too, by the purity of the air and the resiny bituminous beds into which they are pressed. Man is a microcosm, at least our shepherd is, or rather his trousers. These precious overalls are never taken off, and nobody knows how old they are, though one may guess by their thickness and concentric structure. Instead of wearing thin they wear thick, and in their stratification have no small geological significance.

(*My First Summer in the Sierra*)

THE AMOROUS DOG

J
UNE 24. — Our regular allowance of clouds and thunder. Shepherd Billy is in a peck of trouble about the sheep; he de-clares that they are possessed with more of the evil one than any other flock from the beginning of the invention of mutton and wool to the last batch of it. No matter how many are missing, he will not, he says, go a step to seek them, because, as he reasons, while getting back one wanderer he would probably lose ten. Therefore runaway hunting must be Carlo's and mine. Billy's little dog Jack is also giving trouble by leaving camp every night to visit his neighbors up the mountain at Brown's Flat. He is a common-looking cur of no particular breed, but tremendously enterprising in love and war. He has cut all the ropes and leather straps he has been tied with, until his master in desperation, after

climbing the brushy mountain again and again to drag him back, fastened him with a pole attached to his collar under his chin at one end, and to a stout sapling at the other. But the pole gave good leverage, and by constant twisting during the night, the fastening at the sapling end was chafed off, and he set out on his usual journey, dragging the pole through the brush, and reached the Indian settlement in safety. His master followed, and making no allowance, gave him a beating, and swore in bad terms that next evening he would "fix that infatuated pup" by anchoring him unmercifully to the heavy cast-iron lid of our Dutch oven, weighing about as much as the dog. It was linked directly to his collar close up under the chin, so that the poor fellow seemed unable to stir. He stood quite discouraged until after dark, unable to look about him, or even to lie down unless he stretched himself out with his front feet across the lid, and his head close down between his paws. Before morning, however, Jack was heard far up the height howling Excelsior, cast-iron anchor to the contrary notwithstanding. He must have walked, or rather climbed, erect on his hind legs, clasping the heavy lid like a shield against his breast, a formidable iron-clad condition in which to meet his rivals. Next night, dog, pot-lid, and all, were tied up in an old bean-sack, and thus at last angry Billy gained the victory. Just before leaving home, Jack was bitten in the lower jaw by a rattle-snake, and for a week or so his head and neck were swollen to more than double the normal size; nevertheless he ran about as brisk and lively as ever, and is now completely recovered. The only treatment he got was fresh milk — a gallon or two at a time forcibly poured down his sore, poisoned throat.

(*My First Summer in the Sierra*)

The Mossy Boulder
Leaf Shadows

RARELY FOR LONG did Muir follow the beaten path. He continually turned aside, physically or in imagination, for little adventures by the way. Two of many instances of the kind in his Sierra record are these accounts of sleeping on the green bed of a mossy boulder and watching leaf shadows on a rock.

THE MOSSY BOULDER

J UNE 14. — The pool-basins below the falls and cascades hereabouts, formed by the heavy down-plunging currents, are kept nicely clean and clear of detritus. The heavier parts of the material swept over the falls are heaped up a short distance in front of the basins in the form of a dam, thus tending, together with erosion, to increase their size. Sudden changes, however, are effected during the spring floods, when the snow is melting and the upper tributaries are roaring loud from "bank to brae." Then boulders that have fallen into the channels, and which the ordinary summer and winter currents were unable to move, are suddenly swept forward as by a mighty besom, hurled over the falls into these pools, and piled up in a new dam together with part of the old one, while some of the smaller boulders are carried further down stream and variously lodged according to size and shape, all seeking rest where the force of the current is less than the resistance they are able to offer. But the greatest changes made in these relations of fall, pool, and dam are caused, not by the ordinary spring floods, but by extraordinary ones that occur at irregular intervals. The testimony of trees growing on flood boulder deposits shows that a century or more has passed since the last master flood came to awaken everything movable to go swirling and dancing on wonderful journeys. These floods may occur during the summer, when heavy thunder-showers, called "cloudbursts," fall on wide, steeply inclined stream basins furrowed by converging channels, which suddenly gather the waters together into the main trunk in booming torrents of enormous transporting power, though short lived.

One of these ancient flood boulders stands firm in the middle of the stream channel, just below the lower edge of the pool dam at the foot of the fall nearest our camp. It is a nearly cubical mass of granite about eight feet high, plushed with mosses over the top and down the sides to ordinary high-water mark. When I climbed on top of it to-day and lay down to rest, it seemed the most romantic spot I had yet found — the one big stone with its mossy level top and smooth sides standing square and firm and solitary, like an altar, the fall in front of it bathing it lightly with the finest of the spray, just enough to keep its moss cover fresh; the clear green pool beneath, with its foam-bells and its half circle of lilies leaning forward like a band of admirers, and flowering Dogwood and Alder trees leaning over all in sun-sifted arches. How soothingly, restfully cool it is beneath that leafy, translucent ceiling, and how delightful the water music — the deep bass tones of the fall, the clashing, ringing spray, and infinite variety of small low tones of the current gliding past the side of the boulder-island, and glinting against a thousand smaller stones down the ferny channel! All this shut in; every one of these influences acting at short range as if in a quiet room. The place seemed holy, where one might hope to see God.

After dark, when the camp was at rest, I groped my way back to the altar-boulder and passed the night on it — above the water, beneath the leaves and stars — everything still more impressive than by day, the fall seen dimly white, singing Nature's old love song with solemn enthusiasm, while the stars peering through the leaf-roof seemed to join in the white water's song. Precious night, precious day to abide in me forever. Thanks be to God for this immortal gift.

(My First Summer in the Sierra)

LEAF SHADOWS

JUNE 19. — Pure sunshine all day. How beautiful a rock is made by leaf shadows! Those of the Live-oak are particularly clear and distinct, and beyond all art in grace and delicacy, now still as if painted on stone, now gliding softly as if afraid of noise, now dancing, waltzing in swift, merry swirls, or jumping on and off sunny rocks in quick dashes like wave embroidery on seashore cliffs. How true and substantial is this shadow beauty, and with what sublime extravagance is beauty thus multiplied! The big orange lilies are now arrayed in all their glory of leaf and flower. Noble plants, in perfect health, Nature's darlings.

(My First Summer in the Sierra)

The Indian

BOTH IN Wisconsin and California Muir was disappointed in the Indians he met. Only partly did they represent the free wildness he admired. However, one aspect of their traditional way of life appealed to him. This was the manner in which they adapted themselves to their surroundings, fitted in with nature's ways, leaving hardly a scar on the landscape.

J UNE 16. — One of the Indians from Brown's Flat got right into the middle of the camp this morning, unobserved. I was seated on a stone, looking over my notes and sketches, and happening to look up, was startled to see him standing grim and silent within a few steps of me, as motionless and weather-stained as an old tree-stump that had stood there for centuries. All Indians seem to have learned this wonderful way of walking unseen — making themselves invisible like certain spiders I have been observing here, which, in case of alarm, caused, for example, by a bird alighting on the bush their webs are spread upon, immediately bounce themselves up and down on their elastic threads so rapidly that only a blur is visible. The wild Indian power of escaping observation, even where there is little or no cover to hide in, was probably slowly acquired in hard hunting and fighting lessons while trying to approach game, take enemies by surprise, or get safely away when compelled to retreat. And this experience transmitted through many generations seems at length to have become what is vaguely called instinct.

How smooth and changeless seems the surface of the mountains about us! Scarce a track is to be found beyond the range of the sheep except on small open spots on the sides of the streams, or where the forest carpets are thin or wanting. On the smoothest of these open strips and patches deer tracks may be seen, and the great suggestive footprints of bears, which, with those of the many small animals, are scarce enough to answer as a kind of light ornamental stitching or embroidery. Along the main ridges and larger branches of the river Indian trails may be traced, but they are not nearly as distinct as one would expect to find them. How many centuries Indians have roamed these woods nobody knows, probably a great many, extending far beyond the time that Columbus touched our shores, and it seems strange that heavier marks have not been made. Indians walk softly and hurt the landscape hardly more than the birds and squirrels, and their brush and bark huts last hardly longer than those of woodrats, while their more enduring monuments, excepting those wrought on the forests by the fires they made to improve their hunting grounds, vanish in a few centuries.

How different are most of those of the white man, especially on the lower gold region — roads blasted in the solid rock, wild streams dammed and tamed and turned out of their channels and led along the sides of cañons and valleys to work in mines like slaves. Crossing from ridge to ridge, high in the air, on long straddling trestles as if flowing on stilts, or down and up across valleys and hills, imprisoned in iron pipes to strike and wash away hills and miles of the skin of the mountain's face, riddling, stripping every gold gully and flat. These are the white man's marks made in a few feverish years, to say nothing of mills, fields, villages, scattered hundreds of miles along the flank of the Range. Long will it be ere these marks are effaced, though Nature is doing what she can, replanting, gardening, sweeping away old dams and flumes, leveling gravel and boulder piles, patiently trying to heal every raw scar. The main gold-storm is over. Calm enough are the gray old miners scratching a bare living in waste diggings here and there. Thundering underground blasting is still going on to feed the pounding quartz mills, but their influence on the landscape is light as compared with that of the pick-and-shovel storms waged a few years ago. Fortunately for Sierra scenery the gold-bearing slates are mostly restricted to the foothills. The region about our camp is still wild, and higher lies the snow about as trackless as the sky.

(*My First Summer in the Sierra*)

Bread Famine

THOSE WHO accompanied Muir into the mountains often marveled at the manner in which he would go for the better part of a day without thinking of food. One friend recalls a time when a fried trout was placed before him on a camp table after a long day in the mountains. Talking on, Muir forgot all about his food. He failed to notice a companion remove the fish and eat it. A new trout was placed before him. This in turn Muir ignored and another companion ate. Half a dozen times this was repeated while Muir, oblivious to what was taking place, was engrossed in his conversation. On his solo expeditions into the Sierra, he sometimes took oatmeal, which he cooked in little cakes; but the great staple diet of his life was hard bread. Even during his last days at Martinez he was wont to nibble on crusts of French bread while at work writing. Of all foods, he missed bread most. Hence the seriousness, in his eyes, of the bread famine here recounted.

JULY 6. — Mr. Delaney has not arrived, and the bread famine is sore. We must eat mutton a while longer, though it seems hard to get accustomed to it. I have heard of Texas pioneers living without bread or anything made from the cereals for months without suffering, using the breast-meat of wild turkeys for bread. Of this kind they had plenty in the good old days when life, though considered less safe, was fussed over the less. The trappers and fur traders of early days in the Rocky Mountain regions lived on bison and beaver meat for months. Salmon-eaters, too, there are among both Indians and whites who seem to suffer little or not at all from the want of bread. Just at this moment mutton seems the least desirable of food, though of good quality. We pick out the leanest bits, and down they go against heavy disgust, causing nausea and an effort to reject the offensive stuff. Tea makes matters worse, if possible. The stomach begins to assert itself as an independent creature with a will of its own. We should boil lupine leaves, clover, starchy petioles, and saxifrage rootstocks like the Indians. We try to ignore our gastric troubles, rise and gaze about us, turn our eyes to the mountains, and climb doggedly up through brush and rocks into the heart of the scenery. A stifled calm comes on, and the day's duties and even enjoyments are languidly got through with. We chew a few leaves of ceanothus by way of luncheon, and smell or chew the spicy monardella for the dull headache and stomach-ache that now lightens, now comes muffling down upon us and into us like fog. At night more mutton, flesh to flesh, down with it, not too much, and there are the stars shining through the Cedar plumes and branches above our beds.

July 7. — Rather weak and sickish this morning, and all about a piece of bread. Can scarce command attention to my best studies, as if one couldn't take a few days' saunter in the Godful woods without maintaining a base on a wheat-field and grist-mill. Like caged parrots we want a cracker, any of the hundred kinds — the remainder biscuit of a voyage around the world would answer well enough, nor would the wholesomeness of saleratus biscuit be questioned. Bread without flesh is a good diet, as on many botanical excursions I have proved. Tea also may easily be ignored. Just bread and water and delightful toil is all I need — not unreasonably much, yet one ought to be trained and tempered to enjoy life in these brave wilds in full independence of any particular kind of nourishment. That this may be accomplished is manifest, as far as bodily welfare is concerned, in the lives of people of other climes. The Eskimo, for example, gets a living far north of the wheat-line, from oily seals and whales. Meat, berries, bitter weeds, and blubber, or only the last, for months at a time; and yet these people all around the frozen shores of our continent are said to be hearty, jolly, stout, and brave. We hear, too, of fish-eaters, carnivorous as spiders, yet well enough as far as stomachs are concerned, while we are so ridiculously helpless, making wry faces over our fare, looking sheepish in digestive distress amid rumbling, grumbling sounds that might well pass for smothered baas. We have a large supply of sugar, and this evening it occurred to me that these belligerent stomachs might possibly, like complaining children, be coaxed with candy. Accordingly the frying-pan was cleansed, and a lot of sugar cooked in it to a sort of wax, but this stuff only made matters worse.

Man seems to be the only animal whose food soils him, making necessary much washing and shield-like bibs and napkins. Moles living in the earth and eating slimy worms are yet as clean as seals or fishes, whose lives are one perpetual wash. And, as we have seen, the squirrels in these resiny woods keep themselves clean in some mysterious way; not a hair is sticky, though they handle the gummy cones, and glide about apparently without care. The birds, too, are clean, though they seem to make a good deal of fuss washing and cleaning their feathers. Certain flies and ants I see are in a fix, entangled and sealed up in the sugar-wax we threw away, like some of their ancestors in amber. Our stomachs, like tired muscles, are sore with long squirming. Once I was very hungry in the Bonaventure graveyard near Savannah, Georgia, having fasted for several days; then the empty stomach seemed to chafe in much the same way as now, and a somewhat similar tenderness aching was produced, hard to bear, though the pain was not acute. We dream of bread, a sure sign we need it. Like the Indians, we ought to know how to get the starch out of fern and saxifrage stalks, lily bulbs, Pine bark, etc. Our education has been sadly neglected for many generations. Wild rice would be good. I noticed a leersia in wet meadow edges, but the seeds are small. Acorns are not ripe, nor pine-nuts, nor filberts. The inner bark of Pine or Spruce might be tried. Drank tea until half intoxicated. Man seems to crave a stimulant when anything extraordinary is going on, and this is the only one I use. Billy chews great quantities of tobacco, which I suppose helps to stupefy and moderate his misery. We look and listen for the Don every hour. How beautiful upon the mountains his big feet would be!

In the warm, hospitable Sierra, shepherds and mountain men in general, as far as I have seen, are easily satisfied as to food supplies and bedding. Most of them are heartily content to "rough it," ignoring Nature's fineness as bothersome or unmanly. The shepherd's bed is often only the bare ground and a pair of blankets, with a stone, a piece of wood, or a pack-saddle for a pillow. In choosing the spot, he shows less care than the dogs, for they usually deliberate before making up their minds in so important an affair, going from place to place, scraping away loose sticks and pebbles, and trying for comfort by making many changes, while the shepherd casts himself down anywhere, seemingly the least skilled of all rest seekers. His food, too, even when he has all he wants, is usually far from delicate, either in kind or cooking. Beans, bread of any sort, bacon, mutton, dried peaches, and sometimes potatoes and onions, make up his bill-of-fare, the two latter articles being regarded as luxuries on account of their weight as compared with the nourishment they contain; a half-sack or so of each may be put into the pack in setting out from the home ranch and in a few days they are done. Beans are the main stand-by, portable, wholesome, and capable of going far, besides being easily cooked, although curiously enough a great deal of mystery is supposed to lie about the bean-pot. No two cooks quite agree on the methods of making beans do their best, and, after petting and coaxing and nursing the savory mess — well oiled and mellowed with bacon boiled into the heart of it — the proud cook will ask, after dishing out a quart or two for trial, "Well, how do you like *my* beans?" as if by no possibility could they be like any other beans cooked in the same way, but must needs possess some special virtue of which he alone is master. Molasses, sugar, or pepper may be used to give desired flavors; or the first water may be poured off and a spoonful or two of ashes or soda added to dissolve or soften the skins more fully, according to various tastes and notions. But, like casks of wine, no two potfuls are exactly alike to every palate. Some are supposed to be spoiled by the moon, by some unlucky day, by the beans having been grown on soil not suitable; or the whole year may be to blame as not favorable for beans.

Coffee, too, has its marvels in the camp kitchen, but not so many, and not so inscrutable as those that beset the bean-pot. A low complacent grunt follows a mouthful drawn in with a gurgle, and the remark cast forth aimlessly, "That's good coffee." Then another gurgling sip and repetition of the judgment, "*Yes, sir, that is* good coffee." As to tea, there are but two kinds, weak and strong, the stronger the better. The only remark heard is, "That tea's weak," otherwise it is good enough and not worth mentioning. If it has been boiled an hour or two or smoked on a pitchy fire, no matter — who cares for a little tannin or creosote? they make the black beverage all the stronger and more attractive to tobacco-tanned palates.

Sheep-camp bread, like most California camp bread, is baked in Dutch ovens, some of it in the form of yeast powder biscuit, an unwholesome sticky compound leading straight to dyspepsia. The greater part, however, is fermented with sour dough, a handful from each batch being saved and put away in the mouth of the flour sack to inoculate the next. The oven is simply a cast-iron pot, about five inches deep and from twelve to eighteen inches wide. After the batch has been mixed and kneaded in a tin pan, the oven is slightly heated and rubbed with a piece of tallow or pork rind. The dough is then placed in it, pressed out against the sides, and left to rise. When ready for baking a shovelful of coals is spread out by the side of the fire and the oven set upon them, while another shovelful is placed on top of the lid, which is raised from time to time to see that the requisite amount of heat is being kept up. With care good bread may be made in this way, though it is liable to be burned or to be sour, or raised too much, and the weight of the oven is a serious objection.

At last Don Delaney comes doon the lang glen — hunger vanishes, we turn our eyes to the mountains, and to-morrow we go climbing toward cloudland.

(*My First Summer in the Sierra*)

On the Brink of Yosemite Falls

EDGAR ALLAN POE, in the memorable first sentences of "A Descent into the Maelström," produces a sense of dizzying height and an almost physical fear of falling. It is the only other example I recall that compares with this account of John Muir's perilous moments at the very lip of Yosemite Falls. Often, in his wanderings, Muir took chances; but always they were calculated risks. And, in later years, when his wife feared he might fall victim to pneumonia and die alone on one of his solitary journeys among the mountains, he used to answer quite simply and sincerely, "And where could one find a more glorious place to die?"

JULY 15. — Followed the Mono Trail up the eastern rim of the basin nearly to its summit, then turned off southward to a small shallow valley that extends to the edge of the Yosemite, which we reached about noon, and encamped. After luncheon I made haste to high ground, and from the top of the ridge on the west side of Indian Cañon gained the noblest view of the summit peaks I have ever yet enjoyed. Nearly all the upper basin of the Merced was displayed, with its sublime domes and cañons, dark upsweeping forests, and glorious array of white peaks deep in the sky, every feature glowing, radiating beauty that pours into our flesh and bones like heat rays from fire. Sunshine over all; no breath of wind to stir the brooding calm. Never before had I seen so glorious a landscape, so boundless an affluence of sublime mountain beauty. The most extravagant description I might give of this view to any one who has not seen similar landscapes with his own eyes would not so much as hint its grandeur and the spiritual glow that covered it. I shouted and gesticulated in a wild burst of ecstasy, much to the astonishment of St. Bernard Carlo, who came running up to me, manifesting in his intelligent eyes a puzzled concern that was very ludicrous, which had the effect of bringing me to my senses. A brown bear, too, it would seem, had been a spectator of the show I had made of myself, for I had gone but a few yards when I started one from a thicket of brush. He evidently considered me dangerous, for he ran away very fast, tumbling over the tops of the tangled Manzanita bushes in his haste. Carlo drew back, with his ears depressed as if afraid, and kept looking me in the face, as if expecting me to pursue and shoot, for he had seen many a bear battle in his day.

Following the ridge which made a gradual descent to the south, I came at length to the brow of that massive cliff that stands between Indian Cañon and Yosemite Falls, and here the far-famed valley came suddenly into view throughout almost its whole extent. The noble walls — sculptured into endless variety of domes and gables, spires and battlements and plain mural precipices — all a-tremble with the thunder tones of the falling water. The level bottom seemed to be dressed like a garden — sunny meadows here and there, and groves of Pine and Oak; the river of Mercy sweeping in majesty through the midst of them and flashing back the sunbeams. The great Tissiack, or Half Dome, rising at the upper end of the valley to a height of nearly a mile, is nobly proportioned and life-like, the most impressive of all the rocks, holding the eye in devout admiration, calling it back again and again from falls or meadows, or even the mountains beyond — marvelous cliffs, marvelous in sheer dizzy depth and sculpture, types of endurance. Thousands of years have they stood in the sky exposed to rain, snow, frost, earthquake and avalanche, yet they still wear the bloom of youth.

I rambled along the valley rim to the westward; most of it is rounded off on the very brink, so that it is not easy to find places where one may look clear down the face of the wall to the bottom. When such places were found, and I had cautiously set my feet and drawn my body erect, I could not help fearing a little

that the rock might split off and let me down, and what a down!
— more than three thousand feet. Still my limbs did not tremble,
nor did I feel the least uncertainty as to the reliance to be placed
on them. My only fear was that a flake of the granite, which in
some places showed joints more or less open and running parallel
with the face of the cliff, might give way. After withdrawing
from such places, excited with the view I had got, I would say to
myself, "Now don't go out on the verge again." But in the face
of Yosemite scenery cautious remonstrance is vain; under its spell
one's body seems to go where it likes with a will over which we
seem to have scarce any control.

After a mile or so of this memorable cliff work I approached
Yosemite Creek, admiring its easy, graceful, confident gestures as
it comes bravely forward in its narrow channel, singing the last
of its mountain songs on its way to its fate — a few rods more
over the shining granite, then down half a mile in snowy foam
to another world, to be lost in the Merced, where climate, vegetation, inhabitants, all are different. Emerging from its last gorge,
it glides in wide lace-like rapids down a smooth incline into a
pool where it seems to rest and compose its gray, agitated waters
before taking the grand plunge, then slowly slipping over the lip
of the pool basin, it descends another glossy slope with rapidly
accelerated speed to the brink of the tremendous cliff, and with
sublime, fateful confidence springs out free in the air.

I took off my shoes and stockings and worked my way cautiously down alongside the rushing flood, keeping my feet and
hands pressed firmly on the polished rock. The booming, roaring
water, rushing past close to my head, was very exciting. I had
expected that the sloping apron would terminate with the per-
pendicular wall of the valley, and that from the foot of it, where
it is less steeply inclined, I should be able to lean far enough out
to see the forms and behavior of the fall all the way down to the
bottom. But I found that there was yet another small brow over
which I could not see, and which appeared to be too steep for
mortal feet. Scanning it keenly, I discovered a narrow shelf about
three inches wide on the very brink, just wide enough for a rest
for one's heels. But there seemed to be no way of reaching it over

so steep a brow. At length, after careful scrutiny of the surface, I found an irregular edge of a flake of the rock some distance back from the margin of the torrent. If I was to get down to the brink at all that rough edge, which might offer slight finger-holds, was the only way. But the slope beside it looked dangerously smooth and steep, and the swift roaring flood beneath, overhead, and beside me was very nerve-trying. I therefore concluded not to venture farther, but did nevertheless. Tufts of artemisia were growing in clefts of the rock near by, and I filled my mouth with the bitter leaves, hoping they might help to prevent giddiness. Then, with a caution not known in ordinary circumstances, I crept down safely to the little ledge, got my heels well planted on it, then shuffled in a horizontal direction twenty or thirty feet until close to the outplunging current, which, by the time it had descended thus far, was already white. Here I obtained a perfectly free view down into the heart of the snowy, chanting throng of comet-like streamers, into which the body of the fall soon separates.

While perched on that narrow niche I was not distinctly conscious of danger. The tremendous grandeur of the fall in form and sound and motion, acting at close range, smothered the sense of fear, and in such places one's body takes keen care for safety on its own account. How long I remained down there, or how I returned, I can hardly tell. Anyhow I had a glorious time, and got back to camp about dark, enjoying triumphant exhilaration soon followed by dull weariness. Hereafter I'll try to keep from such extravagant, nerve-straining places. Yet such a day is well worth venturing for. My first view of the High Sierra, first view looking down into Yosemite, the death song of Yosemite Creek, and its flight over the vast cliff, each one of these is of itself enough for a great life-long landscape fortune — a most memorable day of days — enjoyment enough to kill if that were possible.

July 16. — My enjoyments yesterday afternoon, especially at the head of the fall, were too great for good sleep. Kept starting up last night in a nervous tremor, half awake, fancying that the foundation of the mountain we were camped on had given way and was falling into Yosemite Valley. In vain I roused myself to make a new beginning for sound sleep. The nerve strain had been too great, and again and again I dreamed I was rushing through the air above a glorious avalanche of water and rocks. One time, springing to my feet, I said, "This time it is real — all must die, and where could mountaineer find a more glorious death!"

(*My First Summer in the Sierra*)

The Bear, the Fly and the Grasshopper

TO MUIR, during this first summer in the Sierra, everything was new and fresh — lily and tree and bear and grasshopper. Everywhere he looked he saw things of interest, small things, large things, some rooted, some winged, some walking the earth. The following entry in his journal, concerning a day with a bear, a fly and a grasshopper, captures for the reader the mood of that time with its zest for life, its fresh delight in each new adventure, its never ending curiosity concerning all the mountain life around him.

J ULY 21. — Sketching on the Dome — no rain; clouds at noon about quarter filled the sky, casting shadows with fine effect on the white mountains at the heads of the streams, and a soothing cover over the gardens during the warm hours.

Saw a common house fly and a grasshopper and a brown bear. The fly and grasshopper paid me a merry visit on the top of the Dome, and I paid a visit to the bear in the middle of a small garden meadow between the Dome and the camp where he was standing alert among the flowers as if willing to be seen to advantage. I had not gone more than half a mile from camp this morning, when Carlo, who was trotting on a few yards ahead of me, came to a sudden, cautious standstill. Down went tail and ears, and forward went his knowing nose, while he seemed to be saying "Ha, what's this? A bear, I guess." Then a cautious advance of a few steps, setting his feet down softly like a hunting cat, and questioning the air as to the scent he had caught until all doubt vanished. Then he came back to me, looked me in the face, and with his speaking eyes reported a bear near by; then led on softly, careful, like an experienced hunter, not to make the slightest noise, and frequently looking back as if whispering "Yes, it's a bear, come and I'll show you." Presently we came to where the sunbeams were streaming through between the purple shafts of the Firs, which showed that we were nearing an open spot, and here Carlo came behind me, evidently sure that the bear was very near. So I crept to a low ridge of moraine boulders on the edge of a narrow garden meadow, and in this meadow I felt pretty sure the bear must be. I was anxious to get a good look at the sturdy mountaineer without alarming him; so drawing myself up noiselessly back of one of the largest of the trees I peered past its bulging buttresses, exposing only a part of my head, and there stood neighbor Bruin within a stone's throw, his hips covered by tall grass and flowers, and his front feet on the trunk of a Fir that had fallen out into the meadow, which raised his head so high that he seemed to be standing erect. He had not yet seen me, but was looking and listening attentively, showing that in some way he was aware of our approach. I watched his gestures and tried to make the most of my opportunity to learn what I could about him, fearing he would catch sight of me and run away. For I had been told that this sort of bear, the cinnamon, always ran from his bad brother man, never showing fight unless wounded or in defense of young. He made a telling picture standing alert in the sunny forest garden. How well he played his part, harmonizing in bulk and color and shaggy hair with the trunks of the trees and lush vegetation, as natural a feature as any other in the landscape. After examining at leisure, noting the sharp muzzle thrust inquiringly forward, the long shaggy hair on his broad chest, the stiff erect ears nearly buried in hair, and the slow heavy way he moved his head, I thought I should like to see his gait in running, so I made a sudden rush at him, shouting and swinging my hat to frighten him, expecting to see him make haste to get away. But to my dismay he did not run or show any sign of running. On the contrary, he stood his ground ready to fight and defend himself, lowered his head, thrust it forward, and looked sharply and fiercely at me. Then I suddenly began to fear that upon me would fall the work of running; but I was afraid to run, and therefore, like the bear, held my ground. We stood staring at each other in solemn silence within a dozen yards or thereabouts, while I fervently hoped that the power of the human eye over wild beasts would prove as great as it is said to be. How long our awfully strenuous interview lasted, I don't know; but at length in the slow fullness of time he pulled his huge paws down off the log, and with magnificent deliberation turned and walked leisurely up the meadow, stopping frequently to look back over his shoulder to see whether I was pursuing him, then moving on again, evidently neither fearing me very much nor trusting me. He was probably about five hundred pounds in weight, a broad rusty bundle of ungovernable wildness, a happy fellow whose lines have fallen in pleasant places. The flowery glade in which I saw him so well, framed like a picture, is one of the best of all I have yet discovered, a conservatory of Nature's precious plant people. Tall lilies were swinging their bells over the bear's back, with geraniums, larkspurs, columbines, and daisies brushing against his sides. A place for angels, one would say, instead of bears.

In the great cañons Bruin reigns supreme. Happy fellow, whom no famine can reach while one of his thousand kinds of food is spared him. His bread is sure at all seasons, ranged on the mountain-shelves like stores in a pantry. From one to the other, up or down he climbs, tasting and enjoying each in turn in different climates, as if he had journeyed thousands of miles to other countries north or south to enjoy their varied productions. I should like to know my hairy brothers better — though after this particular Yosemite bear, my very neighbor, had sauntered out of sight this morning, I reluctantly went back to camp for the Don's rifle to shoot him, if necessary, in defense of the flock. Fortunately I couldn't find him, and after tracking him a mile or two toward Mount Hoffman I bade him Godspeed and gladly returned to my work on the Yosemite dome.

The house fly also seemed at home and buzzed about me as I sat sketching, and enjoying my bear interview now it was over. I wonder what draws house flies so far up the mountains, heavy, gross feeders as they are, sensitive to cold, and fond of domestic ease. How have they been distributed from continent to continent, across seas and deserts and mountain chains, usually so influential in determining boundaries of species both of plants and animals. Beetles and butterflies are sometimes restricted to small areas. Each mountain in a range, and even the different zones of a mountain, may have its own peculiar species. But the house fly seems to be everywhere. I wonder if any island in mid-ocean is flyless. The bluebottle is abundant in these Yosemite woods, ever ready with his marvelous store of eggs to make all dead flesh fly. Bumblebees are here, and are well fed on boundless stores of nectar and pollen. The honeybee, though abundant in the foothills, has not yet got so high. It is only a few years since the first swarm was brought to California.

A queer fellow and a jolly fellow is the grasshopper. Up the mountains he comes on excursions, how high I don't know, but at least as far and high as Yosemite tourists. I was much interested with the hearty enjoyment of the one that danced and sang for me on the Dome this afternoon. He seemed brimful of glad, hilarious energy, manifested by springing into the air to a height of twenty or thirty feet, then diving and springing up again and making a sharp musical rattle just as the lowest point in the descent was reached. Up and down a dozen times or so he danced and sang, then alighted to rest, then up and at it again. The curves he described in the air in diving and rattling resembled those made by cords hanging loosely and attached at the same height at the ends, the loops nearly covering each other. Braver, heartier, keener carefree enjoyment of life I have never seen or heard in any creature, great or small. The life of this comic redlegs, the mountain's merriest child, seems to be made up of pure, condensed gayety. The Douglas Squirrel is the only living creature that I can compare him with in exuberant, rollicking, irrepressible jollity. Wonderful that these sublime mountains are so loudly cheered and brightened by a creature so queer. Nature in him seems to be snapping her fingers in the face of all earthy dejection and melancholy with a boyish hip-hip-hurrah. How the sound is made I do not understand. When he was on the ground he made not the slightest noise, nor when he was simply flying from place to place, but only when diving in curves, the motion seeming to be required for the sound; for the more vigorous the diving the more energetic the corresponding outbursts of jolly rattling. I tried to observe him closely while he was resting in the intervals of his performances; but he would not allow a near approach, always getting his jumping legs ready to spring for immediate flight, and keeping his eyes on me. A fine sermon the little fellow danced for me on the Dome, a likely place to look for sermons in stones, but not for grasshopper sermons. A large and imposing pulpit for so small a preacher. No danger of weakness in the knees of the world while Nature can spring such a rattle as this. Even the bear did not express for me the mountain's wild health and strength and happiness so tellingly as did this comical little hopper. No cloud of care in his day, no winter of discontent in sight. To him every day is a holiday; and when at length his sun sets, I fancy he will cuddle down on the forest floor and die like the leaves and flowers, and like them leave no unsightly remains calling for burial.

Sundown, and I must to camp. Good-night, friends three — brown bear, rugged boulder of energy in groves and gardens fair as Eden; restless fussy fly with gauzy wings stirring the air around all the world; and grasshopper, crisp electric spark of joy enlivening the massy sublimity of the mountains like the laugh of a child. Thank you, thank you all three for your quickening company. Heaven guide every wing and leg. Good night, friends three, good-night.

(My First Summer in the Sierra)

Professor Butler

WHEN, IN 1860, Muir had exhibited his whittled-out inventions at the Wisconsin State Fair, two small boys had volunteered to help demonstrate how his self-rising bed set an occupant on his feet in the morning. One of the boys was the son of James Davie Butler, Professor of Greek and Latin at the University of Wisconsin, a friend and disciple of Ralph Waldo Emerson and one of the most important influences in Muir's life. At the University Muir took courses under him and in his library he first read Emerson and Thoreau. It was Professor Butler who recognized Muir's literary bent. And it was Professor Butler who urged him to keep notebooks of his thoughts and observations during his wanderings. When Muir visited him at Madison, before starting on his thousand-mile walk to the Gulf, his teacher presented him with his own copy of Vergil's bucolic poems. However, Muir declined it with thanks saying he wanted to see nature not through Vergil's eyes but through his own. He did not see his revered friend again until the following remarkable meeting with him in Yosemite Valley.

AUGUST 2. — Clouds and showers, about the same as yesterday. Sketching all day on the North Dome until four or five o'clock in the afternoon, when, as I was busily employed thinking only of the glorious Yosemite landscape, trying to draw every tree and every line and feature of the rocks, I was suddenly, and without warning, possessed with the notion that my friend, Professor J. D. Butler, of the State University of Wisconsin, was below me in the valley, and I jumped up full of the idea of meeting him, with almost as much startling excitement as if he had suddenly touched me to make me look up. Leaving my work without the slightest deliberation, I ran down the western slope of the Dome and along the brink of the valley wall, looking for a way to the bottom, until I came to a side cañon, which, judging by its apparently continuous growth of trees and bushes, I thought might afford a practical way into the valley, and immediately began to make the descent, late as it was, as if drawn irresistibly. But after a little, common sense stopped me and explained that it would be long after dark ere I could possibly reach the hotel, that the visitors would be asleep, that nobody would know me, that I had no money in my pockets, and moreover was without a coat. I therefore compelled myself to stop, and finally succeeded in reasoning myself out of the notion of seeking my friend in the dark, whose presence I only felt in a strange, telepathic way. I succeeded in dragging myself back through the woods to camp, never for a moment wavering, however, in my determination to go down to him next morning. This I think is the most unexplainable notion that ever struck me. Had some one whispered in my ear while I sat on the Dome, where I had spent so many days, that Professor Butler was in the valley, I could not have been more surprised and startled. When I was leaving the University he said, "Now, John, I want to hold you in sight and watch your career. Promise to write me at least once a year." I received a letter from him in July, at our first camp in the Hollow, written in May, in which he said that he might possibly visit California some time this summer, and therefore hoped to meet me. But inasmuch as he named no meeting-place, and gave no directions as to the course he would probably follow, and as I should be in the wilderness all summer, I had not the slightest hope of seeing him, and all thought of the matter had vanished from my mind until this afternoon, when he seemed to be wafted bodily almost against my face. Well, to-morrow I shall see; for, reasonable or unreasonable, I feel I must go.

August 3. — Had a wonderful day. Found Professor Butler as the compass-needle finds the pole. So last evening's telepathy, transcendental revelation, or whatever else it may be called, was true; for, strange to say, he had just entered the valley by way of the Coulterville Trail and was coming up the valley past El Capitan when his presence struck me. Had he then looked toward the North Dome with a good glass when it first came in sight, he might have seen me jump up from my work and run toward him. This seems the one well-defined marvel of my life of the kind called supernatural; for, absorbed in glad Nature, spirit-rappings, second sight, ghost stories, etc., have never interested me since boyhood, seeming comparatively useless and infinitely less wonderful than Nature's open, harmonious, songful, sunny, every-day beauty.

This morning, when I thought of having to appear among tourists at a hotel, I was troubled because I had no suitable clothes, and at best am desperately bashful and shy. I was determined to go, however, to see my old friend after two years among strangers; got on a clean pair of overalls, a cashmere shirt, and a sort of jacket — the best my camp wardrobe afforded — tied my note-book on my belt, and strode away on my strange journey, followed by Carlo. I made my way through the gap discovered last evening, which proved to be Indian Cañon. There was no trail in it, and the rocks and brush were so rough that Carlo frequently called me back to help him down precipitous places. Emerging from the cañon shadows, I found a man making hay on one of the meadows, and asked him whether Professor Butler was in the valley. "I don't know," he replied; "but you can easily find out at the hotel. There are but few visitors in the valley just now. A small party came in yesterday afternoon, and I heard some one called Professor Butler, or Butterfield, or some name like that."

In front of the gloomy hotel I found a tourist party adjusting their fishing tackle. They all stared at me in silent wonderment, as if I had been seen dropping down through the trees from the clouds, mostly, I suppose, on account of my strange garb. Inquiring for the office, I was told it was locked, and that the landlord was away, but I might find the landlady, Mrs. Hutchings, in the parlor. I entered in a sad state of embarrassment, and after I had waited in the big, empty room and knocked at several doors the landlady at length appeared, and in reply to my question said she rather thought Professor Butler *was* in the valley, but to make sure, she would bring the register from the office. Among the names of the last arrivals I soon discovered the Professor's familiar handwriting, at the sight of which bashfulness vanished; and having learned that his party had gone up the valley — probably to the Vernal and Nevada Falls — I pushed on in glad pursuit, my heart now sure of its prey. In less than an hour I reached the head of the Nevada Cañon at the Vernal Fall, and just outside of the spray discovered a distinguished-looking gentleman, who, like everybody else I have seen to-day, regarded me curiously as I approached. When I made bold to inquire if he knew where Professor Butler was, he seemed yet more curious to know what could possibly have happened that required a messenger for the Professor, and instead of answering my question he asked with military sharpness, "Who wants him?" "I want him," I replied with equal sharpness. "Why? Do *you* know him?" "Yes," I said. "Do *you* know him?" Astonished that any one in the mountains could possibly know Professor Butler and find him as soon as he had reached the valley, he came down to meet the strange mountaineer on equal terms, and courteously replied, "Yes, I know Professor Butler very well. I am General Alvord, and we were fellow students in Rutland, Vermont, long ago, when we were both young." "But where is he now?" I persisted, cutting short his story. "He has gone beyond the falls with a companion, to try to climb that big rock, the top of which you see from here." His guide now volunteered the information that it was the Liberty Cap Professor Butler and his companion had gone to climb, and that if I waited at the head of the fall I should be sure to find them on their way down. I therefore climbed the ladders alongside the Vernal Fall, and was pushing forward, determined to go to the top of Liberty Cap rock in my hurry, rather than wait, if I should not meet my friend sooner. So heart-hungry at times may one be to see a friend in the flesh, however happily full and carefree one's life may be. I had gone but a short distance, however, above the brow of the Vernal Fall when I caught sight of him in the brush and rocks, half erect, groping his way, his sleeves rolled up, vest open, hat in his hand, evidently very hot and tired. When he saw me coming he sat down on a boulder to wipe the perspiration from his brow and neck, and taking me for one of the valley guides, he inquired the way to the fall ladders. I pointed out the path marked with little piles of stones, on seeing which he called his companion, saying that the way was found; but he did not yet recognize me. Then I stood directly in front of him, looked him in the face, and held out my hand. He thought I was offering to assist him in rising. "Never mind," he said. Then I said, "Professor Butler, don't you know me?" "I think not," he replied; but catching my eye, sudden recognition followed, and astonishment that I should have found him just when he was lost in the brush and did not know that I was within hundreds of miles of him. "John Muir, John Muir, where have you come from?" Then I told him the story of my feeling his presence when he entered the valley last evening, when he was four or five miles distant, as I sat sketching on the North Dome. This, of course, only made him wonder the more. Below the foot of the Vernal Fall the guide was waiting with his saddle-horse, and I walked along the trail, chatting all the way back to the hotel, talking of schooldays, friends in Madison, of the students, how each had prospered, etc., ever and anon gazing at the stupendous rocks about us, now growing indistinct in the gloaming, and again quoting from the poets — a rare ramble.

It was late ere we reached the hotel, and General Alvord was waiting the Professor's arrival for dinner. When I was introduced he seemed yet more astonished than the Professor at my descent from cloudland and going straight to my friend without knowing in any ordinary way that he was even in California. They had come on direct from the East, had not yet visited any of their friends in the state, and considered themselves undiscoverable. As we sat at dinner, the General leaned back in his chair, and looking down the table, thus introduced me to the dozen guests or so, including the staring fisherman mentioned above: "This man, you know, came down out of these huge, trackless mountains, you know, to find his friend Professor

Butler here, the very day he arrived; and how did he know he was here? He just felt him, he says. This is the queerest case of Scotch farsightedness I ever heard of," etc., etc. While my friend quoted Shakespeare: "More things in heaven and earth, Horatio, than are dreamt of in your philosophy," "As the sun, ere he has risen, sometimes paints his image in the firmament, e'en so the shadows of events precede the events, and in to-day already walks to-morrow."

Had a long conversation, after dinner, over Madison days. The Professor wants me to promise to go with him, sometime, on a camping trip in the Hawaiian Islands, while I tried to get him to go back with me to camp in the High Sierra. But he says, "Not now." He must not leave the General; and I was surprised to learn they are to leave the valley to-morrow or next day. I'm glad I'm not great enough to be missed in the busy world.

August 4. — It seemed strange to sleep in a paltry hotel chamber after the spacious magnificence and luxury of the starry sky and Silver Fir grove. Bade farewell to my friend and the General. The old soldier was very kind, and an interesting talker. He told me long stories of the Florida Seminole war, in which he took part, and invited me to visit him in Omaha. Calling Carlo, I scrambled home through the Indian Cañon gate, rejoicing, pitying the poor Professor and General, bound by clocks, almanacs, orders, duties, etc., and compelled to dwell with lowland care and dust and din, where Nature is covered and her voice smothered, while the poor, insignificant wanderer enjoys the freedom and glory of God's wilderness.

(My First Summer in the Sierra)

IV

THE VALLEY

The Grandeur of Yosemite Falls
Illilouette Falls

"I AM," Muir wrote, "hopelessly and forever a mountaineer." Almost as soon as the Delaney sheep were safely down from the heights at the end of summer, he climbed back to Yosemite Valley. There he found employment with James M. Hutchings, first permanent resident in the valley and owner of the pioneer Hutchings Hotel. Tall and spare, originally a native of Northamptonshire, England, he had come to California in the same year Muir crossed the ocean from Scotland. His Illustrated California Magazine, *published from 1856 to 1861, had done much to spread knowledge of the beauties of the Yosemite region. Muir's job was to design, build and operate a sawmill on Yosemite Creek for cutting up trees that had blown down in the valley. Near the mill, on a bank of the creek, he built a snug shake cabin at a total cost of three dollars. He designed it so part of the stream flowed through a corner of the room, thus providing him with the sound of running water inside as well as outside the cabin. Here he lived for two years. The arrangements with his employer permitted him, when he was not actually engaged in the operation of the mill, to wander where he wished, visiting such spots of beauty as the waterfalls he here describes.*

THE GRANDEUR OF YOSEMITE FALLS

DURING THE TIME of the spring floods the best near view of the fall is obtained from Fern Ledge on the east side above the blinding spray at a height of about four hundred feet above the base of the fall. A climb of about fourteen hundred feet from the valley has to be made, and there is no trail, but to any one fond of climbing this will make the ascent all the more delightful. A narrow part of the ledge extends to the side of the fall and back of it, enabling us to approach it as closely as we wish. When the afternoon sunshine is streaming through the throng of comets, ever wasting, ever renewed, the marvelous fineness, firmness, and variety of their forms are beautifully revealed. At the top of the fall they seem to burst forth in irregular spurts from some grand, throbbing mountain-heart. Now and then one mighty throb sends forth a mass of solid water into the free air far beyond the others, which rushes alone to the bottom of the fall with long streaming tail, like combed silk, while the others, descending in clusters, gradually mingle and lose their identity. But they all rush past us with amazing velocity and display of power, though apparently drowsy and deliberate in their movements when observed from a distance of a mile or two. The heads of these comet-like masses are composed of nearly solid water, and are dense white in color like pressed snow, from the friction they suffer in rushing through the air, the portion worn off forming the tail, between the white lustrous threads and films of which faint, grayish pencilings appear, while the outer, finer sprays of water-dust, whirling in sunny eddies, are pearly gray throughout. At the bottom of the fall there is but little distinction of form visible. It is mostly a hissing, clashing, seething, upwhirling mass of scud and spray, through which the light sifts in gray and purple tones, while at times when the sun strikes at the required angle, the whole wild and apparently lawless, stormy, striving mass is changed to brilliant rainbow hues, manifesting finest harmony. The middle portion of the fall is the most openly beautiful; lower, the various forms into which the waters are wrought are more closely and voluminously veiled, while higher, toward the head, the current is comparatively simple and undivided. But even at the bottom, in the boiling clouds of spray, there is no confusion, while the rainbow light makes all divine, adding glorious beauty and peace to glorious power. This noble fall has far the richest, as well as the most powerful, voice of all the falls of the valley, its tones varying from the sharp hiss and rustle of the wind in the glossy leaves of the Live-oaks and the soft, sifting, hushing tones of the Pines, to the loudest rush and roar of storm-winds and thunder among the crags of the summit peaks. The low bass, booming, reverberating tones, heard under favorable circumstances five or six miles away, are formed by the dashing and exploding of heavy masses mixed with air upon two projecting ledges on the face of the cliff, the one on which we are standing and another about two hundred feet above it. The torrent of massive comets is continuous at time of high water, while the explosive, booming notes are wildly intermittent, because, unless influenced by the wind, most of the heavier masses shoot out from the face of the precipice, and pass the ledges upon which at other times they are exploded. Occasionally the whole fall is swayed away from the front of the cliff, then suddenly dashed flat against it, or vibrated from side to side like a pendulum, giving rise to endless variety of forms and sounds.

(The Yosemite)

ILLILOUETTE FALLS

ONE OF the finest effects of sunlight on falling water I ever saw in Yosemite or elsewhere I found on the brow of this beautiful fall. It was in the Indian summer, when the leaf-colors were ripe and the great cliffs and domes were transfigured in the hazy golden air. I had scrambled up its rugged talus-dammed cañon, oftentimes stopping to take breath and look back to admire the wonderful views to be had there of the great Half Dome, and to enjoy the extreme purity of the water, which in the motionless pools on this stream is almost perfectly invisible; the colored foliage of the Maples, Dogwoods, rubus tangles, etc., and the late goldenrods and asters. The voice of the fall was now low, and the grand spring and summer floods had waned to sifting, drifting gauze and thin-broidered folds of linked and arrowy lace-work. When I reached the foot of the fall sunbeams were glinting across its head, leaving all the rest of it in shadow; and on its illumined brow a group of yellow spangles of singular form and beauty were playing, flashing up and dancing in large flame-shaped masses, wavering at times, then steadying, rising and falling in accord with the shifting forms of the water. But the color of the dancing spangles changed not at all. Nothing in clouds or flowers, on bird wings or the lip of shells, could rival it in fineness. It was the most divinely beautiful mass of rejoicing yellow light I ever beheld — one of Nature's precious gifts that perchance may come to us but once in a lifetime.

(The Yosemite)

The Water Ouzel

ON THE twenty-ninth of June, 1869, while encamped with his 2500 "woolly bundles" on the north fork of the Merced River, Muir had noted in his journal: "I have been making the acquaintance of a very interesting little bird that flits about the falls and rapids . . . " This was his first introduction to the dipper, or water ouzel, of western mountain streams. His leisure time in the Yosemite afforded him a chance to study the bird intensively. Here, and elsewhere, he amassed the observations which later made his chapter on the water ouzel in The Mountains of California "the finest bird biography in existence." Two of the spots in the Sierra where he carried on these studies were later named Ouzel Basin and Ouzel Creek by David Starr Jordan.

THE WATERFALLS of the Sierra are frequented by only one bird — the ouzel or water thrush (*Cinclus Mexicanus,* Sw.). He is a singularly joyous and lovable little fellow, about the size of a robin, clad in a plain waterproof suit of bluish gray, with a tinge of chocolate on the head and shoulders. In form he is about as smoothly plump and compact as a pebble that had been whirled in a pot-hole, the flowing contour of his body being interrupted only by his strong feet and bill, the crisp wing-tips, and the upslanted wren-like tail.

Among all the countless waterfalls I have met in the course of ten years' exploration in the Sierra, whether among the icy peaks, or warm foot-hills, or in the profound yosemitic cañons of the middle region, not one was found without its ouzel. No cañon is too cold for this little bird, none too lonely, provided it be rich in falling water. Find a fall, or cascade, or rushing rapid, any-where upon a clear stream, and there you will surely find its complementary ouzel, flitting about in the spray, diving in foam-ing eddies, whirling like a leaf among beaten foam-bells; ever vigorous and enthusiastic, yet self-contained, and neither seeking nor shunning your company.

If disturbed while dipping about in the margin shallows, he either sets off with a rapid whir to some other feeding-ground up or down the stream, or alights on some half-submerged rock or snag out in the current, and immediately begins to nod and curtsey like a wren, turning his head from side to side with many other odd dainty movements that never fail to fix the attention of the observer.

He is the mountain streams' own darling, the hummingbird of blooming waters, loving rocky ripple slopes and sheets of foam as a bee loves flowers, as a lark loves sunshine and meadows. Among all the mountain birds, none has cheered me so much in my lonely wanderings — none so unfailingly. For both in winter and sum-mer he sings, sweetly, cheerily, independent alike of sunshine and of love, requiring no other inspiration than the stream on which he dwells. While water sings, so must he, in heat or cold, calm or storm, ever attuning his voice in sure accord; low in the drought of summer and the drought of winter, but never silent.

During the golden days of Indian summer, after most of the snow has been melted, and the mountain streams have become feeble — a succession of silent pools, linked together by shallow, transparent currents and strips of silvery lace-work — then the song of the ouzel is at its lowest ebb. But as soon as the winter clouds have bloomed, and the mountain treasuries are once more replenished with snow, the voices of the streams and ouzels in-crease in strength and richness until the flood season of early summer. Then the torrents chant their noblest anthems, and then is the flood-time of our songster's melody. As for weather, dark days and sun days are the same to him. The voices of most song-birds, however joyous, suffer a long winter eclipse; but the ouzel sings on through all the seasons and every kind of storm. Indeed, no storm can be more violent than those of the waterfalls in the midst of which he delights to dwell. However dark and boisterous the weather, snowing, blowing, or cloudy, all the same he sings, and with never a note of sadness. No need of spring sunshine to thaw *his* song, for it never freezes. Never shall you hear anything wintery from *his* warm breast; no pinched cheeping, no wavering notes between sorrow and joy; his mellow, fluty voice is ever tuned to downright gladness, as free from dejection as cock-crowing.

It is pitiful to see wee frost-pinched sparrows on cold mornings in the mountain groves shaking the snow from their feathers, and hopping about as if anxious to be cheery, then hastening back to their hidings out of the wind, puffing out their breast feathers over their toes, and subsiding among the leaves, cold and breakfastless, while the snow continues to fall, and there is no sign of clearing. But the ouzel never calls forth a single touch of pity; not because he is strong to endure, but rather because he seems to live a charmed life beyond the reach of every influence that makes endurance necessary.

One wild winter morning, when Yosemite Valley was swept its length from west to east by a cordial snowstorm, I sallied forth to see what I might learn and enjoy. A sort of gray, gloaming-like darkness filled the valley, the huge walls were out of sight, all ordinary sounds were smothered, and even the loudest booming of the falls was at times buried beneath the roar of the heavy-laden blast. The loose snow was already over five feet deep on the meadows, making extended walks impossible without the aid of snowshoes. I found no great difficulty, however, in making my way to a certain ripple on the river where one of my ouzels lived. He was at home, busily gleaning his breakfast among the pebbles of a shallow portion of the margin, apparently unaware of anything extraordinary in the weather. Presently he flew out to a stone against which the icy current was beating, and turning his back to the wind, sang as delightfully as a lark in springtime.

After spending an hour or two with my favorite, I made my way across the valley, boring and wallowing through the drifts, to learn as definitely as possible how the other birds were spending their time. The Yosemite birds are easily found during the winter because all of them excepting the ouzel are restricted to the sunny north side of the valley, the south side being constantly eclipsed by the great frosty shadow of the wall. And because the Indian Cañon groves, from their peculiar exposure are the warmest, the birds congregate there, more especially in severe weather.

I found most of the robins cowering on the lee side of the larger branches where the snow could not fall upon them, while two or three of the more enterprising were making desperate efforts to reach the mistletoe berries by clinging nervously to the under side of the snow-crowned masses, back downward, like woodpeckers. Every now and then they would dislodge some of the loose fringes of the snow-crown, which would come sifting down on them and send them screaming back to camp, where they would subside among their companions with a shiver, muttering in low, querulous chatter like hungry children.

Some of the sparrows were busy at the feet of the larger trees gleaning seeds and benumbed insects, joined now and then by a robin weary of his unsuccessful attempts upon the snow-covered berries. The brave woodpeckers were clinging to the snowless sides of the larger boles and overarching branches of the camp trees, making short flights from side to side of the grove, pecking now and then at the acorns they had stored in the bark, and chattering aimlessly as if unable to keep still, yet evidently putting in the time in a very dull way, like storm-bound travelers at a country tavern. The hardy nuthatches were threading the open furrows of the trunks in their usual industrious manner, and uttering their quaint notes, evidently less distressed than their neighbors. The Steller's jays were, of course, making more noisy stir than all the other birds combined; ever coming and going with loud bluster, screaming as if each had a lump of melting sludge in his throat, and taking good care to improve the favorable opportunity afforded by the storm to steal from the acorn stores of the woodpeckers. I also noticed one solitary gray eagle braving the storm on the top of a tall Pine stump just outside the main grove. He was standing bolt upright with his back to the wind, a tuft of snow piled on his square shoulders, a monument of passive endurance. Thus every snow-bound bird seemed more or less uncomfortable if not in positive distress. The storm was reflected in every gesture, and not one cheerful note, not to say song, came from a single bill; their cowering, joyless endurance offering a striking contrast to the spontaneous, irrepressible gladness of the ouzel, who could no more help exhaling sweet song than a rose sweet fragrance. He *must* sing, though the heavens fall. I remember noticing the distress of a pair of robins during the violent earthquake of the year 1872, when the Pines of the valley, with strange movements, flapped and waved their branches, and beetling rock brows came thundering down to the meadows in tremendous avalanches. It did not occur to me in the midst of the excitement of other observations to look for the ouzels, but I doubt not they were singing straight on through it all, regarding the terrible rock thunder as fearlessly as they do the booming of the waterfalls.

What may be regarded as the separate songs of the ouzel are exceedingly difficult of description, because they are so variable and at the same time so confluent. Though I have been acquainted with my favorite ten years, and during most of this time have heard him sing nearly every day, I still detect notes and strains that seem new to me. Nearly all of his music is sweet and tender, lapsing from his round breast like water over the smooth lip of a pool, then breaking farther on into a sparkling foam of melodious notes, which glow with subdued enthusiasm, yet without expressing much of the strong, gushing ecstasy of the bobolink or skylark.

The more striking strains are perfect arabesques of melody, composed of a few full, round, mellow notes, embroidered with delicate trills which fade and melt in long slender cadences. In a general way his music is that of the streams refined and spiritualized. The deep booming notes of the falls are in it, the trills of rapids, the gurgling of margin eddies, the low whispering of level reaches, and the sweet tinkle of separate drops oozing from the ends of mosses and falling into tranquil pools.

The ouzel never sings in chorus with other birds, nor with his kind, but only with the streams. And like flowers that bloom beneath the surface of the ground, some of our favorite's best song-blossoms never rise above the surface of the heavier music of the water. I have often observed him singing in the midst of beaten spray, his music completely buried beneath the water's roar; yet I knew he was surely singing by his gestures and the movements of his bill.

His food, as far as I have noticed, consists of all kinds of water insects, which in summer are chiefly procured along shallow margins. Here he wades about ducking his head under water and deftly turning over pebbles and fallen leaves with his bill, seldom choosing to go into deep water where he has to use his wings in diving.

He seems to be especially fond of the larvæ of mosquitoes, found in abundance attached to the bottom of smooth rock channels where the current is shallow. When feeding in such places he wades upstream, and often while his head is under water the swift current is deflected upward along the glossy curves of his neck and shoulders, in the form of a clear, crystalline shell, which fairly incloses him like a bell-glass, the shell being broken and re-formed as he lifts and dips his head; while ever and anon he sidles out to where the too powerful current carries him off his feet; then he dexterously rises on the wing and goes gleaning again in shallower places.

But during the winter, when the stream banks are embossed in snow, and the streams themselves are chilled nearly to the freezing-point, so that the snow falling into them in stormy weather is not wholly dissolved, but forms a thin, blue sludge, thus rendering the current opaque — then he seeks the deeper portions of the main rivers, where he may dive to clear water beneath the sludge. Or he repairs to some open lake or millpond, at the bottom of which he feeds in safety.

When thus compelled to betake himself to a lake, he does not plunge into it at once like a duck, but always alights in the first place upon some rock or fallen Pine along the shore. Then flying out thirty or forty yards, more or less, according to the character of the bottom, he alights with a dainty glint on the surface, swims about, looks down, finally makes up his mind, and disappears with a sharp stroke of his wings. After feeding for two or three minưtes, he suddenly reappears, showers the water from his wings with one vigorous shake, and rises abruptly into the air as if pushed up from beneath, comes back to his perch, sings a few minutes, and goes out to dive again; thus coming and going, singing and diving at the same place for hours.

The ouzel is usually found singly; rarely in pairs, excepting during the breeding-season, and *very* rarely in threes or fours. I once observed three thus spending a winter morning in company, upon a small glacier lake, on the Upper Merced, about seventy-five hundred feet above the level of the sea. A storm had occurred during the night, but the morning sun shone unclouded, and the shadowy lake, gleaming darkly in its setting of fresh snow, lay smooth and motionless as a mirror. My camp chanced to be within a few feet of the water's edge, opposite a fallen Pine, some of the branches of which leaned out over the lake. Here my three dearly welcome visitors took up their station, and at once began to embroider the frosty air with their delicious melody, doubly delightful to me that particular morning, as I had been somewhat apprehensive of danger in breaking my way down through the snow-choked cañons to the lowlands.

The portion of the lake bottom selected for a feeding-ground lies at a depth of fifteen or twenty feet below the surface, and is covered with a short growth of algæ and other aquatic plants — facts I had previously determined while sailing over it on a raft. After alighting on the glassy surface, they occasionally indulged in a little play, chasing one another round about in small circles; then all three would suddenly dive together, and then come ashore and sing.

The ouzel seldom swims more than a few yards on the surface, for, not being web-footed, he makes rather slow progress, but by means of his strong, crisp wings he swims, or rather flies, with celerity under the surface, often to considerable distances. But it is in withstanding the force of heavy rapids that his strength of wing in this respect is most strikingly manifested. The following may be regarded as a fair illustration of his power of sub-aquatic flight. One stormy morning in winter when the Merced River was blue and green with unmelted snow, I observed one of my ouzels perched on a snag out in the midst of a swift-rushing rapid, singing cheerily, as if everything was just to his mind; and while I stood on the bank admiring him, he suddenly plunged into the sludgy current, leaving his song abruptly broken off. After feeding a minute or two at the bottom, and when one would suppose that he must inevitably be swept far downstream, he emerged just where he went down, alighted on the same snag, showered the water beads from his feathers, and continued his unfinished song, seemingly in tranquil ease as if it had suffered no interruption.

The ouzel alone of all birds dares to enter a white torrent. And though strictly terrestrial in structure, no other is so inseparably related to water, not even the duck, or the bold ocean albatross, or the stormy petrel. For ducks go ashore as soon as they finish feeding in undisturbed places, and very often make long flights overland from lake to lake or field to field. The same is true of most other aquatic birds. But the ouzel, born on the brink of a stream, or on a snag or boulder in the midst of it, seldom leaves it for a single moment. For, notwithstanding he is often on the wing, he never flies overland, but whirs with rapid, quail-like beat above the stream, tracing all its windings. Even when the stream is quite small, say from five to ten feet wide, he seldom shortens his flight by crossing a bend, however abrupt it may be; and even when disturbed by meeting some one on the bank, he prefers to fly over one's head, to dodging out over the ground. When, therefore, his flight along a crooked stream is viewed endwise, it appears most strikingly wavered — a description on the air of every curve with lightning-like rapidity.

The vertical curves and angles of the most precipitous torrents he traces with the same rigid fidelity, swooping down the inclines of cascades, dropping sheer over dizzy falls amid the spray, and ascending with the same fearlessness and ease, seldom seeking to lessen the steepness of the acclivity by beginning to ascend before reaching the base of the fall. No matter though it may be several hundred feet in height he holds straight on, as if about to dash headlong into the throng of booming rockets, then darts abruptly upward, and, after alighting at the top of the precipice to rest a moment, proceeds to feed and sing. His flight is solid and impetuous, without any intermission of wing-beats — one homogeneous buzz like that of a laden bee on its way home. And while thus buzzing freely from fall to fall, he is frequently heard giving utterance to a long outdrawn train of unmodulated notes, in no way connected with his song, but corresponding closely with his flight in sustained vigor.

Were the flights of all the ouzels in the Sierra traced on a chart, they would indicate the direction of the flow of the entire system of ancient glaciers, from about the period of the breaking up of the ice-sheet until near the close of the glacial winter; because the streams which the ouzels so rigidly follow are, with the unimportant exceptions of a few side tributaries, all flowing in channels eroded for them out of the solid flank of the range by the vanished glaciers — the streams tracing the ancient glaciers, the ouzels tracing the streams. Nor do we find so complete compliance to glacial conditions in the life of any other mountain bird, or animal of any kind. Bears frequently accept the pathways laid down by glaciers as the easiest to travel; but they often leave them and cross over from cañon to cañon. So also, most of the birds trace the moraines to some extent, because the forests are growing on them. But they wander far, crossing the cañons from grove to grove, and draw exceedingly angular and complicated courses.

The ouzel's nest is one of the most extraordinary pieces of bird architecture I ever saw, odd and novel in design, perfectly fresh and beautiful, and in every way worthy of the genius of the little builder. It is about a foot in diameter, round and bossy in outline, with a neatly arched opening near the bottom, somewhat like an old-fashioned brick oven, or Hottentot's hut. It is built almost exclusively of green and yellow mosses, chiefly the beautiful fronded hypnum that covers the rocks and old drift-logs in the vicinity of waterfalls. These are deftly interwoven, and felted together into a charming little hut; and so situated that many of the outer mosses continue to flourish as if they had not been plucked. A few fine, silky-stemmed grasses are occasionally found interwoven with the mosses, but, with the exception of a thin layer lining the floor, their presence seems accidental, as they are of a species found growing with the mosses and are probably plucked with them. The site chosen for this curious mansion is usually some little rock shelf within reach of the lighter particles of the spray of a waterfall, so that its walls are kept green and growing, at least during the time of high water.

No harsh lines are presented by any portion of the nest as seen in place, but when removed from its shelf, the back and bottom, and sometimes a portion of the top, is found quite sharply angular, because it is made to conform to the surface of the rock upon which and against which it is built, the little architect always taking advantage of slight crevices and protuberances that may chance to offer, to render his structure stable by means of a kind of gripping and dovetailing.

In choosing a building-spot, concealment does not seem to be taken into consideration; yet notwithstanding the nest is large and guilelessly exposed to view, it is far from being easily detected, chiefly because it swells forward like any other bulging moss cushion growing naturally in such situations. This is more especially the case where the nest is kept fresh by being well sprinkled. Sometimes these romantic little huts have their beauty enhanced by rock ferns and grasses that spring up around the mossy walls, or in front of the doorsill, dripping with crystal beads.

Furthermore, at certain hours of the day, when the sunshine is poured down at the required angle, the whole mass of the spray enveloping the fairy establishment is brilliantly irised; and it is through so glorious a rainbow atmosphere as this that some of our blessed ouzels obtain their first peep at the world.

Ouzels seem so completely part and parcel of the streams they inhabit, they scarce suggest any other origin than the streams themselves; and one might almost be pardoned in fancying they come direct from the living waters, like flowers from the ground. At least, from whatever cause, it never occurred to me to look for their nests until more than a year after I had made the acquaintance of the birds themselves, although I found one the very day on which I began the search. In making my way from Yosemite to the glaciers at the heads of the Merced and Tuolumne Rivers, I camped in a particularly wild and romantic portion of the Nevada cañon where in previous excursions I had never failed to enjoy the company of my favorites, who were attracted here, no doubt, by the safe nesting-places in the shelving rocks, and by the abundance of food and falling water. The river, for miles above and below, consists of a succession of small falls from ten to sixty feet in height, connected by flat, plume-like cascades that go flashing from fall to fall, free and almost channelless, over waving folds of glacier-polished granite.

On the south side of one of the falls, that portion of the precipice bathed by the spray presents a series of little shelves and tablets caused by the development of planes of cleavage in the granite, and by the consequent fall of masses through the action of the water. "Now, here," said I, "of all places, is the most charming spot for an ouzel's nest." Then carefully scanning the fretted face of the precipice through the spray, I at length noticed a yellowish moss cushion, growing on the edge of a level tablet within five or six feet of the outer folds of the fall. But apart from the fact of its being situated where one acquainted with the lives of ouzels would fancy an ouzel's nest ought to be, there was nothing in its appearance visible at first sight, to distinguish it from other bosses of rock-moss similarly situated with reference to perennial spray; and it was not until I had scrutinized it again and again, and had removed my shoes and stockings and crept along the face of the rock within eight or ten feet of it, that I could decide certainly whether it was a nest or a natural growth.

In these moss huts three or four eggs are laid, white like foam bubbles; and well may the little birds hatched from them sing water-songs, for they hear them all their lives, and even before they are born.

I have often observed the young just out of the nest making their odd gestures, and seeming in every way as much at home as their experienced parents, like young bees on their first excursions to the flower fields. No amount of familiarity with people and their ways seems to change them in the least. To all appearance their behavior is just the same on seeing a man for the first time, as when they have seen him frequently.

On the lower reaches of the rivers where mills are built, they sing on through the din of the machinery, and all the noisy confusion of dogs, cattle, and workmen. On one occasion, while a wood-chopper was at work on the river-bank, I observed one cheerily singing within reach of the flying chips. Nor does any kind of unwonted disturbance put him in bad humor, or frighten him out of calm self-possession. In passing through a narrow gorge, I once drove one ahead of me from rapid to rapid, disturbing him four times in quick succession where he could not very well fly past me on account of the narrowness of the channel. Most birds under similar circumstances fancy themselves pursued, and become suspiciously uneasy; but, instead of growing nervous about it, he made his usual dippings, and sang one of his most tranquil strains. When observed within a few yards their eyes are seen to express remarkable gentleness and intelligence; but they seldom allow so near a view unless one wears clothing of about the same color as the rocks and trees, and knows how to sit still. On one occasion, while rambling along the shore of a mountain lake, where the birds, at least those born that season, had never seen a man, I sat down to rest on a large stone close to the water's edge, upon which it seemed the ouzels and sandpipers were in the habit of alighting when they came to feed on that part of the shore, and some of the other birds also, when they came down to wash or drink. In a few minutes, along came a whirring ouzel and alighted on the stone beside me, within reach of my hand. Then suddenly observing me, he stooped nervously as if about to fly on the instant, but as I remained as motionless as the stone, he gained confidence, and looked me steadily in the face for about a minute, then flew quietly to the outlet and began to sing. Next came a sandpiper and gazed at me with much the same guileless expression of eye as the ouzel. Lastly, down with a swoop came a Steller's jay out of a Fir tree, probably with the intention of moistening his noisy throat. But instead of sitting confidingly as my other visitors had done, he rushed off at once, nearly tumbling heels over head into the lake in his suspicious confusion, and with loud screams roused the neighborhood.

Love for songbirds, with their sweet human voices, appears

to be more common and unfailing than love for flowers. Every one loves flowers to some extent, at least in life's fresh morning, attracted by them as instinctively as hummingbirds and bees. Even the young Digger Indians have sufficient love for the brightest of those found growing on the mountains to gather them and braid them as decorations for the hair. And I was glad to discover, through the few Indians that could be induced to talk on the subject, that they have names for the wild rose and the lily, and other conspicuous flowers, whether available as food or otherwise. Most men, however, whether savage or civilized, become apathetic toward all plants that have no other apparent use than the use of beauty. But fortunately one's first instinctive love of songbirds is never wholly obliterated, no matter what the influences upon our lives may be. I have often been delighted to see a pure, spiritual glow come into the countenances of hard business men and old miners, when a songbird chanced to alight near them. Nevertheless, the little mouthful of meat that swells out the breasts of some songbirds is too often the cause of their death. Larks and robins in particular are brought to market in hundreds. But fortunately the ouzel has no enemy so eager to eat his little body as to follow him into the mountain solitudes. I never knew him to be chased even by hawks.

An acquaintance of mine, a sort of foot-hill mountaineer, had a pet cat, a great, dozy, overgrown creature, about as broad-shouldered as a lynx. During the winter, while the snow lay deep, the mountaineer sat in his lonely cabin among the Pines smoking his pipe and wearing the dull time away. Tom was his sole companion, sharing his bed, and sitting beside him on a stool with much the same drowsy expression of eye as his master. The good-natured bachelor was content with his hard fare of soda bread and bacon, but Tom, the only creature in the world acknowledging dependence on him, must needs be provided with fresh meat. Accordingly he bestirred himself to contrive squirrel traps, and waded the snowy woods with his gun, making sad havoc among the few winter birds, sparing neither robin, sparrow, nor tiny nuthatch, and the pleasure of seeing Tom eat and grow fat was his great reward.

One cold afternoon, while hunting along the river-bank, he noticed a plain-feathered little bird skipping about in the shallows, and immediately raised his gun. But just then the confiding songster began to sing, and after listening to his summery melody the charmed hunter turned away, saying, "Bless your little heart, I can't shoot you, not even for Tom."

Even so far north as icy Alaska, I have found my glad singer. When I was exploring the glaciers between Mount Fairweather and the Stickeen River, one cold day in November, after trying in vain to force a way through the innumerable icebergs of Sum Dum Bay to the great glaciers at the head of it, I was weary and baffled and sat resting in my canoe convinced at last that I would have to leave this part of my work for another year. Then I began to plan my escape to open water before the young ice which was beginning to form should shut me in. While I thus lingered drifting with the bergs, in the midst of these gloomy forebodings and all the terrible glacial desolation and grandeur, I suddenly heard the well-known whir of an ouzel's wings, and, looking up saw my little comforter coming straight across the ice from the shore. In a second or two he was with me, flying three times round my head with a happy salute, as if saying, "Cheer up, old friend; you see I'm here, and all's well." Then he flew back to the shore, alighted on the topmost jag of a stranded iceberg, and began to nod and bow as though he were on one of his favorite boulders in the midst of a sunny Sierra cascade.

The species is distributed all along the mountain ranges of the Pacific Coast from Alaska to Mexico, and east to the Rocky Mountains. Nevertheless, it is as yet comparatively little known. Audubon and Wilson did not meet it. Swainson was, I believe, the first naturalist to describe a specimen from Mexico. Specimens were shortly afterward procured by Drummond near the sources of the Athabasca River, between the fifty-fourth and fifty-sixth parallels; and it has been collected by nearly all of the numerous exploring expeditions undertaken of late through our Western States and Territories; for it never fails to engage the attention of naturalists in a very particular manner.

Such then, is our little cinclus, beloved of every one who is so fortunate as to know him. Tracing on strong wing every curve of the most precipitous torrents from one extremity of the Sierra to the other; not fearing to follow them through their darkest gorges and coldest snow-tunnels; acquainted with every waterfall, echoing their divine music; and throughout the whole of their beautiful lives interpreting all that we in our unbelief call terrible in the utterances of torrents and storms, as only varied expressions of God's eternal love.

(The Mountains of California)

Emerson at Yosemite

THE GREAT EVENT of Muir's second spring in Yosemite was the arrival in the valley of Ralph Waldo Emerson. In April 1871, Emerson with a party of twelve left Boston for California. A Western Journey with Mr. Emerson, by the historian of the expedition, the Boston lawyer James Bradley Thayer, appeared in 1884. He recalls the accommodations in Yosemite at the time were so simple that one of the party was awakened by the cackling of a hen walking over his bed in search of a place to lay an egg. That spring Muir was thirty-three; Emerson, "in the late Indian Summer of his years," was sixty-eight. Looking up at the Sequoias Muir showed him, he remarked, "These trees have a monstrous talent for being tall." As the party prepared to depart, "M," as Thayer refers to Muir, protested that leaving Yosemite so soon was "as if a photographer should remove his plate before the impression was fully made." Two years after Emerson's visit, Muir bestowed his name on "a grand wide-winged mountain" in the Yosemite region. This peak is now known as Mount Humphreys, and the name Mount Emerson has been transferred to another peak some two and a half miles to the southeast.

DURING MY FIRST years in the Sierra I was ever calling on everybody within reach to admire them, but I found no one half warm enough until Emerson came. I had read his essays, and felt sure that of all men he would best interpret the sayings of these noble mountains and trees. Nor was my faith weakened when I met him in Yosemite. He seemed as serene as a Sequoia, his head in the empyrean; and forgetting his age, plans, duties, ties of every sort, I proposed an immeasurable camping trip back in the heart of the mountains. He seemed anxious to go, but considerately mentioned his party. I said: "Never mind. The mountains are calling; run away, and let plans and parties and dragging lowland duties all 'gang tapsal-teerie.' We'll go up a cañon singing your own song, 'Good-by, proud world! I'm going home,' in divine earnest. Up there lies a new heaven and a new earth; let us go to the show." But alas, it was too late — too near the sundown of his life. The shadows were growing long, and he leaned on his friends. His party, full of indoor philosophy, failed to see the natural beauty and fullness of promise of my wild plan, and laughed at it in good-natured ignorance, as if it were necessarily amusing to imagine that Boston people might be led to accept Sierra manifestations of God at the price of rough camping. Anyhow, they would have none of it, and held Mr. Emerson to the hotels and trails.

After spending only five tourist days in Yosemite he was led away, but I saw him two days more; for I was kindly invited to go with the party as far as the Mariposa big trees. I told Mr. Emerson that I would gladly go to the Sequoias with him, if he would camp in the grove. He consented heartily, and I felt sure that we would have at least one good wild memorable night around a Sequoia camp-fire. Next day we rode through the magnificent forests of the Merced basin, and I kept calling his attention to the Sugar Pines, quoting his wood-notes, "Come listen what the pine tree saith," etc., pointing out the noblest as kings and high priests, the most eloquent and commanding preachers of all the mountain forests, stretching forth their century-old arms in benediction over the worshiping congregations crowded about them. He gazed in devout admiration, saying but little, while his fine smile faded away.

Early in the afternoon, when we reached Clark's Station, I was surprised to see the party dismount. And when I asked if we were not going up into the grove to camp they said: "No; it would never do to lie out in the night air. Mr. Emerson might take cold; and you know, Mr. Muir, that would be a dreadful thing."

In vain I urged, that only in homes and hotels were colds caught, that nobody ever was known to take cold camping in these woods, that there was not a single cough or sneeze in all the Sierra. Then I pictured the big climate-changing, inspiring fire I would make, praised the beauty and fragrance of Sequoia flame, told how the great trees would stand about us transfigured in the purple light, while the stars looked down between the great domes; ending by urging them to come on and make an immortal Emerson night of it. But the house habit was not to be overcome, nor the strange dread of pure night air, though it is only cooled day air with a little dew in it. So the carpet dust and unknowable reeks were preferred. And to think of this being a Boston choice! Sad commentary on culture and the glorious transcendentalism.

Accustomed to reach whatever place I started for, I was going up the mountain alone to camp, and wait the coming of the party next day. But since Emerson was so soon to vanish, I concluded to stop with him. He hardly spoke a word all the evening, yet it was a great pleasure simply to be near him, warming in the light of his face as at a fire. In the morning we rode up the trail through a noble forest of Pine and Fir into the famous Mariposa Grove, and stayed an hour or two, mostly in ordinary tourist fashion — looking at the biggest giants, measuring them with a tape line, riding through prostrate fire-bored trunks, etc., though Mr. Emerson was alone occasionally, sauntering about as if under a spell. As we walked through a fine group, he quoted, "There were giants in those days," recognizing the antiquity of the race. To commemorate his visit, Mr. Galen Clark, the guardian of the grove, selected the finest of the unnamed trees and requested him to give it a name. He named it Samoset, after the New England sachem, as the best that occurred to him.

The poor bit of measured time was soon spent, and while the saddles were being adjusted I again urged Emerson to stay. "You are yourself a Sequoia," I said. "Stop and get acquainted with your big brethren." But he was past his prime, and was now as a child in the hands of his affectionate but sadly civilized friends, who seemed as full of old-fashioned conformity as of bold intellectual independence. It was the afternoon of the day and the afternoon of his life, and his course was now westward down all the mountains into the sunset. The party mounted and rode away in wondrous contentment, apparently, tracing the trail through Ceanothus and Dogwood bushes, around the bases of the Big Trees, up the slope of the Sequoia basin, and over the divide. I followed to the edge of the grove. Emerson lingered in the rear of the train, and when he reached the top of the ridge, after all the rest of the party were over and out of sight, he turned his horse, took off his hat and waved me a last good-by. I felt lonely, so sure had I been that Emerson of all men would be the quickest to see the mountains and sing them. Gazing awhile on the spot where he vanished, I sauntered back into the heart of the grove, made a bed of Sequoia plumes and ferns by the side of a stream, gathered a store of firewood, and then walked about until sundown. The birds, robins, thrushes, warblers, etc., that had kept out of sight, came about me, now that all was quiet, and made cheer. After sundown I built a great fire, and as usual had it all to myself. And though lonesome for the first time in these forests, I quickly took heart again — the trees had not gone to Boston, nor the birds; and as I sat by the fire, Emerson was still with me in spirit, though I never again saw him in the flesh. He sent books and wrote, cheering me on; advised me not to stay too long in solitude. Soon he hoped that my guardian angel would intimate that my probation was at a close. Then I was to roll up my herbariums, sketches, and poems (though I never knew I had any poems), and come to his house; and when I tired of him and his humble surroundings, he would show me to better people.

But there remained many a forest to wander through, many a mountain and glacier to cross, before I was to see his Wachusett and Monadnock, Boston and Concord. It was seventeen years after our parting on the Wawona ridge that I stood beside his grave under a Pine tree on the hill above Sleepy Hollow. He had gone to higher Sierras, and, as I fancied, was again waving his hand in friendly recognition.

(Our National Parks)

The Earthquake

DURING THE WINTER after he met Emerson, while Muir was acting as caretaker at Black's Hotel under Sentinel Rock, Yosemite Valley was shaken by the violent Inyo Earthquake of March 26, 1872. The terror of the inhabitants was increased by the theory advanced by the state geologist, Dr. Josiah Dwight Whitney, that the floor of the valley had dropped down during some ancient cataclysm. Imagining another cataclysm at hand, they upbraided Muir for his unbelief and glacial theories and some, mounting horses and mules, fled to the lowland.

IN YOSEMITE VALLEY, one morning about two o'clock, I was aroused by an earthquake; and though I had never before enjoyed a storm of this sort, the strange, wild thrilling motion and rumbling could not be mistaken, and I ran out of my cabin, near the Sentinel Rock, both glad and frightened, shouting, "A noble earthquake!" feeling sure I was going to learn something. The shocks were so violent and varied, and succeeded one another so closely, one had to balance in walking as if on the deck of a ship among the waves, and it seemed impossible the high cliffs should escape being shattered. In particular, I feared that the sheer-fronted Sentinel Rock, which rises to a height of three thousand feet, would be shaken down, and I took shelter back of a big Pine, hoping I might be protected from outbounding boulders, should any come so far. I was now convinced that an earthquake had been the maker of the taluses and positive proof soon came. It was a calm moonlight night, and no sound was heard for the first minute or two save a low muffled underground rumbling and a slight rustling of the agitated trees, as if, in wrestling with the mountains, Nature were holding her breath. Then, suddenly, out of the strange silence and strange motion there came a tremendous roar. The Eagle Rock, a short distance up the valley, had given way, and I saw it falling in thousands of the great boulders I had been studying so long, pouring to the valley floor in a free curve luminous from friction, making a terribly sublime and beautiful spectacle — an arc of fire fifteen hundred feet span, as true in form and as steady as a rainbow, in the midst of the stupendous roaring rock-storm. The sound was inconceivably deep and broad and earnest, as if the whole earth, like a living creature, had at last found a voice and were calling to her sister planets. It seemed to me that if all the thunder I ever heard were condensed into one roar it would not equal this rock roar at the birth of a mountain talus. Think, then, of the roar that arose to heaven when all the thousands of ancient cañon taluses throughout the length and breadth of the range were simultaneously given birth.

The main storm was soon over, and, eager to see the newborn talus, I ran up the valley in the moonlight and climbed it before the huge blocks, after their wild fiery flight, had come to complete rest. They were slowly settling into their places, chafing, grating against one another, groaning, and whispering; but no motion was visible except in a stream of small fragments pattering down the face of the cliff at the head of the talus. A cloud of dust particles, the smallest of the boulders, floated out across the whole breadth of the valley and formed a ceiling that lasted until after sunrise; and the air was loaded with the odor of crushed Douglas Spruces, from a grove that had been mowed down and mashed like weeds.

Sauntering about to see what other changes had been made, I found the Indians in the middle of the valley, terribly frightened, of course, fearing the angry spirits of the rocks were trying to kill them. The few whites wintering in the valley were assembled in front of the old Hutchings Hotel, comparing notes and meditating flight to steadier ground, seemingly as sorely frightened as the Indians. It is always interesting to see people in dead earnest, from whatever cause, and earthquakes make everybody earnest.

Shortly after sunrise, a low blunt muffled rumbling, like distant thunder, was followed by another series of shocks, which, though not nearly so severe as the first, made the cliffs and domes tremble like jelly, and the big Pines and Oaks thrill and swish and wave their branches with startling effect. Then the groups of talkers were suddenly hushed, and the solemnity on their faces was sublime. One in particular of these winter neighbors, a rather thoughtful, speculative man, with whom I had often conversed, was a firm believer in the cataclysmic origin of the valley; and I now jokingly remarked that his wild tumble-down-and-engulfment hypothesis might soon be proved, since these underground rumblings and shakings might be the forerunners of another Yosemite-making cataclysm, which would perhaps double the depth of the valley by swallowing the floor, leaving the ends of the wagon roads and trails three or four thousand feet in the air. Just then came the second series of shocks, and it was fine to see how awfully silent and solemn he became. His belief in the existence of a mysterious abyss, into which the suspended floor of the valley and all the domes and battlements of the walls might at any moment go roaring down, mightily troubled him. To cheer and tease him into another view of the case, I said: "Come, cheer up; smile a little and clap your hands, now that kind Mother Earth is trotting us on her knee to amuse us and make us good." But the well-meant joke seemed irreverent and utterly failed, as if only prayerful terror could rightly belong to the wild beauty-making business. Even after all the heavier shocks were over, I could do nothing to reassure him. On the contrary, he handed me the keys of his little store, and, with a companion of like mind, fled to the lowlands. In about a month he returned; but a sharp shock occurred that very day, which sent him flying again.

The rocks trembled more or less every day for over two months, and I kept a bucket of water on my table to learn what I could of the movements. The blunt thunder-tones in the depths of the mountains were usually followed by sudden jarring, horizontal thrusts from the northward, often succeeded by twisting, upjolting movements. Judging by its effects, this Yosemite, or Inyo earthquake, as it is sometimes called, was gentle as compared with the one that gave rise to the grand talus system of the range and did so much for the cañon scenery. Nature, usually so deliberate in her operations, then created, as we have seen, a new set of features, simply by giving the mountains a shake — changing not only the high peaks and cliffs, but the streams. As soon as these rock avalanches fell every stream began to sing new songs; for in many places thousands of boulders were hurled into their channels, roughening and half damming them, compelling the waters to surge and roar in rapids where before they were gliding smoothly. Some of the streams were completely dammed, drift-wood, leaves, etc., filling the interstices between the boulders, thus giving rise to lakes and level reaches; and these, again, after being gradually filled in, to smooth meadows, through which the streams now silently meander; while at the same time some of the taluses took the places of old meadows and groves. Thus rough places were made smooth, and smooth places rough. But on the whole, by what at first sight seemed pure confusion and ruin, the landscapes were enriched; for gradually every talus, however big the boulders composing it, was covered with groves and gardens, and made a finely proportioned and ornamental base for the sheer cliffs. In this beauty work, every boulder is prepared and measured and put in its place more thoughtfully than are the stones of temples. If for a moment you are inclined to regard these taluses as mere draggled, chaotic dumps, climb to the top of one of them, tie your mountain shoes firmly over the instep, and with braced nerves run down without any haggling, puttering hesitation, boldly jumping from boulder to boulder with even speed. You will then find your feet playing a tune, and quickly discover the music and poetry of rock-piles — a fine lesson; and all Nature's wildness tells the same story. Storms of every sort, torrents, earthquakes, cataclysms, "convulsions of nature," etc., however mysterious and lawless at first sight they may seem, are only harmonious notes in the song of creation, varied expressions of God's love.

(Our National Parks)

Snow-Banners

DYNAMIC FORCES of nature — glaciers carving out canyons, floods changing the face of a landscape — these had special appeal for Muir. He is one of the few writers to stress the beauty of storms. "The world," he wrote in recounting his adventures in wind and flood at the headwaters of the Feather and Yuba rivers in the winter of 1875, "needs the woods and is beginning to come to them. But it is not yet ready for storms. Nevertheless the world moves onward and 'it is coming yet, for a' that' that the beauty of storms will be as visible as that of calms." This account of snow-banners streaming from the Sierra peaks in the winter winds is one of many glimpses we have of Muir's appreciation of the beauty that often attends the violence of nature.

THE MOST MAGNIFICENT storm phenomenon I ever saw, surpassing in showy grandeur the most imposing effects of clouds, floods, or avalanches, was the peaks of the High Sierra, back of Yosemite Valley, decorated with snow-banners. Many of the starry snow-flowers, out of which these banners are made, fall before they are ripe, while most of those that do attain perfect development as six-rayed crystals glint and chafe against one another in their fall through the frosty air, and are broken into fragments. This dry fragmentary snow is still further prepared for the formation of banners by the action of the wind. For, instead of finding rest at once, like the snow which falls into the tranquil depths of the forests, it is rolled over and over, beaten against rock-ridges, and swirled in pits and hollows, like boulders, pebbles, and sand in the pot-holes of a river, until finally the delicate angles of the crystals are worn off, and the whole mass is reduced to dust. And whenever storm-winds find this prepared snow-dust in a loose condition on exposed slopes, where there is a free upward sweep to leeward, it is tossed back into the sky, and borne onward from peak to peak in the form of banners or cloudy drifts, according to the velocity of the wind and the conformation of the slopes up or around which it is driven. While thus flying through the air, a small portion makes good its escape, and remains in the sky as vapor. But far the greater part, after being driven into the sky again and again, is at length locked fast in bossy drifts, or in the wombs of glaciers, some of it to remain silent and rigid for centuries before it is finally melted and sent singing down the mountain-sides to the sea.

Yet, notwithstanding the abundance of winter snow-dust in the mountains, and the frequency of high winds, and the length of time the dust remains loose and exposed to their action, the occurrence of well-formed banners is, for causes we shall hereafter note, comparatively rare. I have seen only one display of this kind that seemed in every way perfect. This was in the winter of 1873, when the snow-laden summits were swept by a wild "norther." I happened at the time to be wintering in Yosemite Valley, that sublime Sierra temple where every day one may see the grandest sights. Yet even here the wild gala-day of the north wind seemed surpassingly glorious. I was awakened in the morning by the rocking of my cabin and the beating of pine-burs on the roof. Detached torrents and avalanches from the main wind-flood overhead were rushing wildly down the narrow side cañons, and over the precipitous walls, with loud resounding roar, rousing the Pines to enthusiastic action, and making the whole valley vibrate as though it were an instrument being played.

But afar on the lofty exposed peaks of the range standing so high in the sky, the storm was expressing itself in still grander characters, which I was soon to see in all their glory. I had long been anxious to study some points in the structure of the ice-cone that is formed every winter at the foot of the upper Yosemite fall, but the blinding spray by which it is invested had hitherto prevented me from making a sufficiently near approach. This morning the entire body of the fall was torn into gauzy shreds, and blown horizontally along the face of the cliff, leaving the cone dry; and while making my way to the top of an overlooking ledge to seize so favorable an opportunity to examine the interior of the cone, the peaks of the Merced group came in sight over the shoulder of the South Dome, each waving a resplendent banner against the blue sky, as regular in form, and as firm in texture, as if woven of fine silk. So rare and splendid a phenomenon, of course, overbore all other considerations, and I at once let the ice-cone go, and began to force my way out of the valley to some dome or ridge sufficiently lofty to command a general view of the main summits, feeling assured that I should find them bannered still more gloriously; nor was I in the least disappointed. Indian Cañon, through which I climbed, was choked with snow that had been shot down in avalanches from the high cliffs on either side, rendering the ascent difficult; but inspired by the roaring storm, the tedious wallowing brought no fatigue, and in four hours I gained the top of a ridge above the valley, 8000 feet high. And there in bold relief, like a clear painting, appeared a most imposing scene. Innumerable peaks, black and sharp, rose grandly into the dark blue sky, their bases set in solid white, their sides streaked and splashed with snow, like ocean rocks with foam; and from every summit, all free and unconfused, was streaming a beautiful silky silvery banner, from half a mile to a mile in length, slender at the point of attachment, then widening gradually as it extended from the peak until it was about 1000 or 1500 feet in breadth, as near as I could estimate. The cluster of peaks called the "Crown of the Sierra," at the head of the Merced and Tuolumne Rivers — Mounts Dana, Gibbs, Conness, Lyell, Maclure, Ritter, with their nameless compeers — each had its own refulgent banner, waving with a clearly visible motion in the sun-glow, and there was not a single cloud in the sky to mar their simple grandeur. Fancy yourself standing on this Yosemite ridge looking eastward. You notice a strange garish glitter in the air. The gale drives wildly overhead with a fierce, tempestuous roar, but its violence is not felt, for you are looking through a sheltered opening in the woods as through a window. There, in the immediate foreground of your picture, rises a majestic forest of Silver Fir blooming in eternal freshness, the foliage yellow-green, and the snow beneath the trees strewn with their beautiful plumes, plucked off by the wind. Beyond, and extending over all the middle ground, are somber swaths of Pine, interrupted by huge swelling ridges and domes; and just beyond the dark forest you see the monarchs of the High Sierra waving their magnificent banners. They are twenty miles away, but you would not wish them nearer, for every feature is distinct, and the whole glorious show is seen in its right proportions. After this general view, mark how sharply the dark snowless ribs and buttresses and summits of the peaks are defined, excepting the portions veiled by the banners, and how delicately their sides are streaked with snow, where it has come to rest in narrow flutings and gorges. Mark, too, how grandly the banners wave as the wind is deflected against their sides, and how trimly each is attached to the very summit of its peak, like a streamer at a masthead; how smooth and silky they are in texture, and how finely their fading fringes are penciled on the azure sky. See how dense and opaque they are at the point of attachment, and how filmy and translucent toward the end, so that the peaks back of them are seen dimly, as though you were looking through ground glass. Yet again observe how some of the longest, belonging to the loftiest summits, stream perfectly free all the way across intervening notches and passes from peak to peak, while others overlap and partly hide each other. And consider how keenly every particle of this wondrous cloth of snow is flashing out jets of light. These are the main features of the beautiful and terrible picture as seen from the forest window; and it would still be surpassingly glorious were the fore- and middle-grounds obliterated altogether, leaving only the black peaks, the white banners, and the blue sky.

Glancing now in a general way at the formation of snow-banners, we find that the main causes of the wondrous beauty and perfection of those we have been contemplating were the favorable direction and great force of the wind, the abundance of snow-dust, and the peculiar conformation of the slopes of the peaks. It is essential not only that the wind should move with great velocity and steadiness to supply a sufficiently copious and continuous stream of snow-dust, but that it should come from the north. No perfect banner is ever hung on the Sierra peaks by a south wind. Had the gale that day blown from the south, leaving other conditions unchanged, only a dull, confused, fog-like drift would have been produced; for the snow, instead of being spouted up over the tops of the peaks in concentrated currents to be drawn out as streamers, would have been shed off around the sides, and piled down into the glacier wombs. The cause of the concentrated action of the north wind is found in the peculiar form of the north sides of the peaks, where the amphitheaters of the residual glaciers are. In general the south sides are convex and irregular, while the north sides are concave both in their vertical and horizontal sections; the wind in ascending these curves converges toward the summits, carrying the snow in concentrating currents with it, shooting it almost straight up into the air above the peaks, from which it is then carried away in a horizontal direction.

This difference in form between the north and south sides of the peaks was almost wholly produced by the difference in the kind and quantity of the glaciation to which they have been subjected, the north sides having been hollowed by residual shadow-glaciers of a form that never existed on the sun-beaten sides.

It appears, therefore, that shadows in great part determine not only the forms of lofty icy mountains, but also those of the snow-banners that the wild winds hang on them.

(The Mountains of California)

Tracks in the Sand

MUIR'S CONTINUOUS residence in the Yosemite ended in the fall of 1873. But as long as he lived the valley was a loadstone that drew him to it whenever he was free. After climbing Mount Whitney — the first man to reach its summit by the direct eastern approach — Muir began, in November 1873, ten city-bound months in Oakland writing up his Sierra experiences. By the end of summer his health began to be affected by the confinement and the irregular meals at restaurants. Then one September day the call of the mountains became suddenly irresistible. Without even saying goodbye to his friends, he left "time and wheels" behind and hurried toward the valley. His sense of soaring freedom is reflected in this account of his joyous course among tracks and traceries in the sand. It is taken from a long letter written in Yosemite to Mrs. Jeanne C. Carr, wife of Ezra Slocum Carr, Muir's teacher of geology and chemistry at the University of Wisconsin, then a professor at the University of California and later California State Superintendent of Public Instruction. Mrs. Carr was the most helpful of all Muir's friends, the one whose influence was greatest, the one with the most unwavering faith in his genius and destiny. She brought him in contact with leading scientists. And she helped him place his first articles with publications, when at her urging he began to write.

❀

I SLEPT AT TURLOCK and next morning faced the Sierra and set through the sand afoot. The freedom I felt was exhilarating, and the burning heat and thirst and faintness could not make it less. Before I had walked ten miles I was wearied and footsore, but it was real earnest work and I liked it. Any kind of simple natural destruction is preferable to the numb, dumb, apathetic deaths of a town.

Heavy wagon-loads of wheat had been hauled along the road and the wheels had sunk deep and left smooth beveled furrows in the sand. Upon the smooth slopes of these sand furrows I soon observed a most beautiful and varied embroidery, evidently tracks of some kind. At first I thought of mice, but soon saw they were too light and delicate for mice. Then a tiny lizard darted into the stubble ahead of me, and I carefully examined the track he made, but it was entirely unlike the fine-print embroidery I was studying. However I knew that he might make very different tracks if walking leisurely. Therefore I determined to catch one and experiment. I found out in Florida that lizards, however swift, are short-winded, so I gave chase and soon captured a tiny gray fellow and carried him to a smooth sand-bed where he could embroider without getting away into grass tufts or holes. He was so wearied that he couldn't skim and was compelled to walk, and I was excited with delight in seeing an exquisitely beautiful strip of embroidery about five eighths of an inch wide, drawn out in flowing curves behind him as from a loom. The riddle was solved. I knew that mountain boulders moved in music; so also do lizards, and their written music, printed by their feet, moved so swiftly as to be invisible, covers the hot sands with beauty wherever they go.

But my sand-embroidery lesson was by no means done. I speedily discovered a yet more delicate pattern on the sands, woven into that of the lizard. I examined the strange combination of dots and bars. No five-toed lizard had printed that music. I watched narrowly down on my knees, following the strange and beautiful pattern along the wheel-furrows and out into the stubble. Occasionally the pattern would suddenly end in a shallow pit half an inch across and an eighth of an inch deep. I was fairly puzzled, picked up my bundle, and trudged discontentedly away, but my eyes were hungrily awake and I watched all the ground. At length a gray grasshopper rattled and flew up, and the truth flashed upon me that he was the complementary embroiderer of the lizard.

Then followed long careful observation, but I never could see the grasshopper until he jumped, and after he alighted he invariably stood watching me with his legs set ready for another jump in case of danger. Nevertheless I soon made sure that he was my man, for I found that in jumping he made the shallow pits I had observed at the termination of the pattern I had been studying. But no matter how patiently I waited he wouldn't *walk* while I was sufficiently near to observe. They are also nearly the color of the sand, I therefore caught one and lifted his wing-covers and cut off about half of each wing with my penknife, and carried him to a favorable place on the sand. At first he did nothing but jump and make dimples, but soon he became weary and *walked* in common rhythms with all his six legs, and my interest you may guess while I watched the embroidery — the written music laid down in a beautiful ribbon-like strip behind. I glowed with wild joy as if I had found a new glacier — copied specimens of the precious fabric into my note-book, and strode away with my own feet sinking with a dull crunch, crunch, crunch in the hot gray sand, glad to believe that the dark and cloudy vicissitudes of the Oakland period had not dimmed my vision in the least.

Happen what would, fever, thirst, or sun-stroke, my joy for that day was complete. Yet I was to receive still more. A train of curving tracks with a line in the middle next fixed my attention, and almost before I had time to make a guess concerning their author, a small hawk came shooting down vertically out of the sky a few steps ahead of me and picked up something in his talons. After rising thirty or forty feet overhead, he dropped it by the roadside as if to show me what it was. I ran forward and found a little bunchy field mouse and at once suspected him of being embroiderer number three. After an exciting chase through stubble heaps and weed thickets I wearied and captured him without being bitten and turned him free to make his mark in a favorable sand-bed. He also embroidered better than he knew, and at once claimed the authorship of the new track-work.

I soon learned to distinguish the pretty sparrow track from that of the magpie and lark with their three delicate branches and the straight scratch behind made by the back-curving claw, dragged loosely like a spur of a Mexican vaquero. The cushioned elastic feet of the hare frequently were seen mixed with the pattering scratchy prints of the squirrels. I was now wholly trackful. I fancied I could see the air whirling in dimpled eddies from sparrow and lark wings. Earthquake boulders descending in a song of curves, snowflakes glinting songfully hither and thither. "The water in music the oar forsakes." The air in music the wing forsakes. All things move in music and write it. The mouse, lizard, and grasshopper sing together on the Turlock sands, sing with the morning stars.

(*The Life and Letters of John Muir*)

V

FORESTS OF THE WEST

Wind-Storm in the Forest

HENRY FAIRFIELD OSBORN, in his Impressions of Great Naturalists, *observes that Muir "wrote about trees as no one else in the whole history of trees, chiefly because he loved them as he loved men and women." In his youth he penned an elegy to a great oak that he and his brother had to cut on the Wisconsin farm. And in his late manhood he literally went around the world to see the trees, the eucalyptus groves of New Zealand, the araucaria forests of Brazil, the baobab trees of Africa. The journals of these arboreal wanderings, which have never been published, must contain material of intense interest to all who share Muir's love of trees.*

During the time he was making his solitary expeditions into the California mountains, subsisting largely on tea and bread, Muir calculated his living expenses at three dollars a month. The last week of December 1874 found him exploring the high divide between the Yuba and Feather rivers in northern California. When a winter gale struck the forest along one of the tributaries of the Yuba, Muir climbed to the top of a Douglas spruce — now called a Douglas fir — better to enjoy the wild adventure of the storm. Four years later, Scribner's Monthly *published an account of his experience as "A Wind Storm in the Forests of the Yuba" in its issue of November 1878. This later became a chapter in Muir's first book,* The Mountains of California. *Nothing else he ever wrote, with the exception of his dog story,* Stickeen, *brought Muir so many letters from readers.*

❀

T HE MOUNTAIN WINDS, like the dew and rain, sunshine and snow, are measured and bestowed with love on the forests to develop their strength and beauty. However restricted the scope of other forest influences, that of the winds is universal. The snow bends and trims the upper forests every winter, the lightning strikes a single tree here and there, while avalanches mow down thousands at a swoop as a gardener trims out a bed of flowers. But the winds go to every tree, fingering every leaf and branch and furrowed bole; not one is forgotten; the Mountain Pine towering with outstretched arms on the rugged buttresses of the icy peaks, the lowliest and most retiring tenant of the dells; they seek and find them all, caressing them tenderly, bending them in lusty exercise, stimulating their growth, plucking off a leaf or limb as required, or removing an entire tree or grove, now whispering and cooing through the branches like a sleepy child, now roaring like the ocean; the winds blessing the forests, the forests the winds, with ineffable beauty and harmony as the sure result.

After one has seen Pines six feet in diameter bending like grasses before a mountain gale, and ever and anon some giant falling with a crash that shakes the hills, it seems astonishing that any, save the lowest thickset trees, could ever have found a period sufficiently stormless to establish themselves; or, once established, that they should not, sooner or later, have been blown down. But when the storm is over, and we behold the same forests tranquil again, towering fresh and unscathed in erect majesty, and consider what centuries of storms have fallen upon them since they were first planted — hail, to break the tender seedlings; lightning, to scorch and shatter; snow, winds, and avalanches, to crush and overwhelm — while the manifest result of all this wild storm-culture is the glorious perfection we behold; then faith in Nature's forestry is established, and we cease to deplore the violence of her most destructive gales, or of any other storm-implement whatsoever.

There are two trees in the Sierra forests that are never blown down, so long as they continue in sound health. These are the

Juniper and the Dwarf Pine of the summit-peaks. Their stiff, crooked roots grip the storm-beaten ledges like eagles' claws, while their lithe, cord-like branches bend round compliantly, offering but slight holds for winds, however violent. The other alpine conifers — the Needle Pine, Mountain Pine, Two-leaved Pine, and Hemlock Spruce — are never thinned out by this agent to any destructive extent, on account of their admirable toughness and the closeness of their growth. In general the same is true of the giants of the lower zones. The kingly Sugar Pine, towering aloft to a height of more than 200 feet, offers a fine mark to storm-winds; but it is not densely foliaged, and its long, horizontal arms swing round compliantly in the blast, like tresses of green, fluent algæ in a brook; while the Silver Firs in most places keep their ranks well together in united strength. The Yellow or Silver Pine is more frequently overturned than any other tree on the Sierra, because its leaves and branches form a larger mass in proportion to its height, while in many places it is planted sparsely, leaving open lanes through which storms may enter with full force. Furthermore, because it is distributed along the lower portion of the range, which was the first to be left bare on the breaking up of the ice-sheet at the close of the glacial winter, the soil it is growing upon has been longer exposed to post-glacial weathering, and consequently is in a more crumbling, decayed condition than the fresher soils farther up the range, and therefore offers a less secure anchorage for the roots.

While exploring the forest zones of Mount Shasta, I discovered the path of a hurricane strewn with thousands of Pines of this species. Great and small had been uprooted or wrenched off by sheer force, making a clean gap, like that made by a snow avalanche. But hurricanes capable of doing this class of work are rare in the Sierra, and when we have explored the forests from one extremity of the range to the other, we are compelled to believe that they are the most beautiful on the face of the earth, however we may regard the agents that have made them so.

There is always something deeply exciting, not only in the sounds of winds in the woods, which exert more or less influence over every mind, but in their varied water-like flow as manifested by the movements of the trees, especially those of the conifers. By no other trees are they rendered so extensively and impressively visible, not even by the lordly tropic Palms or tree-ferns responsive to the gentlest breeze. The waving of a forest of the giant Sequoias is indescribably impressive and sublime, but the Pines seem to me the best interpreters of winds. They are mighty waving goldenrods, ever in tune, singing and writing wind-music all their long century lives. Little, however, of this noble tree-waving and tree-music will you see or hear in the strictly alpine portion of the forests. The burly Juniper, whose girth sometimes more than equals its height, is about as rigid as the rocks on which it grows. The slender lash-like sprays of the Dwarf Pine stream out in wavering ripples, but the tallest and slenderest are far too unyielding to wave even in the heaviest gales. They only shake in quick, short vibrations. The Hemlock Spruce, however, and the Mountain Pine, and some of the tallest thickets of the Two-leaved species bow in storms with considerable scope and gracefulness. But it is only in the lower and middle zones that the meeting of winds and woods is to be seen in all its grandeur.

One of the most beautiful and exhilarating storms I ever enjoyed in the Sierra occurred in December, 1874, when I happened to be exploring one of the tributary valleys of the Yuba River. The sky and the ground and the trees had been thoroughly rainwashed and were dry again. The day was intensely pure, one of those incomparable bits of California winter, warm and balmy and full of white sparkling sunshine, redolent of all the purest influences of the spring, and at the same time enlivened with one of the most bracing wind-storms conceivable. Instead of camping out, as I usually do, I then chanced to be stopping at the house of a friend. But when the storm began to sound, I lost no time in pushing out into the woods to enjoy it. For on such occasions Nature has always something rare to show us, and the danger to life and limb is hardly greater than one would experience crouching deprecatingly beneath a roof.

It was still early morning when I found myself fairly adrift. Delicious sunshine came pouring over the hills, lighting the tops of the Pines, and setting free a steam of summery fragrance that contrasted strangely with the wild tones of the storm. The air was mottled with pine-tassels and bright green plumes, that went flashing past in the sunlight like birds pursued. But there was not the slightest dustiness, nothing less pure than leaves, and ripe pollen, and flecks of withered bracken and moss. I heard trees falling for hours at the rate of one every two or three minutes; some uprooted, partly on account of the loose, water-soaked condition of the ground; others broken straight across, where some weakness caused by fire had determined the spot. The gestures of the various trees made a delightful study. Young Sugar Pines, light and feathery as squirrel-tails, were bowing almost to the ground; while the grand old patriarchs, whose massive boles had been tried in a hundred storms, waved solemnly above them, their long, arching branches streaming fluently on the gale, and every needle thrilling and ringing and shedding off keen lances of light like a diamond. The Douglas Spruces, with long sprays drawn out in level tresses, and needles massed in a gray, shimmering glow, presented a most striking appearance as they stood in bold relief along the hilltops. The Madroños in the dells, with their red bark and large glossy leaves tilted every way, reflected the sunshine in throbbing spangles like those one so often sees on the rippled surface of a glacier lake. But the Silver Pines were now the most impressively beautiful of all. Colossal spires 200 feet in height waved like supple goldenrods chanting and bowing low as if in worship, while the whole mass of their long, tremulous foliage was kindled into one continuous blaze of white sun-fire. The force of the gale was such that the most steadfast monarch of them all rocked down to its roots with a motion plainly perceptible when one leaned against it. Nature was holding high festival, and every fiber of the most rigid giants thrilled with glad excitement.

I drifted on through the midst of this passionate music and motion, across many a glen, from ridge to ridge; often halting in the lee of a rock for shelter, or to gaze and listen. Even when the grand anthem had swelled to its highest pitch, I could distinctly hear the varying tones of individual trees — Spruce, and Fir, and Pine, and leafless Oak — and even the infinitely gentle rustle of the withered grasses at my feet. Each was expressing itself in its own way — singing its own song, and making its own peculiar gestures — manifesting a richness of variety to be found in no other forest I have yet seen. The coniferous woods of Canada, and the Carolinas, and Florida, are made up of trees that resemble one another about as nearly as blades of grass, and grow close together in much the same way. Coniferous trees, in general, seldom possess individual character, such as is manifest among Oaks and Elms. But the California forests are made up of a greater number of distinct species than any other in the world. And in them we find, not only a marked differentiation into special groups, but also a marked individuality in almost every tree, giving rise to storm effects indescribably glorious.

Toward midday, after a long, tingling scramble through copses of hazel and ceanothus, I gained the summit of the highest ridge in the neighborhood; and then it occurred to me that it would be a fine thing to climb one of the trees to obtain a wider outlook and get my ear close to the Æolian music of its topmost needles. But under the circumstances the choice of a tree was a serious matter. One whose instep was not very strong seemed in danger of being blown down, or of being struck by others in case they should fall; another was branchless to a considerable height above the ground, and at the same time too large to be grasped with arms and legs in climbing; while others were not favorably situated for clear views. After cautiously casting about, I made a choice of the tallest of a group of Douglas Spruces that were growing close together like a tuft of grass, no one of which seemed likely to fall unless all the rest fell with it. Though comparatively young, they were about 100 feet high, and their lithe, brushy tops were rocking and swirling in wild ecstasy. Being accustomed to climb trees in making botanical studies, I experienced no difficulty in reaching the top of this one, and never before did I enjoy so noble an exhilaration of motion. The slender tops fairly flapped and swished in the passionate torrent, bending and swirling backward and forward, round and round, tracing indescribable combinations of vertical and horizontal curves, while I clung with muscles firm braced, like a bobolink on a reed.

In its widest sweeps my tree-top described an arc of from

twenty to thirty degrees, but I felt sure of its elastic temper, having seen others of the same species still more severely tried — bent almost to the ground indeed, in heavy snows — without breaking a fiber. I was therefore safe, and free to take the wind into my pulses and enjoy the excited forest from my superb outlook. The view from here must be extremely beautiful in any weather. Now my eye roved over the piny hills and dales as over fields of waving grain, and felt the light running in ripples and broad swelling undulations across the valleys from ridge to ridge, as the shining foliage was stirred by corresponding waves of air. Oftentimes these waves of reflected light would break up suddenly into a kind of beaten foam, and again, after chasing one another in regular order, they would seem to bend forward in concentric curves, and disappear on some hillside, like sea-waves on a shelving shore. The quantity of light reflected from the bent needles was so great as to make whole groves appear as if covered with snow, while the black shadows beneath the trees greatly enhanced the effect of the silvery splendor.

Excepting only the shadows there was nothing somber in all this wild sea of Pines. On the contrary, notwithstanding this was the winter season, the colors were remarkably beautiful. The shafts of the Pine and Libocedrus were brown and purple, and most of the foliage was well tinged with yellow; the laurel groves, with the pale undersides of their leaves turned upward, made masses of gray; and then there was many a dash of chocolate color from clumps of Manzanita, and jet of vivid crimson from the bark of the Madroños, while the ground on the hillsides, appearing here and there through openings between the groves, displayed masses of pale purple and brown.

The sounds of the storm corresponded gloriously with this wild exuberance of light and motion. The profound bass of the naked branches and boles booming like waterfalls; the quick, tense vibrations of the pine-needles, now rising to a shrill, whistling hiss, now falling to a silky murmur; the rustling of laurel groves in the dells, and the keen metallic click of leaf on leaf — all this was heard in easy analysis when the attention was calmly bent.

The varied gestures of the multitude were seen to fine advantage, so that one could recognize the different species at a distance of several miles by this means alone, as well as by their forms and colors, and the way they reflected the light. All seemed strong and comfortable, as if really enjoying the storm, while responding to its most enthusiastic greetings. We hear much nowadays concerning the universal struggle for existence, but no struggle in the common meaning of the word was manifest here; no recognition of danger by any tree; no deprecation; but rather an invincible gladness as remote from exultation as from fear.

I kept my lofty perch for hours, frequently closing my eyes to enjoy the music by itself, or to feast quietly on the delicious fragrance that was streaming past. The fragrance of the woods was less marked than that produced during warm rain, when so many balsamic buds and leaves are steeped like tea; but, from the chafing of resiny branches against each other, and the incessant attrition of myriads of needles, the gale was spiced to a very tonic degree. And besides the fragrance from these local sources there were traces of scents brought from afar. For this wind came first from the sea, rubbing against its fresh, briny waves, then distilled through the Redwoods, threading rich ferny gulches, and spreading itself in broad undulating currents over many a flower-enameled ridge of the coast mountains, then across the golden plains, up the purple foot-hills, and into these piny woods with the varied incense gathered by the way.

Winds are advertisements of all they touch, however much or little we may be able to read them; telling their wanderings even by their scents alone. Mariners detect the flowery perfume of land-winds far at sea, and sea-winds carry the fragrance of dulse and tangle far inland, where it is quickly recognized, though mingled with the scents of a thousand land-flowers. As an illustration of this, I may tell here that I breathed sea-air on the Firth of Forth, in Scotland, while a boy; then was taken to Wisconsin, where I remained nineteen years; then, without in all this time having breathed one breath of the sea, I walked quietly, alone, from the middle of the Mississippi Valley to the Gulf of Mexico, on a botanical excursion, and while in Florida, far from the coast, my attention wholly bent on the splendid tropical vegetation about me, I suddenly recognized a sea-breeze, as it came sifting through the Palmettos and blooming vine-tangles, which at once awakened and set free a thousand dormant associations, and made me a boy again in Scotland, as if all the intervening years had been annihilated.

Most people like to look at mountain rivers, and bear them in mind; but few care to look at the winds, though far more beautiful and sublime, and though they become at times about as visible as flowing water. When the north winds in winter are making upward sweeps over the curving summits of the High Sierra, the fact is sometimes published with flying snow-banners a mile long. Those portions of the winds thus embodied can scarce be wholly invisible, even to the darkest imagination. And when we look around over an agitated forest, we may see something of the wind that stirs it, by its effects upon the trees. Yonder it descends in a rush of water-like ripples, and sweeps over the bending Pines from hill to hill. Nearer, we see detached plumes and leaves, now speeding by on level currents, now whirling in eddies, or, escaping over the edges of the whirls, soaring aloft on grand, upswelling domes of air, or tossing on flame-like crests. Smooth, deep currents, cascades, falls, and swirling eddies, sing around every tree and leaf, and over all the varied topography of the region with telling changes of form, like mountain rivers conforming to the features of their channels.

After tracing the Sierra streams from their fountains to the plains, marking where they bloom white in falls, glide in crystal plumes, surge gray and foam-filled in boulder-choked gorges, and slip through the woods in long, tranquil reaches — after thus learning their language and forms in detail, we may at length hear them chanting all together in one grand anthem, and comprehend them all in clear inner vision, covering the range like lace. But even this spectacle is far less sublime and not a whit more substantial than what we may behold of these storm-streams of air in the mountain woods.

We all travel the milky way together, trees and men; but it never occurred to me until this storm-day, while swinging in the wind, that trees are travelers, in the ordinary sense. They make many journeys, not extensive ones, it is true; but our own little journeys, away and back again, are only little more than tree-wavings — many of them not so much.

When the storm began to abate, I dismounted and sauntered down through the calming woods. The storm-tones died away, and, turning toward the east, I beheld the countless hosts of the forests hushed and tranquil, towering above one another on the slopes of the hills like a devout audience. The setting sun filled them with amber light, and seemed to say, while they listened, "My peace I give unto you."

As I gazed on the impressive scene, all the so-called ruin of the storm was forgotten, and never before did these noble woods appear so fresh, so joyous, so immortal.

(*The Mountains of California*)

The Dwarf Pine
Song of the Silver Pine

IN REPLY to a correspondent who asked him to name his favorite tree, John Muir wrote on January 10, 1913: "I can't tell which of all God's trees I like best, though I should write a big book trying to." All trees were to him living things to be respected and revered. Once when his friend Charles S. Sargent of Harvard proposed changing the name of the magnolia from Magnolia grandifolia *to* Magnolia foetida *because of the prior use of the latter name, Muir's indignation was intense. "Why inflict upon a beautiful and defenseless plant for all time the stigma of such a name as* Magnolia foetida?" *he demanded. "You yourself would not like it to have your name changed from Charles S. Sargent to The Malodorous Sargent!" The following accounts of two mountain pines and the long enduring dwarf pine of the bleak, windswept heights illustrate Muir's feeling of fellowship for trees.*

THE DWARF PINE

THIS SPECIES forms the extreme edge of the timber-line nearly the whole extent of the range on both flanks. It is first met growing in company with *Pinus contorta,* var. *Murrayana,* on the upper margin of the belt, as an erect tree from fifteen to thirty feet high and from one to two feet in thickness; thence it goes straggling up the flanks of the summit peaks, upon moraines or crumbling ledges, wherever it can obtain a foothold, to an elevation of from 10,000 to 12,000 feet, where it dwarfs to a mass of crumpled, prostrate branches, covered with slender, upright shoots, each tipped with a short, close-packed tassel of leaves. The bark is smooth and purplish, in some places almost white. The fertile cones grow in rigid clusters upon the upper branches, dark chocolate in color while young, and bear beautiful pearly seeds about the size of peas, most of which are eaten by two species of tamias and the notable Clark Crow. The staminate cones occur in clusters, about an inch wide, down among the leaves, and, as they are colored bright rose-purple, they give rise to a lively, flowery appearance little looked for in such a tree.

Pines are commonly regarded as sky-loving trees that must necessarily aspire or die. This species forms a marked exception, creeping lowly, in compliance with the most rigorous demands of climate, yet enduring bravely to a more advanced age than many of its lofty relatives in the sun-lands below. Seen from a distance, it would never be taken for a tree of any kind. Yonder, for example, is Cathedral Peak, some three miles away, with a scattered growth of this Pine creeping like mosses over the roof and around the beveled edges of the north gable, nowhere giving any hint of an ascending axis. When approached quite near it still appears matted and healthy, and is so low that one experiences no great difficulty in walking over the top of it. Yet it is seldom absolutely prostrate, at its lowest usually attaining a height of three or four feet, with a main trunk, and branches outspread and intertangled above it, as if in ascending they had been checked by a ceiling, against which they had grown and been compelled to spread horizontally. The winter snow is indeed such a ceiling, lasting half the year; while the pressed, shorn surface is made yet smoother by violent winds, armed with cutting sand-grains, that beat down any shoot that offers to rise much above the general level, and carve the dead trunks and branches in beautiful patterns.

During stormy nights I have often camped snugly beneath the interlacing arches of this little Pine. The needles, which have accumulated for centuries, make fine beds, a fact well known to other mountaineers, such as deer and wild sheep, who paw out oval hollows and lie beneath the larger trees in safe and comfortable concealment.

The longevity of this lowly dwarf is far greater than would be guessed. Here, for example, is a specimen, growing at an elevation of 10,700 feet, which seems as though it might be plucked up by the roots, for it is only three and a half inches in diameter, and its topmost tassel is hardly three feet above the ground. Cutting it half through and counting the annual rings with the aid of a lens, we find its age to be no less than 255 years. Here is another telling specimen about the same height, 426 years old, whose trunk is only six inches in diameter; and one of its supple branchlets, hardly an eighth of an inch in diameter inside the bark, is seventy-five years old, and so filled with oily balsam, and so well seasoned by storms, that we may tie it in knots like a whip-cord.

(*The Mountains of California*)

SONG OF THE SILVER PINE

I HAVE OFTENTIMES feasted on the beauty of these noble trees when they were towering in all their winter grandeur, laden with snow — one mass of bloom; in summer, too, when the brown, staminate clusters hang thick among the shimmering needles, and the big purple burs are ripening in the mellow light; but it is during cloudless wind-storms that these colossal Pines are most impressively beautiful. Then they bow like Willows, their leaves streaming forward all in one direction, and, when the sun shines upon them at the required angle, entire groves glow as if every leaf were burnished silver. The fall of tropic light on the royal crown of a Palm is a truly glorious spectacle, the fervid sun-flood breaking upon the glossy leaves in long lance-rays, like mountain water among boulders. But to me there is something more impressive in the fall of light upon these Silver Pines. It seems beaten to the finest dust, and is shed off in myriads of minute sparkles that seem to come from the very heart of the trees, as if, like rain falling upon fertile soil, it had been absorbed, to reappear in flowers of light.

This species also gives forth the finest music to the wind. After listening to it in all kinds of winds, night and day, season after season, I think I could approximate to my position on the mountains by this Pine-music alone. If you would catch the tones of separate needles, climb a tree. They are well tempered, and give forth no uncertain sound, each standing out, with no interference excepting during heavy gales; then you may detect the click of one needle upon another, readily distinguishable from their free, wing-like hum. Some idea of their temper may be drawn from the fact that, notwithstanding they are so long, the vibrations that give rise to the peculiar shimmering of the light are made at the rate of about two hundred and fifty per minute.

When a Sugar Pine and one of this species equal in size are observed together, the latter is seen to be far more simple in manners, more lithely graceful, and its beauty is of a kind more easily appreciated; but then, it is, on the other hand, much less dignified and original in demeanor. The Silver Pine seems eager to shoot aloft. Even while it is drowsing in autumn sun-gold, you may still detect a skyward aspiration. But the Sugar Pine seems too unconsciously noble, and too complete in every way, to leave room for even a heavenward care.

(The Mountains of California)

The Douglas Squirrel

IT WAS the whole of forest life that absorbed Muir. The trees were a never ending delight. But so were the squirrels that lived in the trees, the birds that flew from branch to branch, the wildflowers that grew in the shade. The breadth of his interest encompassed all the interrelationships of life in the woods. And whether he wrote of sequoias or water ouzels or, as in the following selection, of Douglas squirrels, whatever Muir set down on paper was based on his own long and careful observations.

THE DOUGLAS SQUIRREL is by far the most interesting and influential of the California sciuridæ, surpassing every other species in force of character, numbers, and extent of range, and in the amount of influence he brings to bear upon the health and distribution of the vast forests he inhabits.

Go where you will throughout the noble woods of the Sierra Nevada, among the giant Pines and Spruces of the lower zones, up through the towering Silver Firs to the storm-bent thickets of the summit peaks, you everywhere find this little squirrel the master-existence. Though only a few inches long, so intense is his fiery vigor and restlessness, he stirs every grove with wild life, and makes himself more important than even the huge bears that shuffle through the tangled underbrush beneath him. Every wind is fretted by his voice, almost every bole and branch feels the sting of his sharp feet. How much the growth of the trees is stimulated by this means it is not easy to learn, but his action in manipulating their seeds is more appreciable. Nature has made him master forester and committed most of her coniferous crops to his paws. Probably over fifty per cent of all the cones ripened on the Sierra are cut off and handled by the Douglas alone, and of those of the Big Trees perhaps ninety per cent pass through his hands: the greater portion is of course stored away for food to last during the winter and spring, but some of them are tucked separately into loosely covered holes, where some of the seeds germinate and become trees. But the Sierra is only one of the many provinces over which he holds sway, for his dominion extends over all the Redwood Belt of the Coast Mountains, and far northward throughout the majestic forests of Oregon, Washington, and British Columbia. I make haste to mention these facts, to show upon how substantial a foundation the importance I ascribe to him rests.

The Douglas is closely allied to the Red Squirrel or Chickaree of the eastern woods. Ours may be a lineal descendant of this species, distributed westward to the Pacific by way of the Great Lakes and the Rocky Mountains, and thence southward along our forested ranges. This view is suggested by the fact that our species becomes redder and more Chickaree-like in general, the farther it is traced back along the course indicated above. But whatever their relationship, and the evolutionary forces that have acted upon them, the Douglas is now the larger and more beautiful animal.

From the nose to the root of the tail he measures about eight inches; and his tail, which he so effectively uses in interpreting his feelings, is about six inches in length. He wears dark bluish-gray over the back and halfway down the sides, bright buff on the belly, with a stripe of dark gray, nearly black, separating the upper and under colors; this dividing stripe, however, is not very sharply defined. He has long black whiskers, which gives him a rather fierce look when observed closely, strong claws, sharp as fishhooks, and the brightest of bright eyes, full of telling speculation.

A King's River Indian told me that they call him "Pillillooeet," which, rapidly pronounced with the first syllable heavily accented, is not unlike the lusty exclamation he utters on his way up a tree when excited. Most mountaineers in California call him the Pine

Squirrel; and when I asked an old trapper whether he knew our
little forester, he replied with brightening countenance: "Oh, yes,
of course I know him; everybody knows him. When I'm huntin'
in the woods, I often find out where the deer are by his barkin'
at 'em. I call 'em Lightnin' Squirrels, because they're so mighty
quick and peert."

All the true squirrels are more or less birdlike in speech and
movements; but the Douglas is preëminently so, possessing, as he
does, every attribute peculiarly squirrelish enthusiastically concentrated. He is the squirrel of squirrels, flashing from branch to
branch of his favorite evergreens crisp and glossy and undiseased
as a sunbeam. Give him wings and he would outfly any bird in
the woods. His big gray cousin is a looser animal, seemingly light
enough to float on the wind; yet when leaping from limb to limb,
or out of one tree-top to another, he sometimes halts to gather
strength, as if making efforts concerning the upshot of which he
does not always feel exactly confident. But the Douglas, with his
denser body, leaps and glides in hidden strength, seemingly as independent of common muscles as a mountain stream. He threads
the tasseled branches of the Pines, stirring their needles like a
rustling breeze; now shooting across openings in arrowy lines;
now launching in curves, glinting deftly from side to side in sudden zigzags, and swirling in giddy loops and spirals around the
knotty trunks; getting into what seem to be the most impossible
situations without sense of danger; now on his haunches, now on
his head; yet ever graceful, and punctuating his most irrepressible
outbursts of energy with little dots and dashes of perfect repose.
He is, without exception, the wildest animal I ever saw — a fiery,
sputtering little bolt of life, luxuriating in quick oxygen and the
woods' best juices. One can hardly think of such a creature being
dependent, like the rest of us, on climate and food. But, after all,
it requires no long acquaintance to learn he is human, for he works
for a living. His busiest time is in the Indian summer. Then he
gathers burs and hazel-nuts like a plodding farmer, working con-
tinuously every day for hours; saying not a word; cutting off the
ripe cones at the top of his speed, as if employed by the job, and
examining every branch in regular order, as if careful that not one

should escape him; then, descending, he stores them away beneath logs and stumps, in anticipation of the pinching hunger days of winter. He seems himself a kind of coniferous fruit — both fruit and flower. The resiny essences of the Pines pervade every pore of his body, and eating his flesh is like chewing gum.

One never tires of this bright chip of nature — this brave little voice crying in the wilderness — of observing his many works and ways, and listening to his curious language. His musical, piny gossip is as savory to the ear as balsam to the palate; and, though he has not exactly the gift of song, some of his notes are as sweet as those of a linnet — almost flute-like in softness, while others prick and tingle like thistles. He is the mocking-bird of squirrels, pouring forth mixed chatter and song like a perennial fountain; barking like a dog, screaming like a hawk, chirping like a black-bird or a sparrow; while in bluff, audacious noisiness he is a very jay.

In descending the trunk of a tree with the intention of alighting on the ground, he preserves a cautious silence, mindful, perhaps, of foxes and wildcats; but while rocking safely at home in the Pine tops there is no end to his capers and noise; and woe to the gray squirrel or chipmunk that ventures to set foot on his favorite tree! No matter how slyly they trace the furrows of the bark, they are speedily discovered, and kicked downstairs with comic vehemence, while a torrent of angry notes comes rushing from his whiskered lips that sounds remarkably like swearing. He will even attempt at times to drive away dogs and men, especially if he has had no previous knowledge of them. Seeing a man for the first time, he approaches nearer and nearer, until within a few feet; then, with an angry outburst, he makes a sudden rush, all teeth and eyes, as if about to eat you up. But, finding that the big, forked animal doesn't scare, he prudently beats a retreat, and sets himself up to reconnoiter on some overhanging branch, scru-tinizing every movement you make with ludicrous solemnity. Gathering courage, he ventures down the trunk again, churring and chirping, and jerking nervously up and down in curious loops, eyeing you all the time, as if showing off and demanding your admiration. Finally, growing calmer, he settles down in a com-

fortable posture on some horizontal branch commanding a good
view, and beats time with his tail to a steady "Chee-up! chee-up!"
or, when somewhat less excited, "Pee-ah!" with the first syllable
keenly accented, and the second drawn out like the scream of a
hawk — repeating this slowly and more emphatically at first, then
gradually faster, until a rate of about 150 words a minute is
reached; usually sitting all the time on his haunches, with paws
resting on his breast, which pulses visibly with each word. It is
remarkable, too, that, though articulating distinctly, he keeps his
mouth shut most of the time, and speaks through his nose. I have
occasionally observed him even eating Sequoia seeds and nibbling
a troublesome flea without ceasing or in any way confusing his
"Pee-ah! pee-ah!" for a single moment.

While ascending trees all his claws come into play, but in descending the weight of his body is sustained chiefly by those of
the hind feet; still in neither case do his movements suggest effort,
though if you are near enough you may see the bulging strength
of his short, bear-like arms, and note his sinewy fists clinched in
the bark.

Whether going up or down, he carries his tail extended at full
length in line with his body, unless it be required for gestures. But
while running along horizontal limbs or fallen trunks, it is frequently folded forward over the back, with the airy tip daintily
upcurled. In cool weather it keeps him warm. Then, after he has
finished his meal, you may see him crouched close on some level
limb with his tail-robe neatly spread and reaching forward to his
ears, the electric, outstanding hairs quivering in the breeze like
pine-needles. But in wet or very cold weather he stays in his nest,
and while curled up there his comforter is long enough to come
forward around his nose. It is seldom so cold, however, as to prevent his going out to his stores when hungry.

Once as I lay storm-bound on the upper edge of the timber line
on Mount Shasta, the thermometer nearly at zero and the sky
thick with driving snow, a Douglas came bravely out several times
from one of the lower hollows of a Dwarf Pine near my camp,
faced the wind without seeming to feel it much, frisked lightly
about over the mealy snow, and dug his way down to some hidden

seeds with wonderful precision, as if to his eyes the thick snow-covering were glass.

No other of the Sierra animals of my acquaintance is better fed, not even the deer, amid abundance of sweet herbs and shrubs, or the mountain sheep, or omnivorous bears. His food consists of grass-seeds, berries, hazel-nuts, chinquapins, and the nuts and seeds of all the coniferous trees without exception — Pine, Fir, Spruce, Libocedrus, Juniper, and Sequoia — he is fond of them all, and they all agree with him, green or ripe. No cone is too large for him to manage, none so small as to be beneath his notice. The smaller ones, such as those of the Hemlock, and the Douglas Spruce, and the Two-leaved Pine, he cuts off and eats on a branch of the tree, without allowing them to fall; beginning at the bottom of the cone and cutting away the scales to expose the seeds; not gnawing by guess, like a bear, but turning them round and round in regular order, in compliance with their spiral arrangement.

When thus employed, his location in the tree is betrayed by a dribble of scales, shells, and seed-wings, and, every few minutes, by the fall of the stripped axis of the cone. Then of course he is ready for another, and if you are watching you may catch a glimpse of him as he glides silently out to the end of a branch and see him examining the cone-clusters until he finds one to his mind; then, leaning over, pull back the springy needles out of his way, grasp the cone with his paws to prevent its falling, snip it off in an incredibly short time, seize it with jaws grotesquely stretched, and return to his chosen seat near the trunk. But the immense size of the cones of the Sugar Pine — from fifteen to twenty inches in length — and those of the Jeffrey variety of the Yellow Pine compel him to adopt a quite different method. He cuts them off without attempting to hold them, then goes down and drags them from where they have chanced to fall up to the bare, swelling ground around the instep of the tree, where he demolishes them in the same methodical way, beginning at the bottom and following the scale-spirals to the top.

From a single Sugar Pine cone he gets from two to four hundred seeds about half the size of a hazel-nut, so that in a few minutes he can procure enough to last a week. He seems, however, to prefer those of the two Silver Firs above all others; perhaps because they are most easily obtained, as the scales drop off when ripe without needing to be cut. Both species are filled with an exceedingly pungent, aromatic oil, which spices all his flesh, and is of itself sufficient to account for his lightning energy.

You may easily know this little workman by his chips. On sunny hillsides around the principal trees they lie in big piles — bushels and basketfuls of them, all fresh and clean, making the most beautiful kitchen-middens imaginable. The brown and yellow scales and nut-shells are as abundant and as delicately penciled and tinted as the shells along the sea-shore; while the beautiful red and purple seed-wings mingled with them would lead one to fancy that innumerable butterflies had there met their fate.

He feasts on all the species long before they are ripe, but is wise enough to wait until they are matured before he gathers them into his barns. This is in October and November, which with him are the two busiest months of the year. All kinds of burs, big and little, are now cut off and showered down alike, and the ground is speedily covered with them. A constant thudding and bumping is kept up; some of the larger cones chancing to fall on old logs make the forest reëcho with the sound. Other nut-eaters less industrious know well what is going on, and hasten to carry away the cones as they fall. But however busy the harvester may be, he is not slow to descry the pilferers below, and instantly leaves his work to drive them away. The little striped tamias is a thorn in his flesh, stealing persistently, punish him as he may. The large gray squirrel gives trouble also, although the Douglas has been accused of stealing from him. Generally, however, just the opposite is the case.

The excellence of the Sierra evergreens is well known to nurserymen throughout the world, consequently there is considerable demand for the seeds. The greater portion of the supply has hitherto been procured by chopping down the trees in the more accessible sections of the forest alongside of bridle-paths that cross the range. Sequoia seeds at first brought from twenty to thirty dollars per pound, and therefore were eagerly sought after.

Some of the smaller fruitful trees were cut down in the groves not protected by government, especially those of Fresno and King's River. Most of the Sequoias, however, are of so gigantic a size that the seedsmen have to look for the greater portion of their supplies to the Douglas, who soon learns he is no match for these freebooters. He is wise enough, however, to cease working the instant he perceives them, and never fails to embrace every opportunity to recover his burs whenever they happen to be stored in any place accessible to him, and the busy seedsman often finds on returning to camp that the little Douglas has exhaustively spoiled the spoiler. I know one seed-gatherer who, whenever he robs the squirrels, scatters wheat or barley beneath the trees as conscience-money.

The want of appreciable life remarked by so many travelers in the Sierra forests is never felt at this time of year. Banish all the humming insects and the birds and quadrupeds, leaving only Sir Douglas, and the most solitary of our so-called solitudes would still throb with ardent life. But if you should go impatiently even into the most populous of the groves on purpose to meet him, and walk about looking up among the branches, you would see very little of him. But lie down at the foot of one of the trees and straightway he will come. For, in the midst of the ordinary forest sounds, the falling of burs, piping of quails, the screaming of the Clark Crow, and the rustling of deer and bears among the chaparral, he is quick to detect your strange footsteps, and will hasten to make a good, close inspection of you as soon as you are still. First, you may hear him sounding a few notes of curious inquiry, but more likely the first intimation of his approach will be the prickly sounds of his feet as he descends the tree overhead, just before he makes his savage onrush to frighten you and proclaim your presence to every squirrel and bird in the neighborhood. If you remain perfectly motionless, he will come nearer and nearer, and probably set your flesh a-tingle by frisking across your body. Once, while I was seated at the foot of a Hemlock Spruce in one of the most inaccessible of the San Joaquin yosemites engaged in sketching, a reckless fellow came up behind me, passed under my bended arm, and jumped on my paper. And one warm afternoon, while an old friend of mine was reading out in the shade of his cabin, one of his Douglas neighbors jumped from the gable upon his head, and then with admirable assurance ran down over his shoulder and on to the book he held in his hand.

Our Douglas enjoys a large social circle; for, besides his numerous relatives, *Sciurus fossor, Tamias quadrivitatus, T. Townsendii, Spermophilus Beecheyi, S. Douglasii,* he maintains intimate relations with the nut-eating birds, particularly the Clark Crow (*Picicorvus Columbianus*) and the numerous woodpeckers and jays. The two spermophiles are astonishingly abundant in the lowlands and lower foot-hills, but more and more sparingly distributed up through the Douglas domains — seldom venturing higher than six or seven thousand feet above the level of the sea. The gray sciurus ranges but little higher than this. The little striped tamias alone is associated with him everywhere. In the lower and middle zones, where they all meet, they are tolerably harmonious — a happy family, though very amusing skirmishes may occasionally be witnessed. Wherever the ancient glaciers have spread forest soil there you find our wee hero, most abundant where depth of soil and genial climate have given rise to a corresponding luxuriance in the trees, but following every kind of growth up the curving moraines to the highest glacial fountains.

Though I cannot of course expect all my readers to sympathize fully in my admiration of this little animal, few, I hope, will think this sketch of his life too long. I cannot begin to tell here how much he has cheered my lonely wanderings during all the years I have been pursuing my studies in these glorious wilds; or how much unmistakable humanity I have found in him. Take this for example: One calm, creamy Indian summer morning, when the nuts were ripe, I was camped in the upper Pine woods of the south fork of the San Joaquin, where the squirrels seemed to be about as plentiful as the ripe burs. They were taking an early breakfast before going to their regular harvest-work. While I was busy with my own breakfast I heard the thudding fall of two or three heavy cones from a Yellow Pine near me. I stole noiselessly forward within about twenty feet of the base of it to observe. In a few moments down came the Douglas. The breakfast-burs he had cut off had rolled on the gently sloping ground into a clump of ceanothus bushes, but he seemed to know exactly where they were, for he found them at once, apparently without searching for them. They were more than twice as heavy as himself, but after turning them into the right position for getting a good hold with his long sickle-teeth he managed to drag them up to the foot of the tree from which he had cut them, moving backward. Then seating himself comfortably, he held them on end, bottom up, and demolished them at his ease. A good deal of nibbling had to be done before he got anything to eat, because the lower scales are barren, but when he had patiently worked his way up to the fertile ones he found two sweet nuts at the base of each, shaped like trimmed hams, and spotted purple like birds' eggs. And notwithstanding these cones were dripping with soft balsam, and covered with prickles, and so strongly put together that a boy would be puzzled to cut them open with a jackknife, he accomplished his meal with easy dignity and cleanliness, making less effort apparently than a man would in eating soft cookery from a plate.

Breakfast done, I whistled a tune for him before he went to work, curious to see how he would be affected by it. He had not seen me all this while; but the instant I began to whistle he darted up the tree nearest to him, and came out on a small dead limb opposite me, and composed himself to listen. I sang and whistled more than a dozen airs, and as the music changed his eyes sparkled, and he turned his head quickly from side to side, but made no other response. Other squirrels, hearing the strange sounds, came around on all sides, also chipmunks and birds. One of the birds, a handsome, speckle-breasted thrush, seemed even more interested than the squirrels. After listening for a while on one of the lower dead sprays of a Pine, he came swooping forward within a few feet of my face, and remained fluttering in the air for half a minute or so, sustaining himself with whirring wing-beats, like a humming bird in front of a flower, while I could look into his eyes and see his innocent wonder.

By this time my performance must have lasted nearly half an hour. I sang or whistled "Bonnie Doon," "Lass o' Gowrie," "O'er the Water to Charlie," "Bonnie Woods o' Cragie Lee," etc., all of which seemed to be listened to with bright interest, my first Douglas sitting patiently through it all, with his telling eyes fixed upon me until I ventured to give the "Old Hundredth," when he screamed his Indian name, Pillillooeet, turned tail, and darted with ludicrous haste up the tree out of sight, his voice and actions in the case leaving a somewhat profane impression, as if he had said, "I'll be hanged if you get me to hear anything so solemn and un-piny." This acted as a signal for the general dispersal of the whole hairy tribe, though the birds seemed willing to wait further developments, music being naturally more in their line.

What there can be in that grand old church-tune that is so offensive to birds and squirrels I can't imagine. A year or two after this High Sierra concert, I was sitting one fine day on a hill in the Coast Range where the common Ground Squirrels were abundant. They were very shy on account of being hunted so much; but after I had been silent and motionless for half an hour or so they began to venture out of their holes and to feed on the seeds of the grasses and thistles around me as if I were no more to be feared than a tree-stump. Then it occurred to me that this was a good opportunity to find out whether they also disliked "Old Hundredth." Therefore I began to whistle as nearly as I could remember the same familiar airs that had pleased the mountaineers of the Sierra. They at once stopped eating, stood erect, and listened patiently until I came to "Old Hundredth," when with ludicrous haste every one of them rushed to their holes and bolted in, their feet twinkling in the air for a moment as they vanished.

No one who makes the acquaintance of our forester will fail to admire him; but he is far too self-reliant and warlike ever to be taken for a darling.

How long the life of a Douglas Squirrel may be, I don't know. The young seem to sprout from knot-holes, perfect from the first, and as enduring as their own trees. It is difficult, indeed, to realize that so condensed a piece of sun-fire should ever become dim or die at all. He is seldom killed by hunters, for he is too small to encourage much of their attention, and when pursued in settled regions becomes excessively shy, and keeps close in the furrows of the highest trunks, many of which are of the same color as himself. Indian boys, however, lie in wait with unbounded patience to shoot them with arrows. In the lower and middle zones a few fall a prey to rattlesnakes. Occasionally he is pursued by hawks and wildcats, etc. But, upon the whole, he dwells safely in the deep bosom of the woods, the most highly favored of all his happy tribe. May his tribe increase!

(*The Mountains of California*)

Sequoia

ACCOMPANIED BY a long-suffering mule, Brownie, John Muir undertook the first intensive study of the sequoia belt of the high Sierra in September 1875. Starting from Yosemite Valley, he worked his way south to Kern Basin, roaming for more than 200 miles through the realm of the Big Trees. "The wonder is that we can see these trees and not wonder more," Ralph Waldo Emerson had said when Muir first showed him the sequoias. To the local Indians, the sequoia was sacred and was called "Wawona." Stephen Powers, in his Tribes of California, *published by the U. S. Department of Interior in 1877, records that the natives tried to persuade the pioneer white men to spare the ancient trees and when they met teamsters hauling lumber made from the sequoia they would cry out and warn them that they would be visited by bad luck. Because of the difficulty of sawing through the trunks, the towering trees were often blasted down with dynamite, thus increasing the waste and destruction. When Muir lived in Yosemite Valley, he sometimes used fluid obtained from the sequoia for ink in writing letters. Rich in tannin, the fluid produced writing that remained perfectly legible for more than half a century.*

ONE OF MY OWN best excursions among the Sequoias was made in the autumn of 1875, when I explored the then unknown or little known Sequoia region south of the Mariposa Grove for comprehensive views of the belt, and to learn what I could of the peculiar distribution of the species and its history in general. In particular I was anxious to try to find out whether it had ever been more widely distributed since the glacial period; what conditions favorable or otherwise were affecting it; what were its relations to climate, topography, soil, and the other trees growing with it, etc.; and whether, as was generally supposed, the species was nearing extinction. I was already acquainted in a general way with the northern groves, but excepting some passing glimpses gained on excursions into the High Sierra about the head-waters of King's and Kern Rivers I had seen nothing of the south end of the belt.

Nearly all my mountaineering has been done on foot, carrying as little as possible, depending on camp-fires for warmth, that so I might be light and free to go wherever my studies might lead. On this Sequoia trip, which promised to be long, I was persuaded to take a small wild mule with me to carry provisions and a pair of blankets. The friendly owner of the animal, having noticed that I sometimes looked tired when I came down from the peaks to replenish my bread-sack, assured me that his "little Brownie mule" was just what I wanted, tough as a knot, perfectly untirable, low and narrow, just right for squeezing through brush, able to climb like a chipmunk, jump from boulder to boulder like a wild sheep, and go anywhere a man could go. But tough as he was and accomplished as a climber, many a time in the course of our journey when he was jaded and hungry, wedged fast in rocks or struggling in chaparral like a fly in a spiderweb, his troubles were sad to see, and I wished he would leave me and find his way home alone.

We set out from Yosemite about the end of August and our first camp was made in the well-known Mariposa Grove. Here and in the adjacent Pine woods I spent nearly a week, carefully examining the boundaries of the grove for traces of its greater extension without finding any. Then I struck out into the majestic trackless forest to the southeastward, hoping to find new groves or traces of old ones in the dense Silver Fir and Pine woods about the head of Big Creek, where soil and climate seemed most favorable to their growth, but not a single tree or old monument of any sort came to light until I climbed the high rock called Wamellow by the Indians. Here I obtained telling views of the fertile forest-filled basin of the upper Fresno. Innumerable spires of the noble Yellow Pine were displayed rising above one another on the braided slopes, and yet nobler Sugar Pines with superb arms outstretched in the rich autumn light, while away toward the southwest, on the verge of the glowing horizon, I discovered the majestic dome-like crowns of Big Trees towering high over all, singly and in close grove congregations. There is something wonderfully attractive in this king tree, even when beheld from afar, that draws us to it with indescribable enthusiasm; its superior height and massive smoothly rounded outlines proclaiming its character in any company; and when one of the oldest attains full stature on some commanding ridge it seems the very god of the woods. I ran back to camp, packed Brownie, steered over the divide and down into the heart of the Fresno Grove. Then choosing a camp on the side of a brook where the grass was good, I made a cup of tea, and set off free among the brown giants, glorying in the abundance of new work about me. One of the first special things that caught my attention was an extensive land-slip. The ground on the side of a stream had given way to a depth of about fifty feet and with all its trees had been launched into the bottom of the stream ravine. Most of the trees — Pines, Firs, Incense Cedar, and Sequoia — were still standing erect and uninjured, as if unconscious that anything out of the common had happened. Tracing the ravine alongside the avalanche, I saw many trees whose roots had been laid bare, and in one instance discovered a Sequoia about fifteen feet in diameter growing above an old prostrate trunk that seemed to belong to a former generation. This slip had occurred seven or eight years ago, and I was glad to find that not only were most of the Big Trees uninjured, but that many companies of hopeful seedlings and saplings were growing confidently on the fresh soil along the broken front of the avalanche. These young trees were already eight or ten feet high, and were shooting up vigorously, as if sure of eternal life, though young Pines, Firs, and Libocedrus were running a race with them for the sunshine with an even start. Farther down the ravine I counted five hundred and thirty-six promising young Sequoias on a bed of rough bouldery soil not exceeding two acres in extent.

The Fresno Big Trees covered an area of about four square miles, and while wandering about surveying the boundaries of the grove, anxious to see every tree, I came suddenly on a handsome log cabin, richly embowered and so fresh and unweathered it was still redolent of gum and balsam like a newly felled tree. Strolling forward, wondering who could have built it, I found an old, weary-eyed, speculative, gray-haired man on a bark stool by the door, reading a book. The discovery of his hermitage by a stranger seemed to surprise him, but when I explained that I was only a tree-lover sauntering along the mountains to study Sequoia, he bade me welcome, made me bring my mule down to a little slanting meadow before his door and camp with him, promising to show me his pet trees and many curious things bearing on my studies.

After supper, as the evening shadows were falling, the good hermit sketched his life in the mines, which in the main was like that of most other pioneer gold-hunters — a succession of intense experiences full of big ups and downs like the mountain topography. Since " '49" he had wandered over most of the Sierra, sinking innumerable prospect holes like a sailor making soundings, digging new channels for streams, sifting gold-sprinkled boulder and gravel beds with unquenchable energy, life's noon the meanwhile passing unnoticed into late afternoon shadows. Then, health and gold gone, the game played and lost, like a wounded deer creeping into this forest solitude, he awaits the sundown call. How sad the undertones of many a life here, now the noise of the first big gold battles has died away! How many interesting wrecks lie drifted and stranded in hidden nooks of the gold region! Perhaps no other range contains the remains of so many rare and interesting men. The name of my hermit friend is John A. Nelder, a fine kind man, who in going into the woods has at last gone home; for he loves nature truly, and realizes that these last shadowy days with scarce a glint of gold in them are the best of all. Birds, squirrels, plants get loving, natural recognition, and delightful it was to see how sensitively he responds to the silent influences of the woods. His eyes brightened as he gazed on the trees that stand guard around his little home; squirrels and mountain quail came to his call to be fed, and he tenderly stroked the little snow-bent sapling Sequoias, hoping they yet might grow straight to the sky and rule the grove. One of the greatest of his trees stands a little way back of his cabin, and he proudly led me to it, bidding me admire its colossal proportions and measure it to see if in all the forest there could be another so grand. It proved to be only twenty-six feet in diameter, and he seemed distressed to learn that the Mariposa Grizzly Giant was larger. I tried to comfort him by observing that his was the taller, finer formed, and perhaps the more favorably situated. Then he led me to some noble ruins, remnants of gigantic trunks of trees that he supposed must have been larger than any now standing, and though they had lain on the damp ground exposed to fire and the weather for centuries, the wood was perfectly sound. Sequoia timber is not only beautiful in color, rose-red when fresh, and as easily worked as Pine, but it is almost absolutely unperishable. Build a house of Big Tree logs on granite and that house will last about as long as its foundation. Indeed fire seems to be the only agent that has any appreciable effect on it. From one of these ancient trunk remnants I cut a specimen of the wood, which neither in color, strength, nor soundness could be distinguished from specimens cut from living trees, although it had certainly lain on the damp forest floor for more than three hundred and eighty years, probably more than thrice as long. The time in this instance was determined as follows: when the tree from which the specimen was derived fell it sunk itself into the ground, making a ditch about two hundred feet long and five or six feet deep; and in the middle of this ditch, where a part of the fallen trunk had been burned, a Silver Fir four feet in diameter and three hundred and eighty years old was growing, showing that the Sequoia trunk had lain on the ground three hundred and eighty years plus the unknown time that it lay before the part whose place had been taken by the Fir was burned out of the way, and that which had elapsed ere the seed from which the monumental Fir sprang fell into the prepared soil and took root. Now because Sequoia trunks are never wholly consumed in one forest fire and these fires recur only at considerable intervals, and because Sequoia ditches, after being cleared, are often left unplanted for centuries, it becomes evident that the trunk remnant in question may have been on the ground a thousand years or more. Similar vestiges are common, and together with the root-bowls and long straight ditches of the fallen monarchs, throw a sure light back on the post-glacial history of the species, bearing on its distribution. One of the most interesting features of this grove is the apparent ease and strength and comfortable independence in which the trees occupy their place in the general forest. Seedlings, saplings, young and middle-aged trees are grouped promisingly around the old patriarchs, betraying no sign of approach to extinction. On the contrary, all seem to be saying, "Everything is to our mind and we mean to live forever." But, sad to tell, a lumber company was building a large mill and flume near by, assuring widespread destruction.

In the cones and sometimes in the lower portion of the trunk and roots there is a dark gritty substance which dissolves readily in water and yields a magnificent purple color. It is a strong astringent, and is said to be used by the Indians as a big medicine. Mr. Nelder showed me specimens of ink he had made from it, which I tried and found good, flowing freely and holding its color well. Indeed everything about the tree seems constant. With these interesting trees, forming the largest of the northern groves, I stopped only a week, for I had far to go before the fall of the snow. The hermit seemed to cling to me and tried to make me promise to winter with him after the season's work was done. Brownie had to be got home, however, and other work awaited me, therefore I could only promise to stop a day or two on my way back to Yosemite and give him the forest news.

The next two weeks were spent in the wide basin of the San Joaquin, climbing innumerable ridges and surveying the far-extending sea of Pine and Firs. But not a single Sequoia crown appeared among them all, nor any trace of a fallen trunk, until I had crossed the south divide of the basin, opposite Dinky Creek, one of the northmost tributaries of King's River. On this stream there is a small grove, said to have been discovered a few years before my visit by two hunters in pursuit of a wounded bear. Just as I was fording one of the branches of Dinky Creek I met a shepherd, and when I asked him whether he knew anything about the Big Trees of the neighborhood he replied, "I know all about them, for I visited them only a few days ago and pastured my sheep in the grove." He was fresh from the East, and as this was his first summer in the Sierra I was curious to learn what impression the Sequoias had made on him. When I asked whether it was true that the Big Trees were really so big as people say, he warmly replied, "Oh, yes sir, you bet. They're whales. I never used to believe half I heard about the awful size of California trees, but they're monsters and no mistake. One of them over here, they tell me, is the biggest tree in the whole world, and I guess it is, for it's forty foot through and as many good long paces around." He was very earnest, and in fullness of faith offered to guide me to the grove that I might not miss seeing this biggest tree. A fair measurement four feet from the ground, above the main swell of the roots, showed a diameter of only thirty-two feet, much to the young man's disgust. "Only thirty-two feet," he lamented, "only thirty-two, and I always thought it was forty!" Then with a sigh of relief, "No matter, that's a big tree, anyway; no fool of a tree, sir, that you can cut a plank out of thirty feet broad, straight-edged, no bark, all good wood, sound and solid. It would make the brag White Pine planks from old Maine look like laths." A good many other fine specimens are distributed along three small branches of the creek, and I noticed several thrifty moderate-sized Sequoias growing on a granite ledge, apparently as independent of deep soil as the Pines and Firs, clinging to seams and fissures and sending their roots far abroad in search of moisture.

The creek is very clear and beautiful, gliding through tangles of shrubs and flower-beds, gay bee and butterfly pastures, the grove's own stream, pure Sequoia water, flowing all the year, every drop filtered through moss and leaves and the myriad spongy rootlets of the giant trees. One of the most interesting features of the grove is a small waterfall with a flowery, ferny, clear brimming pool at the foot of it. How cheerily it sings the songs of the wilderness, and how sweet its tones! You seem to taste as well as hear them, while only the subdued roar of the river in the deep cañon reaches up into the grove, sounding like the sea and the winds. So charming a fall and pool in the heart of so glorious a forest good pagans would have consecrated to some lovely nymph.

Hence down into the main King's River cañon, a mile deep, I led and dragged and shoved my patient, much-enduring mule through miles and miles of gardens and brush, fording innumerable streams, crossing savage rock slopes and taluses, scrambling, sliding through gulches and gorges, then up into the grand Sequoia forests of the south side, cheered by the royal crowns displayed on the narrow horizon. In a day and a half we reached the Sequoia woods in the neighborhood of the old Thomas' Mill Flat. Thence striking off northeastward I found a magnificent forest nearly six miles long by two in width, composed mostly of Big Trees, with outlying groves as far east as Boulder Creek. Here five or six days were spent, and it was delightful to learn from countless trees, old and young, how comfortably they were settled down in concordance with climate and soil and their noble neighbors.

Imbedded in these majestic woods there are numerous meadows, around the sides of which the Big Trees press close together in beautiful lines, showing their grandeur openly from the ground to their domed heads in the sky. The young trees are still more numerous and exuberant than in the Fresno and Dinky groves, standing apart in beautiful family groups, or crowding around the old giants. For every venerable lightning-stricken tree, there is one or more in all the glory of prime, and for each of these, many young trees and crowds of saplings. The young trees express the grandeur of their race in a way indefinable by any words at my command. When they are five or six feet in diameter and a hundred and fifty feet high, they seem like mere baby saplings as many inches in diameter, their juvenile habit and gestures completely veiling their real size, even to those who from long experience, are able to make fair approximation in their measurements of common trees. One morning I noticed three airy, spiry, quick-growing babies on the side of a meadow, the largest of which I took to be about eight inches in diameter. On measuring it, I found to my astonishment it was five feet six inches in diameter, and about a hundred and forty feet high.

On a bed of sandy ground fifteen yards square, which had been occupied by four Sugar Pines, I counted ninety-four promising seedlings, an instance of Sequoia gaining ground from its neighbors. Here also I noted eighty-six young Sequoias from one to fifty feet high on less than half an acre of ground that had been cleared and prepared for their reception by fire. This was a small bay burned into dense chaparral, showing that fire, the great destroyer of tree-life, is sometimes followed by conditions favorable for new growths. Sufficient fresh soil, however, is furnished for the constant renewal of the forest by the fall of old trees without the help of any other agent — burrowing animals, fire, flood, land-slip, etc — for the ground is thus turned and stirred as well as cleared, and in every roomy, shady hollow beside the walls of upturned roots many hopeful seedlings spring up.

The largest, and as far as I know the oldest, of all the King's River trees that I saw is the majestic stump, already referred to, about a hundred and forty feet high, which above the swell of the roots is thirty-five feet and eight inches inside the bark, and over four thousand years old. It was burned nearly half through at the base, and I spent a day in chopping off the charred surface, cutting into the heart, and counting the wood-rings with the aid of a lens. I made out a little over four thousand without difficulty or doubt, but I was unable to get a complete count, owing to confusion in the rings where wounds had been healed over. Judging by what is left of it, this was a fine, tall, symmetrical tree nearly forty feet in diameter before it lost its bark. In the last sixteen hundred and seventy-two years the increase in diameter was ten feet. A short distance south of this forest lies a beautiful grove, now mostly included in the General Grant National Park. I found many shake-makers at work in it, access to these magnificent woods having been made easy by the old mill wagon road. The Park is only two miles square, and the largest of its many fine trees is the General Grant, so named before the date of my

first visit, twenty-eight years ago, and said to be the largest tree
in the world, though above the craggy bulging base the diameter
is less than thirty feet. The Sanger Lumber Company owns nearly
all the King's River groves outside the Park, and for many years
the mills have been spreading desolation without any advantage.

One of the shake-makers, directed me to an "old snag biggeren
Grant." It proved to be a huge black charred stump thirty-two
feet in diameter, the next in size to the grand monument mentioned above.

I found a scattered growth of Big Trees extending across the
main divide to within a short distance of Hyde's Mill, on a tributary of Dry Creek. The mountain ridge on the south side of the
stream was covered from base to summit with a most superb
growth of Big Trees. What a picture it made! In all my wide
forest wanderings I had seen none so sublime. Every tree of all
the mighty host seemed perfect in beauty and strength, and their
majestic domed heads, rising above one another on the mountain
slope, were most imposingly displayed, like a range of bossy upswelling cumulus clouds on a calm sky.

In this glorious forest the mill was busy, forming a sore, sad
center of destruction, though small as yet, so immensely heavy was
the growth. Only the smaller and most accessible of the trees
were being cut. The logs, from three to ten or twelve feet in
diameter, were dragged or rolled with long strings of oxen into
a chute and sent flying down the steep mountain-side to the mill
flat, where the largest of them were blasted into manageable
dimensions for the saws. And as the timber is very brash, by this
blasting and careless felling on uneven ground, half or three
fourths of the timber was wasted.

I spent several days exploring the ridge and counting the annual
wood-rings on a large number of stumps in the clearings, then
replenished my bread-sack and pushed on southward. All the way
across the broad rough basins of the Kaweah and Tule Rivers
Sequoia ruled supreme, forming an almost continuous belt for
sixty or seventy miles, waving up and down in huge massy moun-
tain-billows in compliance with the grand glacier-ploughed topography.

Day after day, from grove to grove, cañon to cañon, I made a long, wavering way, terribly rough in some places for Brownie, but cheery for me, for Big Trees were seldom out of sight. We crossed the rugged, picturesque basins of Redwood Creek, the North Fork of the Kaweah, and Marble Fork gloriously forested, and full of beautiful cascades and falls, sheer and slanting, infinitely varied with broad curly foam fleeces and strips of embroidery in which the sunbeams revel. Thence we climbed into the noble forest on the Marble and Middle Fork Divide. After a general exploration of the Kaweah basin, this part of the Sequoia belt seemed to me the finest, and I then named it "the Giant Forest." It extends, a magnificent growth of giants grouped in pure temple groves, ranged in colonnades along the sides of meadows, or scattered among the other trees, from the granite headlands overlooking the hot foot-hills and plains of the San Joaquin back to within a few miles of the old glacier-fountains at an elevation of 5000 to 8400 feet above the sea.

When I entered this sublime wilderness the day was nearly done, the trees with rosy, glowing countenances seemed to be hushed and thoughtful, as if waiting in conscious religious dependence on the sun, and one naturally walked softly and awe-stricken among them. I wandered on, meeting nobler trees where all are noble, subdued in the general calm, as if in some vast hall pervaded by the deepest sanctities and solemnities that sway human souls. At sundown the trees seemed to cease their worship and breathe free. I heard the birds going home. I too sought a home for the night on the edge of a level meadow where there is a long, open view between the evenly ranked trees standing guard along its sides. Then after a good place was found for poor Brownie, who had had a hard, weary day sliding and scrambling across the Marble Cañon, I made my bed and supper and lay on my back looking up to the stars through pillared arches finer far than the pious heart of man, telling its love, ever reared. Then I took a walk up the meadow to see the trees in the pale light. They seemed still more marvelously massive and tall than by day, heaving their colossal heads into the depths of the sky, among the stars, some of which appeared to be sparkling on their branches like flowers. I built a big fire that vividly illumined the huge brown boles of the nearest trees and the little plants and cones and fallen leaves at their feet, keeping up the show until I fell asleep to dream of boundless forests and trail-building for Brownie.

Joyous birds welcomed the dawn; and the squirrels, now their food-cones were ripe and had to be quickly gathered and stored for winter, began their work before sunrise. My tea-and-bread-crumb breakfast was soon done, and leaving jaded Brownie to feed and rest I sauntered forth to my studies. In every direction Sequoia ruled the woods. Most of the other big conifers were present here and there, but not as rivals or companions. They only served to thicken and enrich the general wilderness. Trees of every age cover craggy ridges as well as the deep moraine-soiled slopes, and plant their magnificent shafts along every brookside and meadow. Bogs and meadows are rare or entirely wanting in the isolated groves north of King's River; here there is a beautiful series of them lying on the broad top of the main dividing ridge, imbedded in the very heart of the mammoth woods as if for ornament, their smooth, plushy bosoms kept bright and fertile by streams and sunshine.

Resting awhile on one of the most beautiful of them when the sun was high, it seemed impossible that any other forest picture in the world could rival it. There lay the grassy, flowery lawn, three fourths of a mile long, smoothly outspread, basking in mellow autumn light, colored brown and yellow and purple, streaked with lines of green along the streams, and ruffled here and there with patches of ledum and scarlet vaccinium. Around the margin there is first a fringe of azalea and willow bushes, colored orange-yellow, enlivened with vivid dashes of red cornel, as if painted. Then up spring the mighty walls of verdure three hundred feet high, the brown fluted pillars so thick and tall and strong they seem fit to uphold the sky; the dense foliage, swelling forward in rounded bosses on the upper half, variously shaded and tinted, that of the young trees dark green, of the old yellowish. An aged lightning-smitten patriarch standing a little forward be-yond the general line with knotty arms outspread was covered with gray and yellow lichens and surrounded by a group of saplings whose slender spires seemed to lack not a single leaf or spray in their wondrous perfection. Such was the Kaweah meadow picture that golden afternoon, and as I gazed every color seemed to deepen and glow as if the progress of the fresh sun-work were visible from hour to hour, while every tree seemed religious and conscious of the presence of God. A free man revels in a scene like this and time goes by unmeasured. I stood fixed in silent wonder or sauntered about shifting my points of view, studying the physiognomy of separate trees, and going out to the different color patches to see how they were put on and what they were made of, giving free expression to my joy, exulting in Nature's wild immortal vigor and beauty, never dreaming any other human being was near. Suddenly the spell was broken by dull bumping, thudding sounds, and a man and horse came in sight at the farther end of the meadow, where they seemed sadly out of place. A good big bear or mastodon or megatherium would have been more in keeping with the old mammoth forest. Nevertheless, it is always pleasant to meet one of our own species after solitary rambles, and I stepped out where I could be seen and shouted, when the rider reined in his galloping mustang and waited my approach. He seemed too much surprised to speak until, laughing in his puzzled face, I said I was glad to meet a fellow mountaineer in so lonely a place. Then he abruptly asked, "What are you doing? How did you get here?" I explained that I came across the cañons from Yosemite and was only looking at the trees. "Oh then, I know," he said, greatly to my surprise, "you must be John Muir." He was herding a band of horses that had been driven up a rough trail from the lowlands to feed on these forest meadows. A few handfuls of crumb detritus was all that was left in my bread-sack, so I told him that I was nearly out of provision and asked whether he could spare me a little flour. "Oh yes, of course you can have anything I've got," he said. "Just take my track and it will lead you to my camp in a big hollow log on the side of a meadow two or three miles from here. I must ride after some strayed horses, but I'll be back before night; in the mean time make yourself at home." He galloped away to the northward, I returned to my own camp, saddled Brownie, and by the middle of the afternoon discovered his noble den in a fallen Sequoia hollowed by fire — a spacious log house of one log, carbon-lined, centuries old yet sweet and fresh, weather proof, earthquake proof, likely to outlast the most durable stone castle, and commanding views of garden and grove grander far than the richest king ever enjoyed. Brownie found plenty of grass and I found bread, which I ate with views from the big round, ever-open door. Soon the good Samaritan mountaineer came in, and I enjoyed a famous rest listening to his observations on trees, animals, adventures, etc., while he was busily preparing supper. In answer to inquiries concerning the distribution of the Big Trees he gave a good deal of particular information of the forest we were in, and he had heard that the species extended a long way south, he knew not how far. I wandered about for several days within a radius of six or seven miles of the camp, surveying boundaries, measuring trees, and climbing the highest points for general views. From the south side of the divide I saw telling ranks of Sequoia-crowned headlands stretching far into the hazy distance, and plunging vaguely down into profound cañon depths foreshadowing weeks of good work. I had now been out on the trip more than a month, and I began to fear my studies would be interrupted by snow, for winter was drawing nigh. "Where there isn't a way make a way" is easily said when no way at the time is needed, but to the Sierra explorer with a mule traveling across the cañon lines of drainage the brave old phrase becomes heavy with meaning. There are ways across the Sierra graded by glaciers, well marked, and followed by men and beasts and birds, and one of them even by locomotives; but none natural or artificial along the range, and the explorer who would thus travel at right angles to the glacial ways must traverse cañons and ridges extending side by side in endless succession, roughened by side gorges and gulches and stubborn chaparral, and defended by innumerable sheer-fronted precipices. My own ways are easily made in any direction, but Brownie, though one of the toughest and most skillful of his race, was oftentimes discouraged for want of hands, and caused endless work. Wild at first, he was tame enough now; and when turned loose he not only refused to run away, but as his troubles increased came to depend on me in such a pitiful, touching way, I became attached to him and helped him as if he were a good-natured boy in distress, and then the labor grew lighter. Bidding good-by to the kind Sequoia cave-dweller, we vanished again in the wilderness, drifting slowly southward, Sequoias on every ridge-top beckoning and pointing the way.

In the forest between the Middle and East forks of the Kaweah, I met a great fire, and as fire is the master scourge and controller of the distribution of trees, I stopped to watch it and learn what I could of its works and ways with the giants. It came racing up the steep chaparral-covered slopes of the East Fork cañon with passionate enthusiasm in a broad cataract of flames, now bending down low to feed on the green bushes, devouring acres of them at a breath, now towering high in the air as if looking abroad to choose a way, then stooping to feed again, the lurid flapping surges and the smoke and terrible rushing and roaring hiding all that is gentle and orderly in the work. But as soon as the deep forest was reached the ungovernable flood became calm like a torrent entering a lake, creeping and spreading beneath the trees where the ground was level or sloped gently, slowly nibbling the cake of compressed needles and scales with flames an inch high, rising here and there to a foot or two on dry twigs and clumps of small bushes and brome grass. Only at considerable intervals were fierce bonfires lighted, where heavy branches broken off by snow had accumulated, or around some venerable giant whose head had been stricken off by lightning.

I tethered Brownie on the edge of a little meadow beside a stream a good safe way off, and then cautiously chose a camp for myself in a big stout hollow trunk not likely to be crushed by the fall of burning trees, and made a bed of ferns and boughs in it. The night, however, and the strange wild fireworks were too beautiful and exciting to allow much sleep. There was no danger of being chased and hemmed in, for in the main forest belt of the Sierra, even when swift winds are blowing, fires seldom or never sweep over the trees in broad all-embracing sheets as they do in the dense Rocky Mountain woods and in those of the Cascade Mountains of Oregon and Washington. Here they creep from tree to tree with tranquil deliberation, allowing close observation, though caution is required in venturing around the burning giants to avoid falling limbs and knots and fragments from dead shattered tops. Though the day was best for study, I sauntered about night after night, learning what I could and admiring the wonderful show vividly displayed in the lonely darkness, the ground-fire advancing in long crooked lines gently grazing and smoking on the close-pressed leaves, springing up in thousands of little jets of pure flame on dry tassels and twigs, and tall spires and flat sheets with jagged flapping edges dancing here and there on grass tufts and bushes, big bonfires blazing in perfect storms of energy where heavy branches mixed with small ones lay smashed together in hundred cord piles, big red arches between spreading root-swells and trees growing close together, huge fire-mantled trunks on the hill-slopes glowing like bars of hot iron, violet-colored fire running up the tall trees, tracing the furrows of the bark in quick quivering rills, and lighting magnificent torches on dry shattered tops, and ever and anon, with a tremendous roar and burst of light, young trees clad in low-descending feathery branches vanishing in one flame two or three hundred feet high.

One of the most impressive and beautiful sights was made by the great fallen trunks lying on the hillsides all red and glowing like colossal iron bars fresh from a furnace, two hundred feet long some of them, and ten to twenty feet thick. After repeated burnings have consumed the bark and sapwood, the sound charred surface, being full of cracks and sprinkled with leaves, is quickly overspread with a pure, rich, furred, ruby glow almost flameless and smokeless, producing a marvelous effect in the night. Another grand and interesting sight are the fires on the tops of the largest living trees flaming above the green branches at a height of perhaps two hundred feet, entirely cut off from the ground-fires, and looking like signal beacons on watch towers. From one standpoint I sometimes saw a dozen or more, those in the distance looking like great stars above the forest roof. At first I could not imagine how these Sequoia lamps were lighted, but the very first night, strolling about waiting and watching, I saw the thing done again and again. The thick, fibrous bark of old trees is divided by deep, nearly continuous furrows, the sides of which are bearded with the bristling ends of fibers broken by the growth swelling of the trunk, and when the fire comes creeping around the feet of the trees, it runs up these bristly furrows in lovely pale blue quivering, bickering rills of flame with a low, earnest whispering sound to the lightning-shattered top of the trunk, which, in the dry Indian summer, with perhaps leaves and twigs and squirrel-gnawed cone-scales and seed-wings lodged in it, is readily ignited. These lamp-lighting rills, the most beautiful fire streams I ever saw, last only a minute or two, but the big lamps burn with varying brightness for days and weeks, throwing off sparks like the spray of a fountain, while ever and anon a shower of red coals comes sifting down through the branches, followed at times with startling effect by a big burned-off chunk weighing perhaps half a ton.

The immense bonfires where fifty or a hundred cords of peeled, split, smashed wood has been piled around some old giant by a single stroke of lightning is another grand sight in the night. The light is so great I fcund I could read common print three hundred yards from them, and the illumination of the circle of onlooking trees is indescribably impressive. Other big fires, roaring and booming like waterfalls, were blazing on the upper sides of trees on hill-slopes, against which limbs broken off by heavy snow had rolled, while branches high overhead, tossed and shaken by the ascending air current, seemed to be writhing in pain. Perhaps the most startling phenomenon of all was the quick death of childlike Sequoias only a century or two of age. In the midst of the other comparatively slow and steady fire work one of these tall, beautiful saplings, leafy and branchy, would be seen blazing up suddenly, all in one heaving, booming, passionate flame reaching from the ground to the top of the tree and fifty to a hundred feet or more above it, with a smoke column bending forward and streaming away on the upper, free-flowing wind. To burn these green trees a strong fire of dry wood beneath them is required, to send up a current of air hot enough to distill inflammable gases from the leaves and sprays; then instead of the lower limbs gradually catching fire and igniting the next and next in succession, the whole tree seems to explode almost simultaneously, and with awful roaring and throbbing a round, tapering flame shoots up two or three hundred feet, and in a second or two is quenched, leaving the green spire a black, dead mast, bristled and roughened with down-curling boughs. Nearly all the trees that have been burned down are lying with their heads uphill, because they are burned far more deeply on the upper side, on account of broken limbs rolling down against them to make hot fires, while only leaves and twigs accumulate on the lower side and are quickly consumed without injury to the tree. But green, resinless Sequoia wood burns very slowly, and many successive fires are required to burn down a large tree. Fires can run only at intervals of several years, and when the ordinary amount of firewood that has rolled against the gigantic trunk is consumed, only a shallow scar is made, which is slowly deepened by recurring fires until far beyond the center of gravity, and when at last the tree falls, it of course falls uphill. The healing folds of wood layers on some of the deeply burned trees show that centuries have elapsed since the last wounds were made.

When a great Sequoia falls, its head is smashed into fragments about as small as those made by lightning, which are mostly de-voured by the first running, hunting fire that finds them, while the trunk is slowly wasted away by centuries of fire and weather. One of the most interesting fire actions on the trunk is the boring of those great tunnel-like hollows through which horsemen may gallop. All of these famous hollows are burned out of the solid wood, for no Sequoia is ever hollowed by decay. When the tree falls the brash trunk is often broken straight across into sections as if sawed; into these joints the fire creeps, and, on account of the great size of the broken ends, burns for weeks or even months without being much influenced by the weather. After the great glowing ends fronting each other have burned so far apart that their rims cease to burn, the fire continues to work on in the centers, and the ends become deeply concave. Then heat being ra-diated from side to side, the burning goes on in each section of the trunk independent of the other, until the diameter of the bore is so great that the heat radiated across from side to side is not suffi-cient to keep them burning. It appears, therefore, that only very large trees can receive the fire-auger and have any shell rim left.

Fire attacks the large trees only at the ground, consuming the fallen leaves and humus at their feet, doing them but little harm unless considerable quantities of fallen limbs happen to be piled about them, their thick mail of spongy, unpitchy, almost unburnable bark affording strong protection. Therefore the oldest and most perfect unscarred trees are found on ground that is nearly level, while those growing on hillsides, against which falling branches roll, are always deeply scarred on the upper side, and as we have seen are sometimes burned down. The saddest thing of all was to see the hopeful seedlings, many of them crinkled and bent with the pressure of winter snow, yet bravely aspiring at the top, helplessly perishing, and young trees, perfect spires of verdure and naturally immortal, suddenly changed to dead masts. Yet the sun looked cheerily down the openings in the forest roof, turning the black smoke to a beautiful brown, as if all was for the best.

(Our National Parks)

Nevada Nut Pines

WHEN THE COAST and Geodetic Survey sent a party into the highlands of Nevada during the summer of 1878, John Muir was invited to accompany it. His letters home, during this expedition, tell of such adventures as seeing a dozen cloudbursts falling at the same time from different portions of the sky. On another occasion his presence with the party undoubtedly saved the lives of at least two of the members when they ventured fifty miles from the nearest water and came close to perishing of thirst. An important aspect of the trip from Muir's point of view was the opportunity it gave him to study the remarkable nut pine, so important in the economy of the Indians of the region. The seeds of the cones of this pine are rich in food value and sweet and delicate in flavor.

THE HEIGHT of the timber-line in eastern Nevada, near the middle of the Great Basin, is about eleven thousand feet above sea-level; consequently the forests, in a dwarfed, storm-beaten condition, pass over the summits of nearly every range in the State, broken here and there only by mechanical conditions of the surface rocks.

In a rambling mountaineering journey of eighteen hundred miles across the state, I have met nine species of coniferous trees — four Pines, two Spruces, two Junipers, and one Fir, — about one third the number found in California. By far the most abundant and interesting of these is the *Pinus Fremontiana*, or Nut Pine. In the number of individual trees and extent of range this curious little conifer surpasses all the others combined. Nearly every mountain in the State is planted with it from near the base to a height of from eight thousand to nine thousand feet above the sea. Some are covered from base to summit by this one species, with only a sparse growth of Juniper on the lower slopes to break the continuity of these curious woods, which, though dark-looking at a little distance, are yet almost shadeless, and without any hint of the dark glens and hollows so characteristic of other Pine woods. Tens of thousands of acres occur in one continuous belt. Indeed, viewed comprehensively, the entire State seems to be pretty evenly divided into mountain ranges covered with Nut Pines and plains covered with sage — now a swath of Pines stretching from north to south, now a swath of sage; the one black, the other gray; one severely level, the other sweeping on complacently over ridge and valley and lofty crowning dome.

The real character of a forest of this sort would never be guessed by the inexperienced observer. Traveling across the sage levels in the dazzling sunlight, you gaze with shaded eyes at the mountains rising along their edges, perhaps twenty miles away, but no invitation that is at all likely to be understood is discernible. Every mountain, however high it swells into the sky, seems utterly barren. Approaching nearer, a low brushy growth is seen, strangely black in aspect, as though it had been burned. This is a Nut Pine forest, the bountiful orchard of the red man. When you ascend into its midst you find the ground beneath the trees, and in the openings also, nearly naked, and mostly rough on the surface — a succession of crumbling ledges of lava, limestones, slate, and quartzite, coarsely strewn with soil weathered from them. Here and there occurs a bunch of sage or linosyris, or a purple aster, or a tuft of dry bunch-grass.

The harshest mountain-sides, hot and waterless, seem best adapted to the Nut Pine's development. No slope is too steep, none too dry; every situation seems to be gratefully chosen, if only it be sufficiently rocky and firm to afford secure anchorage for the tough, grasping roots. It is a sturdy, thickset little tree, usually about fifteen feet high when full grown, and about as broad as high, holding its knotty branches well out in every direction in stiff zigzags, but turning them gracefully upward at the ends in rounded bosses. Though making so dark a mass in the distance, the foliage is a pale grayish green, in stiff, awl-shaped fascicles. When examined closely these round needles seem inclined to be two-leaved, but they are mostly held firmly togther, as if to guard against evaporation. The bark on the older sections is nearly black, so that the boles and branches are clearly traced against the prevailing gray of the mountains on which they delight to dwell.

The value of this species to Nevada is not easily overestimated. It furnishes fuel, charcoal, and timber for the mines, and, together with the enduring Juniper, so generally associated with it, supplies the ranches with abundance of firewood and rough fencing. Many a square mile has already been denuded in supplying these demands, but, so great is the area covered by it, no appreciable loss has as yet been sustained. It is pretty generally known that this tree yields edible nuts, but their importance and excellence as human food is infinitely greater than is supposed. In fruitful seasons like this one, the pine-nut crop of Nevada is, perhaps, greater than the entire wheat crop of California, concerning which so much is said and felt throughout the food-markets of the world.

The Indians alone appreciate this portion of Nature's bounty and celebrate the harvest home with dancing and feasting. The cones, which are a bright grass-green in color and about two inches long by one and a half in diameter, are beaten off with poles just before the scales open, gathered in heaps of several bushels, and lightly scorched by burning a thin covering of brushwood over them. The resin, with which the cones are bedraggled, is thus burned off, the nuts slightly roasted, and the scales made to open. Then they are allowed to dry in the sun, after which the nuts are easily thrashed out and are ready to be stored away. They are about half an inch long by a quarter of an inch in diameter, pointed at the upper end, rounded at the base, light-brown in general color, and handsomely dotted with purple, like birds' eggs. The shells are thin, and may be crushed between the thumb and finger. The kernels are white and waxy-looking, becoming brown by roasting, sweet and delicious to every palate, and are eaten by birds, squirrels, dogs, horses, and man. When the crop is abundant the Indians bring in large quantities for sale; they are eaten around every fireside in the State, and oftentimes fed to horses instead of barley.

Looking over the whole continent, none of Nature's bounties seems to me so great as this in the way of food, none so little appreciated. Fortunately for the Indians and wild animals that gather around Nature's board, this crop is not easily harvested in a monopolizing way. If it could be gathered like wheat the whole would be carried away and dissipated in towns, leaving the brave inhabitants of these wilds to starve.

Long before the harvest-time, which is in September and October, the Indians examine the trees with keen discernment, and inasmuch as the cones require two years to mature from the first appearance of the little red rosettes of the fertile flowers, the scarcity or abundance of the crop may be predicted more than a year in advance. Squirrels, and worms, and Clark Crows, make haste to begin the harvest. When the crop is ripe the Indians make ready their long beating-poles; baskets, bags, rags, mats, are gotten together. The squaws out among the settlers at service, washing and drudging, assemble at the family huts; the men leave their ranch work; all, old and young, are mounted on ponies, and set off in great glee to the nut-lands, forming cavalcades curiously picturesque. Flaming scarfs and calico skirts stream loosely over the knotty ponies, usually two squaws astride of each, with the small baby midgets bandaged in baskets slung on their backs, or balanced upon the saddle-bow, while the nut-baskets and water-jars project from either side, and the long beating-poles, like old-fashioned lances, angle out in every direction.

Arrived at some central point already fixed upon, where water and grass is found, the squaws with baskets, the men with poles, ascend the ridges to the laden trees, followed by the children; beating begins with loud noise and chatter; the burs fly right and left, lodging against stones and sagebrush; the squaws and children gather them with fine natural gladness; smoke-columns speedily mark the joyful scene of their labors as the roasting-fires are kindled; and, at night, assembled in circles, garrulous as jays, the first grand nut feast begins. Sufficient quantities are thus obtained in a few weeks to last all winter.

(Steep Trails)

Any Fool Can Destroy a Tree

MUIR'S LIFELONG dream of visiting the araucaria forests of the Amazon was realized in 1911, at the age of seventy-three. Who else has traveled as far as John Muir to revel in the strength and beauty of trees? Who else has looked with appreciative eyes on as many different species of the trees of the world? And who else has been as influential in arousing people to come to the defense of beautiful, helpless species in America? The effectiveness of Muir's pleading for trees is illustrated in these final words of Our National Parks, *his second book, published in 1901.*

ANY FOOL can destroy trees. They cannot run away; and if they could, they would still be destroyed — chased and hunted down as long as fun or a dollar could be got out of their bark hides, branching horns, or magnificent bole backbones. Few that fell trees plant them; nor would planting avail much toward getting back anything like the noble primeval forests. During a man's life only saplings can be grown, in the place of the old trees — tens of centuries old — that have been destroyed. It took more than three thousand years to make some of the trees in these Western woods — trees that are still standing in perfect strength and beauty, waving and singing in the mighty forests of the Sierra. Through all the wonderful, eventful centuries since Christ's time — and long before that — God has cared for these trees, saved them from drought, disease, avalanches, and a thousand straining, leveling tempests and floods; but he cannot save them from fools — only Uncle Sam can do that.

(*Our National Parks*)

VI

GLACIER PIONEER

Discovery of the Sierra Glaciers

WHEN MUIR BEGAN his tremendous, self-imposed task of exploring every canyon and peak in the Yosemite region, in the year 1871, no one knew of the existence of living glaciers among these mountains. He discovered them. When he proposed that the ice-plows of glaciers of the past had gouged out the spectacular Yosemite Valley, entrenched scientific opinion still clung to the cataclysmic theory of Josiah Dwight Whitney. Only after Muir, by exhaustive study, had amassed his proof was the world convinced. In the history of glacier-study in America, both in California and Alaska, John Muir was one of the important pioneers.

That he never tired of talking of glaciers those who remember him will attest. An amusing sidelight in this connection is contained in an article in Yosemite Nature Notes *for October 1950. Fred P. Clatworthy recalls how he obtained his often published picture of "John o' the Birds and John o' the Mountains" — John Burroughs and John Muir — at Yosemite. Just as he was about to snap the shutter, Muir said to Burroughs, "See that valley below us? That's the effect of a glacier." Burroughs, who had heard all he wanted to about glaciers, replied; "Yes, if a bumblebee were to light on yonder rock, there would be* some *effect." Both men chuckled at this sally and the camera caught them in a relaxed and jovial mood.*

P RIOR TO THE AUTUMN of 1871 the glaciers of the Sierra were unknown. In October of that year I discovered the Black Mountain Glacier in a shadowy amphitheater between Black and Red Mountains, two of the peaks of the Merced group. This group is the highest portion of a spur that straggles out from the main axis of the range in the direction of Yosemite Valley. At the time of this interesting discovery I was exploring the *névé* amphitheaters of the group, and tracing the courses of the ancient glaciers that once poured from its ample fountains through the Illilouette Basin and the Yosemite Valley, not expecting to find any active glaciers so far south in the land of sunshine.

Beginning on the northwestern extremity of the group, I explored the chief tributary basins in succession, their moraines, *roches moutonnées*, and splendid glacier pavements, taking them in regular succession without any reference to the time consumed in their study. The monuments of the tributary that poured its ice from between Red and Black Mountains I found to be the most interesting of them all; and when I saw its magnificent moraines extending in majestic curves from the spacious amphitheater between the mountains, I was exhilarated with the work that lay before me. It was one of the golden days of the Sierra Indian summer, when the rich sunshine glorifies every landscape however rocky and cold, and suggests anything rather than glaciers. The path of the vanished glacier was warm now, and shone in many places as if washed with silver. The tall Pines growing on the moraines stood transfigured in the glowing light, the Poplar groves on the levels of the basin were masses of orange-yellow, and the late-blooming goldenrods added gold to gold. Pushing on over my rosy glacial highway, I passed lake after lake set in solid basins of granite, and many a thicket and meadow watered by a stream that issues from the amphitheater and links the lakes together; now wading through plushy bogs knee-deep in yellow and purple sphagnum; now passing over bare rock. The main lateral moraines that bounded the view on either hand are from 100 to nearly 200 feet high, and about as regular as artificial embankments, and covered with a superb growth of Silver Fir and Pine. But this garden and forest luxuriance was speedily left behind. The trees were dwarfed as I ascended; patches of the alpine bryanthus and cassiope began to appear, and arctic willows pressed into flat carpets by the winter snow. The lakelets, which a few miles down the valley were so richly embroidered with flowery meadows, had here, at an elevation of 10,000 feet, only small brown mats of carex, leaving bare rocks around more than half their shores. Yet amid this alpine suppression the Mountain Pine bravely tossed his storm-beaten branches on the ledges and buttresses of Red Mountain, some specimens being over 100 feet high, and 24 feet in circumference, seemingly as fresh and vigorous as the giants of the lower zones.

Evening came on just as I got fairly within the portal of the main amphitheater. It is about a mile wide, and a little less than two miles long. The crumbling spurs and battlements of Red Mountain bound it on the north, the somber, rudely sculptured precipices of Black Mountain on the south, and a hacked, splintery *col*, curving around from mountain to mountain, shuts it in on the east.

I chose a camping-ground on the brink of one of the lakes where a thicket of Hemlock Spruce sheltered me from the night wind. Then, after making a tin-cupful of tea, I sat by my campfire reflecting on the grandeur and significance of the glacial records I had seen. As the night advanced the mighty rock walls of my mountain mansion seemed to come nearer, while the starry sky in glorious brightness stretched across like a ceiling from wall to wall, and fitted closely down into all the spiky irregularities of the summits. Then, after a long fireside rest and a glance at my note-book, I cut a few leafy branches for a bed, and fell into the clear, death-like sleep of the tired mountaineer.

Early next morning I set out to trace the grand old glacier that had done so much for the beauty of the Yosemite region back to its farthest fountains, enjoying the charm that every explorer feels in Nature's untrodden wildernesses. The voices of the mountains were still asleep. The wind scarce stirred the pine-needles. The sun was up, but it was yet too cold for the birds and the few burrowing animals that dwell here. Only the stream, cascading from pool to pool, seemed to be wholly awake. Yet the spirit of the opening day called to action. The sunbeams came streaming gloriously through the jagged openings of the *col*, glancing on the burnished pavements and lighting the silvery lakes, while every sun-touched rock burned white on its edges like melting iron in a furnace. Passing round the north shore of my camp lake I followed the central stream past many cascades from lakelet to lakelet. The scenery became more rigidly arctic, the Dwarf Pines and Hemlocks disappeared, and the stream was bordered with icicles. As the sun rose higher rocks were loosened on shattered portions of the cliffs, and came down in rattling avalanches, echoing wildly from crag to crag.

The main lateral moraines that extend from the jaws of the amphitheater into the Illilouette Basin are continued in straggling masses along the walls of the amphitheater, while separate boulders, hundreds of tons in weight, are left stranded here and there out in the middle of the channel. Here, also, I observed a series of small terminal moraines ranged along the south wall of the amphitheater, corresponding in size and form with the shadows cast by the highest portions. The meaning of this correspondence between moraines and shadows was afterward made plain. Tracing the stream back to the last of its chain of lakelets, I noticed a deposit of fine gray mud on the bottom except where the force of the entering current had prevented its settling. It looked like the mud worn from a grindstone, and I at once suspected its glacial origin, for the stream that was carrying it came gurgling out of the base of a raw moraine that seemed in process of formation. Not a plant or weather-stain was visible on its rough, unsettled surface. It is from 60 to 100 feet high, and plunges forward at an angle of 38°. Cautiously picking my way, I gained the top of the moraine and was delighted to see a small but well-characterized glacier swooping down from the gloomy precipices of Black Mountain in a finely graduated curve to the moraine on which I stood. The compact ice appeared on all the lower portions of the glacier, though gray with dirt and stones embedded in it. Farther up the ice disappeared beneath coarse granulated snow. The surface of the glacier was further characterized by dirt-bands and the outcropping edges of the blue veins, showing the laminated structure of the ice. The uppermost crevasse, or "bergschrund," where the *névé* was attached to the mountain, was from 12 to 14 feet wide, and was bridged in a few places by the remains of snow avalanches. Creeping along the edge of the schrund, holding on with benumbed fingers, I discovered clear sections where the bedded structure was beautifully revealed. The surface-snow, though sprinkled with stones shot down from the cliffs, was in some places almost pure, gradually becoming crystalline and changing to whitish porous ice of different shades of color, and this again changing at a depth of 20 or 30 feet to blue ice, some of the ribbon-like bands of which were nearly pure, and blended with the paler bands in the most gradual and delicate manner imaginable. A series of rugged zigzags enabled me to make my way down into the weird under-world of the crevasse. Its chambered hollows were hung with a multitude of clustered icicles, amid which pale, subdued light pulsed and shimmered with indescribable loveliness. Water dripped and tinkled overhead, and from far below came strange, solemn murmurings from currents that were feeling their way through veins and fissures in the dark. The chambers of a glacier are perfectly enchanting, notwithstanding one feels out of place in their frosty beauty. I was soon cold in my shirt-sleeves, and the leaning wall threatened to engulf me; yet it was hard to leave the delicious music of the water and the lovely light. Coming again to the surface, I noticed boulders of every size on their journeys to the terminal moraine — journeys of more than a hundred years, without a single stop, night or day, winter or summer.

The sun gave birth to a network of sweet-voiced rills that ran gracefully down the glacier, curling and swirling in their shining channels, and cutting clear sections through the porous surface-ice into the solid blue, where the structure of the glacier was beautifully illustrated.

The series of small terminal moraines which I had observed in the morning, along the south wall of the amphitheater, correspond in every way with the moraine of this glacier, and their distribution with reference to shadows was now understood. When the climatic changes came on that caused the melting and retreat of the main glacier that filled the amphitheater, a series of residual glaciers were left in the cliff shadows, under the protection of which they lingered, until they formed the moraines we are studying. Then, as the snow became still less abundant, all of them vanished in succession, except the one just described; and the cause of its longer life is sufficiently apparent in the greater area of snow-basin it drains, and its more perfect protection from wasting sunshine. How much longer this little glacier will last depends, of course, on the amount of snow it receives from year to year, as compared with melting waste.

After this discovery, I made excursions over all the High Sierra, pushing my explorations summer after summer, and discovered that what at first sight in the distance looked like extensive snow-fields, were in great part glaciers, busily at work completing the sculpture of the summit-peaks so grandly blocked out by their giant predecessors.

(The Mountains of California)

Shadow Lake

SHADOW LAKE LIES at an elevation of more than 7300 feet some eight miles from Yosemite Valley. One of a number of glacial lakes Muir encountered in the high Sierra, it has also been known as Lake Nevada and Lake Washburn. The latter is its present name.

THE COLOR-BEAUTY about Shadow Lake during the Indian summer is much richer than one could hope to find in so young and so glacial a wilderness. Almost every leaf is tinted then, and the goldenrods are in bloom; but most of the color is given by the ripe grasses, Willows, and Aspens. At the foot of the lake you stand in a trembling Aspen grove, every leaf painted like a butterfly, and away to right and left round the shores sweeps a curving ribbon of meadow, red and brown dotted with pale yellow, shading off here and there into hazy purple. The walls, too, are dashed with bits of bright color that gleam out on the neutral granite gray. But neither the walls, nor the margin meadow, nor yet the gay, fluttering grove in which you stand, nor the lake itself, flashing with spangles, can long hold your attention; for at the head of the lake there is a gorgeous mass of orange-yellow, belonging to the main Aspen belt of the basin, which seems the very fountain whence all the color below it had flowed, and here your eye is filled and fixed. This glorious mass is about 30 feet high, and extends across the basin nearly from wall to wall. Rich bosses of Willow flame in front of it, and from the base of these the brown meadow comes forward to the water's edge, the whole being re-

lieved against the unyielding green of the coniferæ, while thick
sun-gold is poured over all.

During these blessed color-days no cloud darkens the sky, the
winds are gentle, and the landscape rests, hushed everywhere, and
indescribably impressive. A few ducks are usually seen sailing on
the lake, apparently more for pleasure than anything else, and the
ouzels at the head of the rapids sing always; while robins, gros-
beaks, and the Douglas Squirrels are busy in the groves, making
delightful company, and intensifying the feeling of grateful se-
questration without ruffling the deep, hushed calm and peace.
This autumnal mellowness usually lasts until the end of November. Then come days of quite another kind. The winter clouds
grow, and bloom, and shed their starry crystals on every leaf and
rock, and all the colors vanish like a sunset. The deer gather and
hasten down their well-known trails, fearful of being snow-bound.
Storm succeeds storm, heaping snow on the cliffs and meadows,
and bending the slender Pines to the ground in wide arches, one
over the other, clustering and interlacing like lodged wheat. Avalanches rush and boom from the shelving heights, piling immense
heaps upon the frozen lake, and all the summer glory is buried and
lost. Yet in the midst of this hearty winter the sun shines warm at
times, calling the Douglas Squirrel to frisk in the snowy Pines and
seek out his hidden stores; and the weather is never so severe as
to drive away the grouse and little nuthatches and chickadees.

Toward May, the lake begins to open. The hot sun sends down
innumerable streams over the cliffs, streaking them round and
round with foam. The snow slowly vanishes, and the meadows
show tintings of green. Then spring comes on apace; flowers and
flies enrich the air and the sod, and the deer come back to the
upper groves like birds to an old nest.

I first discovered this charming lake in the autumn of 1872,
while on my way to the glaciers at the head of the river. It was
rejoicing then in its gayest colors, untrodden, hidden in the glorious wildness like unmined gold. Year after year I walked its
shores without discovering any other trace of humanity than the
remains of an Indian camp-fire, and the thigh-bones of a deer that
had been broken to get at the marrow. It lies out of the regular

ways of Indians, who love to hunt in more accessible fields adjacent to trails. Their knowledge of deer-haunts had probably enticed them here some hunger-time when they wished to make sure of a feast; for hunting in this lake-hollow is like hunting in a fenced park. I had told the beauty of Shadow Lake only to a few friends, fearing it might come to be trampled and "improved" like Yosemite. On my last visit, as I was sauntering along the shore on the strip of sand between the water and sod, reading the tracks of the wild animals that live here, I was startled by a human track, which I at once saw belonged to some shepherd; for each step was turned out 35° or 40° from the general course pursued, and was also run over in an uncertain sprawling fashion at the heel, while a row of round dots on the right indicated the staff that shepherds carry. None but a shepherd could make such a track, and after tracing it a few minutes I began to fear that he might be seeking pasturage; for what else could he be seeking? Returning from the glaciers shortly afterward, my worst fears were realized. A trail had been made down the mountain-side from the north, and all the gardens and meadows were destroyed by a horde of hoofed locusts, as if swept by a fire. The money-changers were in the temple.

(*The Mountains of California*)

A Fall in the Mountains

THE ONE SERIOUS FALL Muir sustained in the mountains occurred during his glacier studies in the winter of 1872. Late in December, just after returning to Yosemite Valley after two "weary municipal weeks" in Oakland and San Francisco, he started out to traverse the whole length of the Tenaya Canyon. This was a feat no one had ever achieved before. Muir succeeded. But as he was working his way around a glacier-polished shoulder of Mount Watkins, above a thousand-foot gorge, he lost his balance and fell backward. A fringe of frail spirea and live-oak bushes at the edge of the abyss saved his life.

AFTER I HAD PASSED the tall groves that stretch a mile above Mirror Lake, and scrambled around the Tenaya Fall, which is just at the head of the lake groves, I crept through the dense and spiny chaparral that plushes the roots of the mountains here for miles in warm green, and was ascending a precipitous rock-front, smoothed by glacial action, when I suddenly fell — for the first time since I touched foot to Sierra rocks. After several somersaults, I became insensible from the shock, and when consciousness returned I found myself wedged among short, stiff bushes, trembling as if cold, not injured in the slightest.

Judging by the sun, I could not have been insensible very long; probably not a minute, possibly an hour; and I could not remember what made me fall, or where I had fallen from; but I saw that if I had rolled a little further, my mountain-climbing would have been finished, for just beyond the bushes the cañon wall steepened and I might have fallen to the bottom. "There," said I, addressing my feet, to whose separate skill I had learned to trust night and day on any mountain, "that is what you get by intercourse with stupid town stairs, and dead pavements." I felt degraded and worthless. I had not yet reached the most difficult portion of the cañon, but I determined to guide my humbled body over the most nerve-trying places I could find; for I was now awake, and felt confident that the last of the town fog had been shaken from both head and feet.

I camped at the mouth of a narrow gorge which is cut into the bottom of the main cañon, determined to take earnest exercise next day. No plushy boughs did my ill-behaved bones enjoy that night, nor did my bumped head get a spicy Cedar plume pillow mixed with flowers. I slept on a naked boulder, and when I awoke all my nervous trembling was gone.

(Steep Trails)

Mount Ritter

MUIR'S GLACIER–STUDIES in the high Sierra reached a climax in the fall of 1872 with his ascent of Mount Ritter. This 13,300-foot peak is, as Muir phrased it, "king of the mountains of the middle portion of the Sierra." So far as is known, it had never been scaled before Muir reached the top. Of Muir's mountain writings Lord James Bryce once said: "The very air of the granite peaks, the very fragrance of the deep and solemn forest, seem to breathe around us and soothe our senses as we read the description of his lonely wanderings in the Sierra when their majesty was first revealed."

AT A DISTANCE of less than 3000 feet below the summit of Mount Ritter you may find tributaries of the San Joaquin and Owen's Rivers, bursting forth from the ice and snow of the glaciers that load its flanks; while a little to the north of here are found the highest affluents of the Tuolumne and Merced. Thus, the fountains of four of the principal rivers of California are within a radius of four or five miles.

Lakes are seen gleaming in all sorts of places — round, or oval, or square, like very mirrors; others narrow and sinuous, drawn close around the peaks like silver zones, the highest reflecting only rocks, snow, and the sky. But neither these nor the glaciers, nor the bits of brown meadow and moorland that occur here and there, are large enough to make any marked impression upon the mighty wilderness of mountains. The eye, rejoicing in its freedom, roves about the vast expanse, yet returns again and again to the fountain-peaks. Perhaps some one of the multitude excites special attention, some gigantic castle with turret and battlement, or some Gothic cathedral more abundantly spired than Milan's. But, generally, when looking for the first time from an all-embracing standpoint like this, the inexperienced observer is oppressed by the incomprehensible grandeur, variety, and abundance of the mountains rising shoulder to shoulder beyond the reach of vision; and it is only after they have been studied one by one, long and lovingly, that their far-reaching harmonies become manifest. Then, penetrate the wilderness where you may, the main telling features, to which all the surrounding topography is subordinate, are quickly perceived, and the most complicated clusters of peaks stand revealed harmoniously correlated and fashioned like works of art — eloquent monuments of the ancient ice-rivers that brought them into relief from the general mass of the range. The cañons, too, some of them a mile deep, mazing wildly through the mighty host of mountains, however lawless and ungovernable at first sight they appear, are at length recognized as the necessary effects of causes which followed each other in harmonious sequence — Nature's poems carved on tables of stone — the simplest and most emphatic of her glacial compositions.

Could we have been here to observe during the glacial period, we should have overlooked a wrinkled ocean of ice as continuous as that now covering the landscapes of Greenland; filling every valley and cañon with only the tops of the fountain-peaks rising darkly above the rock-encumbered ice-waves like islets in a stormy sea — those islets the only hints of the glorious landscapes now smiling in the sun. Standing here in the deep, brooding silence all the wilderness seems motionless, as if the work of creation were done. But in the midst of this outer steadfastness we know there is incessant motion and change. Ever and anon, avalanches are falling from yonder peaks. These cliff-bound glaciers, seemingly wedged and immovable, are flowing like water and grinding the rocks beneath them. The lakes are lapping their granite shores and wearing them away, and every one of these rills and young rivers is fretting the air into music, and carrying the mountains to the plains. Here are the roots of all the life of the valleys, and here more simply than elsewhere is the eternal flux of Nature manifested. Ice changing to water, lakes to meadows, and mountains to plains. And while we thus contemplate Nature's methods of landscape creation, and, reading the records she has carved on the rocks, reconstruct, however imperfectly, the landscapes of the past, we also learn that as these we now behold have succeeded those of the pre-glacial age, so they in turn are withering and vanishing to be succeeded by others yet unborn.

But in the midst of these fine lessons and landscapes, I had to remember that the sun was wheeling far to the west, while a new way down the mountain had to be discovered to some point on the timber-line where I could have a fire; for I had not even burdened myself with a coat. I first scanned the western spurs, hoping some way might appear through which I might reach the northern glacier, and cross its snout; or pass around the lake into which it flows, and thus strike my morning track. This route was soon sufficiently unfolded to show that, if practicable at all, it would require so much time that reaching camp that night would be out of the question. I therefore scrambled back eastward, descending the southern slopes obliquely at the same time. Here the crags seemed less formidable, and the head of a glacier that flows northeast came in sight, which I determined to follow as far as possible, hoping thus to make my way to the foot of the peak on the east side, and thence across the intervening cañons and ridges to camp.

The inclination of the glacier is quite moderate at the head, and, as the sun had softened the *névé*, I made safe and rapid progress, running and sliding, and keeping up a sharp outlook for crevasses. About half a mile from the head, there is an ice-cascade, where the glacier pours over a sharp declivity and is shattered into massive blocks separated by deep, blue fissures. To thread my way through the slippery mazes of this crevassed portion seemed impossible, and I endeavored to avoid it by climbing off to the shoulder of the mountain. But the slopes rapidly steepened and at length fell away in sheer precipices, compelling a return to the ice. Fortunately, the day had been warm enough to loosen the ice-crystals so as to admit of hollows being dug in the rotten portions of the blocks, thus enabling me to pick my way with far less difficulty than I had anticipated. Continuing down over the snout, and along the left lateral moraine, was only a confident saunter, showing that the ascent of the mountain by way of this glacier is easy, provided one is armed with an axe, to cut steps here and there.

The lower end of the glacier was beautifully waved and barred by the outcropping edges of the bedded ice-layers which represent the annual snowfalls, and to some extent the irregularities of structure caused by the weathering of the walls of crevasses, and by separate snowfalls which have been followed by rain, hail, thawing and freezing, etc. Small rills were gliding and swirling over the melting surface with a smooth, oily appearance, in channels of pure ice — their quick, compliant movements contrasting most impressively with the rigid, invisible flow of the glacier itself, on whose back they all were riding.

Night drew near before I reached the eastern base of the mountain, and my camp lay many a rugged mile to the north; but ultimate success was assured. It was now only a matter of endurance and ordinary mountain-craft. The sunset was, if possible, yet more beautiful than that of the day before. The Mono landscape seemed to be fairly saturated with warm, purple light. The peaks marshaled along the summit were in shadow, but through every notch and pass streamed vivid sunfire, soothing and irradiating their rough, black angles, while companies of small, luminous clouds hovered above them like very angels of light.

Darkness came on, but I found my way by the trends of the cañons and the peaks projected against the sky. All excitement died with the light, and then I was weary. But the joyful sound of the waterfall across the lake was heard at last, and soon the stars were seen reflected in the lake itself. Taking my bearings from these, I discovered the little Pine thicket in which my nest was, and then I had a rest such as only a tired mountaineer may enjoy. After lying loose and lost for a while, I made a sunrise fire, went down to the lake, dashed water on my head, and dipped a cupful for tea. The revival brought about by bread and tea was as complete as the exhaustion from excessive enjoyment and toil. Then I crept beneath the pine-tassels to bed. The wind was frosty and the fire burned low, but my sleep was none the less sound, and the evening constellations had swept far to the west before I awoke.

After thawing and resting in the morning sunshine, I sauntered home — that is, back to the Tuolumne camp — bearing away toward a cluster of peaks that hold the fountain snows of one of the north tributaries of Rush Creek. Here I discovered a group of beautiful glacier lakes, nestled together in a grand amphitheater. Toward evening, I crossed the divide separating the Mono waters from those of the Tuolumne, and entered the glacier-basin that now holds the fountain-snows of the stream that forms the upper Tuolumne cascades. This stream I traced down through its many dells and gorges, meadows and bogs, reaching the brink of the main Tuolumne at dusk.

(*The Mountains of California*)

A Perilous Night on Mount Shasta

TWO ASCENTS of Mount Shasta are recorded in this selection taken from Muir's posthumous book, Steep Trails. *The first occurred late in the autumn of 1874, after his ten months in Oakland had ended and he was free to roam once more. The second came five months later, in April 1875. This in reality was a double ascent, for Muir led a Coast and Geodetic Survey party to the summit of the 14,161-foot volcanic peak on April 28 and returned again, with one companion, on April 30. It was on this perilous latter climb that he so nearly lost his life.*

Two years afterwards Muir camped on the slopes of Mount Shasta with Asa Gray and Sir Joseph Hooker. In these cool mountain woods he found a plant he had sought for years, a plant named in honor of Carl Linnaeus, Linnaea borealis. "In Linnaean woods," he wrote, "I always feel willing to encamp forever and forego even heaven." It was on his wandering return from this trip that he floated down the Merced River in a skiff he fashioned with a stone hammer out of sun-twisted fence boards. Finally, 250 miles from the start, he reached Martinez, on the San Joaquin. Here he visited the ranch of the Polish refugee, Dr. John Theophile Strenzel, and met Louie Wanda Strenzel, whom, three years later, he married.

Toward the end of summer, after a light, open winter, one may reach the summit of Mount Shasta without passing over much snow, by keeping on the crest of a long narrow ridge, mostly bare, that extends from near the camp-ground at the timber-line. But on my first excursion to the summit the whole mountain, down to its low swelling base, was smoothly laden with loose fresh snow, presenting a most glorious mass of winter mountain scenery, in the midst of which I scrambled and reveled or lay snugly snow-bound, enjoying the fertile clouds and the snow-bloom in all their growing, drifting grandeur.

I had walked from Redding, sauntering leisurely from station to station along the old Oregon stage-road, the better to see the rocks and plants, birds and people, by the way, tracing the rushing Sacramento to its fountains around icy Shasta. The first rains had fallen on the lowlands, and the first snows on the mountains, and everything was fresh and bracing, while an abundance of balmy sunshine filled all the noonday hours. It was the calm afterglow that usually succeeds the first storm of the winter. I met many of the birds that had reared their young and spent their summer in the Shasta woods and chaparral. They were then on their way south to their winter homes, leading their young full-fledged and about as large and strong as the parents. Squirrels, dry and elastic after the storms, were busy about their stores of pine-nuts, and the latest goldenrods were still in bloom, though it was now past the middle of October. The grand color glow — the autumnal jubilee of ripe leaves — was past prime, but, freshened by the rain, was still making a fine show along the banks of the river and in the ravines and the dells of the smaller streams.

At the salmon-hatching establishment on the McCloud River I halted a week to examine the limestone belt, grandly developed there, to learn what I could of the inhabitants of the river and its banks and to give time for the fresh snow that I knew had fallen on the mountain to settle somewhat, with a view to making the ascent. A pedestrian on these mountain roads, especially so late in the year, is sure to excite curiosity, and many were the interrogations concerning my ramble. When I said that I was simply taking a walk, and that icy Shasta was my mark, I was invariably admonished that I had come on a dangerous quest. The time was far too late, the snow was too loose and deep to climb, and I should be lost in drifts and slides. When I hinted that new snow was beautiful and storms not so bad as they were called, my advisers shook their heads in token of superior knowledge and declared the ascent of "Shasta Butte" through loose snow impossible. Nevertheless, before noon of the second of November I was in the frosty azure of the utmost summit.

When I arrived at Sisson's everything was quiet. The last of the summer visitors had flitted long before, and the deer and bears also were beginning to seek their winter homes. My barometer and the sighing winds and filmy, half-transparent clouds that dimmed the sunshine gave notice of the approach of another storm, and I was in haste to be off and get myself established somewhere in the midst of it, whether the summit was to be attained or not. Sisson, who is a mountaineer, speedily fitted me out for storm or calm as only a mountaineer could, with warm blankets and a week's provisions so generous in quantity and kind that they easily might have been made to last a month in case of my being closely snow-bound. Well I knew the weariness of snow-climbing, and the frosts, and the dangers of mountaineering so late in the year; therefore I could not ask a guide to go with me, even had one been willing. All I wanted was to have blankets and provisions deposited as far up in the timber as the snow would permit a pack-animal to go. There I could build a storm-nest and lie warm, and make raids up and around the mountain in accordance with the weather.

Setting out on the afternoon of November first, with Jerome Fay, mountaineer and guide, in charge of the animals, I was soon plodding wearily upward through the muffled winter woods, the snow of course growing steadily deeper and looser, so that we had to break a trail. The animals began to get discouraged, and after night and darkness came on they became entangled in a bed of rough lava, where, breaking through four or five feet of mealy snow, their feet were caught between angular boulders. Here they were in danger of being lost, but after we had removed packs and saddles and assisted their efforts with ropes, they all escaped to the side of a ridge about a thousand feet below the timber-line.

To go farther was out of the question, so we were compelled to camp as best we could. A pitch-pine fire speedily changed the temperature and shed a blaze of light on the wild lava-slope and the straggling storm-bent Pines around us. Melted snow answered for coffee, and we had plenty of venison to roast. Toward midnight I rolled myself in my blankets, slept an hour and a half, arose and ate more venison, tied two days' provisions to my belt, and set out for the summit, hoping to reach it ere the coming storm should fall. Jerome accompanied me a little distance above camp and indicated the way as well as he could in the darkness. He seemed loath to leave me, but, being reassured that I was at home and required no care he bade me good-by and returned to camp, ready to lead his animals down the mountain at daybreak.

After I was above the Dwarf Pines, it was fine practice pushing up the broad unbroken slopes of snow, alone in the solemn silence of the night. Half the sky was clouded; in the other half the stars sparkled icily in the keen, frosty air; while everywhere the glorious wealth of snow fell away from the summit of the cone in flowing folds, more extensive and continuous than any I had ever seen before. When day dawned the clouds were crawling slowly and becoming more massive, but gave no intimation of immediate danger, and I pushed on faithfully, though holding myself well in hand, ready to return to the timber; for it was easy to see that the storm was not far off. The mountain rises ten thousand feet above the general level of the country, in blank exposure to the deep upper currents of the sky, and no labyrinth of peaks and cañons I had ever been in seemed to me so dangerous as these immense slopes, bare against the sky.

The frost was intense, and drifting snow-dust made breathing at times rather difficult. The snow was as dry as meal, and the finer particles drifted freely, rising high in the air, while the larger portions of the crystals rolled like sand. I frequently sank to my armpits between buried blocks of loose lava, but generally only to my knees. When tired with walking I still wallowed slowly upward on all fours. The steepness of the slope — 35° in some places — made any kind of progress fatiguing, while small avalanches were being constantly set in motion in the steepest places. But the bracing air and the sublime beauty of the snowy expanse thrilled every nerve and made absolute exhaustion impossible. I seemed to be walking and wallowing in a cloud; but, holding steadily onward, by half-past ten o'clock I had gained the highest summit.

I held my commanding foothold in the sky for two hours, gazing on the glorious landscapes spread maplike around the immense horizon, and tracing the outlines of the ancient lava-streams extending far into the surrounding plains, and the pathways of vanished glaciers of which Shasta had been the center. But, as I had left my coat in camp for the sake of having my limbs free in climbing, I soon was cold. The wind increased in violence, raising the snow in magnificent drifts that were drawn out in the form of wavering banners glowing in the sun. Toward the end of my stay a succession of small clouds struck against the summit rocks like drifting icebergs, darkening the air as they passed, and producing a chill as definite and sudden as if ice-water had been dashed in my face. This is the kind of cloud in which snow-flowers grow, and I turned and fled.

Finding that I was not closely pursued, I ventured to take time on the way down for a visit to the head of the Whitney Glacier and the "Crater Butte." After I reached the end of the main summit ridge the descent was but little more than one continuous soft, mealy, muffled slide, most luxurious and rapid, though the hissing, swishing speed attained was obscured in great part by flying snow-dust — a marked contrast to the boring seal-wallowing upward struggle. I reached camp about an hour before dusk, hollowed a strip of loose ground in the lee of a large block of red lava, where firewood was abundant, rolled myself in my blankets, and went to sleep.

Next morning, having slept little the night before the ascent and being weary with climbing after the excitement was over, I slept late. Then, awaking suddenly, my eyes opened on one of the most beautiful and sublime scenes I ever enjoyed. A boundless wilderness of storm-clouds of different degrees of ripeness were congregated over all the lower landscape for thousands of square miles, colored gray, and purple, and pearl, and deep-glowing white, amid which I seemed to be floating; while the great white cone of the mountain above was all aglow in the free, blazing sunshine. It seemed not so much an ocean as a *land* of clouds — undulating hill and dale, smooth purple plains, and silvery mountains of cumuli range over range, diversified with peak and dome and hollow fully brought out in light and shade.

I gazed enchanted, but cold gray masses, drifting like dust on a wind-swept plain, began to shut out the light, forerunners of the coming storm I had been so anxiously watching. I made haste to gather as much wood as possible, snugging it as a shelter around my bed. The storm side of my blankets was fastened down with stakes to reduce as much as possible the sifting-in of drift and the danger of being blown away. The precious bread-sack was placed safely as a pillow, and when at length the first flakes fell I was exultingly ready to welcome them. Most of my firewood was more than half rosin and would blaze in the face of the fiercest drifting; the winds could not demolish my bed, and my bread could be made to last indefinitely; while in case of need I had the means of making snowshoes and could retreat or hold my ground as I pleased.

Presently the storm broke forth into full snowy bloom, and the thronging crystals darkened the air. The wind swept past in hissing floods, grinding the snow into meal and sweeping down into the hollows in enormous drifts all the heavier particles, while the finer dust was sifted through the sky, increasing the icy gloom. But my fire glowed bravely as if in glad defiance of the drift to quench it, and, notwithstanding but little trace of my nest could be seen after the snow had leveled and buried it, I was snug and warm, and the passionate uproar produced a glad excitement.

Day after day the storm continued, piling snow on snow in weariless abundance. There were short periods of quiet, when the sun would seem to look eagerly down through rents in the clouds, as if to know how the work was advancing. During these calm intervals I replenished my fire — sometimes without leaving the nest, for fire and woodpile were so near this could easily be done — or busied myself with my note-book, watching the gestures of the trees in taking the snow, examining separate crystals under a lens, and learning the methods of their deposition as an enduring fountain for the streams. Several times, when the storm ceased for a few minutes, a Douglas Squirrel came frisking from the foot of a clump of Dwarf Pines, moving in sudden interrupted spurts over the bossy snow; then, without any apparent guidance, he would dig rapidly into the drift where were buried some grains of barley that the horses had left. The Douglas Squirrel does not strictly belong to these upper woods, and I was surprised to see him out in such weather. The mountain sheep also, quite a large flock of them, came to my camp and took shelter beside a clump of matted Dwarf Pines a little above my nest.

The storm lasted about a week, but before it was ended Sisson became alarmed and sent up the guide with animals to see what had become of me and recover the camp outfit. The news spread that "there was a man on the mountain," and he must surely have perished, and Sisson was blamed for allowing any one to attempt climbing in such weather; while I was as safe as anybody in the lowlands, lying like a squirrel in a warm, fluffy nest, busied about by own affairs and wishing only to be let alone. Later, however, a trail could not have been broken for a horse, and some of the camp furniture would have had to be abandoned. On the fifth day I returned to Sisson's, and from that comfortable base made excursions, as the weather permitted, to the Black Butte, to the foot of the Whitney Glacier, around the base of the mountain, to Rhett and Klamath Lakes, to the Modoc region and elsewhere, developing many interesting scenes and experiences.

But the next spring, on the other side of this eventful winter, I saw and felt still more of the Shasta snow. For then it was my fortune to get into the very heart of a storm, and to be held in it for a long time.

On the 28th of April [1875] I led a party up the mountain for the purpose of making a survey of the summit with reference to the location of the Geodetic monument. On the 30th, accompanied by Jerome Fay, I made another ascent to make some barometrical observations, the day intervening between the two ascents being devoted to establishing a camp on the extreme edge of the timber-line. Here, on our red trachyte bed, we obtained two hours of shallow sleep broken for occasional glimpses of the keen, starry night. At two o'clock we rose, breakfasted on a warmed tin-cupful of coffee and a piece of frozen venison broiled on the coals, and started for the summit. Up to this time there was nothing in sight that betokened the approach of a storm; but on gaining the summit, we saw toward Lassen's Butte hundreds of square miles of white cumuli boiling dreamily in the sunshine far beneath us, and causing no alarm.

The slight weariness of the ascent was soon rested away, and our glorious morning in the sky promised nothing but enjoyment. At 9 A.M. the dry thermometer stood at 34° in the shade and rose steadily until at 1 P.M. it stood at 50°, probably influenced somewhat by radiation from the sun-warmed cliffs. A common bumblebee, not at all benumbed, zigzagged vigorously about our heads for a few moments, as if unconscious of the fact that the nearest honey flower was a mile beneath him.

In the mean time clouds were growing down in Shasta Valley — massive swelling cumuli, displaying delicious tones of purple and gray in the hollows of their sun-beaten bosses. Extending gradually southward around on both sides of Shasta, these at length united with the older field toward Lassen's Butte, thus encircling Mount Shasta in one continuous cloud-zone. Rhett and Klamath Lakes were eclipsed beneath clouds scarcely less brilliant than their own silvery disks. The Modoc Lava Beds, many a snow-laden peak far north in Oregon, the Scott and Trinity and Siskiyou Mountains, the peaks of the Sierra, the blue Coast Range, Shasta Valley, the dark forests filling the valley of the Sacramento, all in turn were obscured or buried, leaving the lofty cone on which we stood solitary in the sunshine between two skies — a sky of spotless blue above, a sky of glittering cloud beneath. The creative sun shone glorious on the vast expanse of cloudland; hill and dale, mountain and valley springing into existence responsive to his rays and steadily developing in beauty and individuality. One huge mountain-cone of cloud, corresponding to Mount Shasta in these newborn cloud-ranges, rose close alongside with a visible motion, its firm, polished bosses seeming so near and substantial that we almost fancied we might leap down upon them from where we stood and make our way to the lowlands. No hint was given, by anything in their appearance, of the fleeting character of these most sublime and beautiful cloud-mountains. On the contrary they impressed one as being lasting additions to the landscape.

The weather of the springtime and summer, throughout the Sierra in general, is usually varied by slight local rains and dustings of snow, most of which are obviously far too joyous and life-giving to be regarded as storms — single clouds growing in the sunny sky, ripening in an hour, showering the heated landscape, and passing away like a thought, leaving no visible bodily remains to stain the sky. Snowstorms of the same gentle kind abound among the high peaks, but in spring they not unfrequently attain larger proportions, assuming a violence and energy of expression scarcely surpassed by those bred in the depths of winter. Such was the storm now gathering about us.

It began to declare itself shortly after noon, suggesting to us the idea of at once seeking our safe camp in the timber and abandoning the purpose of making an observation of the barometer at 3 P.M., — two having already been made, at 9 A.M., and 12 P.M., while simultaneous observations were made at Strawberry Valley. Jerome peered at short intervals over the ridge, contemplating the rising clouds with anxious gestures in the rough wind, and at length declared that if we did not make a speedy escape we should be compelled to pass the rest of the day and night on the summit. But anxiety to complete my observations stifled my own instinctive promptings to retreat, and held me to my work. No inexperienced person was depending on me, and I told Jerome that we two mountaineers should be able to make our way down through any storm likely to fall.

Presently thin, fibrous films of cloud began to blow directly over the summit from north to south, drawn out in long fairy webs like carded wool, forming and dissolving as if by magic. The wind twisted them into ringlets and whirled them in a succession of graceful convolutions like the outside sprays of Yosemite Falls in flood-time; then, sailing out into the thin azure over the precipitous brink of the ridge they were drifted together like wreaths of foam on a river. These higher and finer cloud fabrics were evidently produced by the chilling of the air from its own expansion caused by the upward deflection of the wind against the slopes of the mountain. They steadily increased on the north rim of the cone, forming at length a thick, opaque, ill-defined embankment from the icy meshes of which snow-flowers began to fall, alternating with hail. The sky speedily darkened, and just as I had completed my last observation and boxed my instruments ready for the descent, the storm began in serious earnest. At first the cliffs were beaten with hail, every stone of which, as far as I could see, was regular in form, six-sided pyramids with rounded base, rich and sumptuous-looking, and fashioned with loving care, yet seemingly thrown away on those desolate crags down which they went rolling, falling, sliding in a network of curious streams.

After we had forced our way down the ridge and past the group of hissing fumaroles, the storm became inconceivably violent. The thermometer fell 22° in a few minutes, and soon dropped below zero. The hail gave place to snow, and darkness came on like night. The wind, rising to the highest pitch of violence, boomed and surged amid the desolate crags; lightning-flashes in quick succession cut the gloomy darkness; and the thunders, the most tremendously loud and appalling I ever heard, made an almost continuous roar, stroke following stroke in quick, passionate succession, as though the mountain were being rent to it foundations and the fires of the old volcano were breaking forth again.

Could we at once have begun to descend the snow-slopes leading to the timber, we might have made good our escape, however dark and wild the storm. As it was, we had first to make our way along a dangerous ridge nearly a mile and a half long, flanked in many places by steep ice-slopes at the head of the Whitney Glacier on one side and by shattered precipices on the other. Apprehensive of this coming darkness, I had taken the precaution, when the storm began, to make the most dangerous points clear to my mind, and to mark their relations with reference to the direction of the wind. When, therefore, the darkness came on, and the bewildering drift, I felt confident that we could force our way through it with no other guidance. After passing the "Hot Springs" I halted in the lee of a lava-block to let Jerome, who had fallen a little behind, come up. Here he opened a council in which, under circumstances sufficiently exciting but without evincing any bewilderment, he maintained, in opposition to my views, that it was impossible to proceed. He firmly refused to make the venture to find the camp, while I, aware of the dangers that would necessarily attend our efforts, and conscious of being the cause of his present peril, decided not to leave him.

Our discussions ended, Jerome made a dash from the shelter of the lava-block and began forcing his way back against the wind to the "Hot Springs," wavering and struggling to resist being carried away, as if he were fording a rapid stream. After waiting and watching in vain for some flaw in the storm that might be urged as a new argument in favor of attempting the descent, I was compelled to follow. "Here," said Jerome, as we shivered in the midst of the hissing, sputtering fumaroles, "we shall be safe from frost." "Yes," said I, "we can lie in this mud and steam and sludge, warm at least on one side; but how can we protect our lungs from the acid gases, and how, after our clothing is saturated, shall we be able to reach camp without freezing, even after the storm is over? We shall have to wait for sunshine, and when will it come?"

The tempered area to which we had committed ourselves extended over about one fourth of an acre; but it was only about an eighth of an inch in thickness, for the scalding gas-jets were shorn off close to the ground by the oversweeping flood of frosty wind. And how lavishly the snow fell only mountaineers may know. The crisp crystal flowers seemed to touch one another and fairly to thicken the tremendous blast that carried them. This was the bloom-time, the summer of the cloud, and never before have I seen even a mountain-cloud flowering so profusely.

When the bloom of the Shasta chaparral is falling, the ground is sometimes covered for hundreds of square miles to a depth of half an inch. But the bloom of this fertile snow-cloud grew and matured and fell to a depth of two feet in a few hours. Some crystals landed with their rays almost perfect, but most of them were worn and broken by striking against one another, or by rolling on the ground. The touch of these snow-flowers in calm weather is infinitely gentle — glinting, swaying, settling silently in the dry mountain air, or massed in flakes soft and downy. To lie out alone in the mountains of a still night and be touched by the first of these small silent messengers from the sky is a memorable experience, and the fineness of that touch none will forget. But the storm-blast laden with crisp, sharp snow seems to crush and bruise and stupefy with its multitude of stings, and compels the bravest to turn and flee.

The snow fell without abatement until an hour or two after what seemed to be the natural darkness of the night. Up to the time the storm first broke on the summit its development was remarkably gentle. There was a deliberate growth of clouds, a weaving of translucent tissue above, then the roar of the wind and the thunder, and the darkening flight of snow. Its subsidence was not less sudden. The clouds broke and vanished, not a crystal was left in the sky, and the stars shone out with pure and tranquil radiance.

During the storm we lay on our backs so as to present as little surface as possible to the wind, and to let the drift pass over us. The mealy snow sifted into the folds of our clothing and in many places reached the skin. We were glad at first to see the snow packing about us, hoping it would deaden the force of the wind, but it soon froze into a stiff, crusty heap as the temperature fell, rather augmenting our novel misery.

When the heat became unendurable, on some spot where steam was escaping through the sludge, we tried to stop it with snow and mud, or shifted a little at a time by shoving with our heels; for to stand in blank exposure to the fearful wind in our frozen-and-broiled condition seemed certain death. The acrid incrustations sublimed from the escaping gases frequently gave way, opening new vents to scald us; and, fearing that if at any time the wind should fall, carbonic acid, which often formed a considerable portion of the gaseous exhalations of volcanoes, might collect in sufficient quantities to cause sleep and death, I warned Jerome against forgetting himself for a single moment, even should his sufferings admit of such a thing.

Accordingly, when during the long, dreary watches of the night we roused from a state of half-consciousness, we called each other by name in a frightened, startled way, each fearing the other might be benumbed or dead. The ordinary sensations of cold give but a faint conception of that which comes on after hard climbing with want of food and sleep in such exposure as this. Life is then seen to be a fire, that now smoulders, now brightens, and may be easily quenched. The weary hours wore away like dim half-forgotten years, so long and eventful they seemed, though we did nothing but suffer. Still the pain was not always of that bitter, intense kind that precludes thought and takes away all capacity for enjoyment. A sort of dreamy stupor came on at times in which we fancied we saw dry, resinous logs suitable for camp-fires, just as after going days without food men fancy they see bread.

Frozen, blistered, famished, benumbed, our bodies seemed lost to us at times — all dead but the eyes. For the duller and fainter we became the clearer was our vision, though only in momentary glimpses. Then, after the sky cleared, we gazed at the stars, blessed immortals of light, shining with marvelous brightness with long lance-rays, near-looking and new-looking, as if never seen before. Again they would look familiar and remind us of star-gazing at home. Oftentimes imagination coming into play would present charming pictures of the warm zone below, mingled with others near and far. Then the bitter wind and the drift would break the blissful vision and dreary pains cover us like clouds. "Are you suffering much?" Jerome would inquire with pitiful faintness. "Yes," I would say, striving to keep my voice brave, "frozen and burned; but never mind, Jerome, the night will wear away at last, and to-morrow we go a-Maying, and what camp-fires we will make, and what sun-baths we will take!"

The frost grew more and more intense, and we became icy and covered over with a crust of frozen snow, as if we had lain cast away in the drift all winter. In about thirteen hours — every hour like a year — day began to dawn but it was long ere the summit's rocks were touched by the sun. No clouds were visible from where we lay, yet the morning was dull and blue, and bitterly frosty; and hour after hour passed by while we eagerly watched the pale light stealing down the ridge to the hollow where we lay.

But there was not a trace of that warm, flushing sunrise splendor we so long had hoped for.

As the time drew near to make an effort to reach camp, we became concerned to know what strength was left us, and whether or no we could walk; for we had lain flat all this time without once rising to our feet. Mountaineers, however, always find in themselves a reserve of power after great exhaustion. It is a kind of second life, available only in emergencies like this; and, having proved its existence, I had no great fear that either of us would fail, though one of my arms was already benumbed and hung powerless.

At length, after the temperature was somewhat mitigated on this memorable first of May, we arose and began to struggle homeward. Our frozen trousers could scarcely be made to bend at the knee, and we waded the snow with difficulty. The summit ridge was fortunately wind-swept and nearly bare, so we were not compelled to lift our feet high, and on reaching the long home-slopes laden with loose snow we made rapid progress, sliding and shuffling and pitching headlong, our feebleness accelerating rather than diminishing our speed. When we had descended some three thousand feet the sunshine warmed our backs and we began to revive. At 10 A.M. we reached the timber and were safe.

Half an hour later we heard Sisson shouting down among the Firs, coming with horses to take us to the hotel. After breaking a trail through the snow as far as possible he had tied his animals and walked up. We had been so long without food that we cared but little about eating, but we eagerly drank the coffee he prepared for us. Our feet were frozen, and thawing them was painful, and had to be done very slowly by keeping them buried in soft snow for several hours, which avoided permanent damage. Five thousand feet below the summit we found only three inches of new snow, and at the base of the mountain only a slight shower of rain had fallen, showing how local our storm had been, notwithstanding its terrific fury. Our feet were wrapped in sacking, and we were soon mounted and on our way down into the thick sunshine — "God's Country," as Sisson calls the Chaparral Zone. In two hours' ride the last snow-bank was left behind. Violets appeared along the edges of the trail, and the chaparral was coming into bloom, with young lilies and larkspurs about the open places in rich profusion. How beautiful seemed the golden sunbeams streaming through the woods between the warm brown boles of the Cedars and Pines! All my friends among the birds and plants seemed like *old* friends, and we felt like speaking to every one of them as we passed, as if we had been a long time away in some far, strange country.

In the afternoon we reached Strawberry Valley and fell asleep. Next morning we seemed to have risen from the dead. My bedroom was flooded with sunshine, and from the window I saw the great white Shasta cone clad in forests and clouds and bearing them loftily in the sky. Everything seemed full and radiant with the freshness and beauty and enthusiasm of youth. Sisson's children came in with flowers and covered my bed, and the storm on the mountain-top vanished like a dream.

(Steep Trails)

Discovery of Glacier Bay

THE SUMMER before his marriage Muir sailed north on the first of his five voyages to study the glaciers of Alaska. In company with an adventurous Presbyterian missionary, the Reverend S. Hall Young, he set out from Fort Wrangell in mid-October 1879, and traveled with native paddlers northward to Glacier Bay, whose existence he was the first to announce. While the rest of the party remained in camp during a Sunday rest, Muir "stretched his legs" by climbing a 1500-foot ridge. Spreading away to the north below him he saw a dim, mysterious solitude of ice and snow. Thus he was the first white explorer to see legendary Glacier Bay. Forty-six years later, on February 25, 1925, the area became a national monument.

Another achievement of this 1879 trip was the discovery of the great ice river now known as Muir Glacier. Twice in later years, 1890 and 1899, Muir returned to explore it. Thomas H. Kearney, Jr., who accompanied Muir on the 1899 Harriman Expedition, once told me that when the party reached this ice field Muir, with the unrestrained emotion that sometimes embarrassed his conservative friends, got down on his hands and knees and kissed the ice of the glacier that was his namesake. In 1879 the freezing of the fiords made a close inspection of the glacier impossible and Muir had to be content with sketching and studying its main features from a distance. To the native paddlers who accompanied him, Muir was "The Great Ice Chief."

❁

W E GOT UNDER WAY about 10 A.M. The wind was in our favor, but a cold rain pelted us, and we could see but little of the dreary, treeless wilderness which we had now fairly entered. The bitter blast, however, gave us good speed; our bedraggled canoe rose and fell on the waves as solemnly as a big ship. Our course was northwestward, up the southwest side of the bay, near the shore of what seemed to be the mainland, smooth marble islands being on our right. About noon we discovered the first of the great glaciers, the one I afterwards named for James Geikie, the noted Scotch geologist. Its lofty blue cliffs, looming through the draggled skirts of the clouds, gave a tremendous impression of savage power, while the roar of the newborn icebergs thick-ened and emphasized the general roar of the storm. An hour and a half beyond the Geikie Glacier we ran into a slight harbor where the shore is low, dragged the canoe beyond the reach of drifting icebergs, and, much against my desire to push ahead, encamped, the guide insisting that the big ice-mountain at the head of the bay could not be reached before dark, that the landing there was dangerous even in daylight, and that this was the only safe harbor on the way to it. While camp was being made, I strolled along the shore to examine the rocks and the fossil timber that abounds here. All the rocks are freshly glaciated, even below the sea-level, nor have the waves as yet worn off the surface polish, much less the heavy scratches and grooves and lines of glacial con-tour.

The next day being Sunday, the minister wished to stay in camp; and so, on account of the weather, did the Indians. I there-fore set out on an excursion, and spent the day alone on the mountain-slopes above the camp, and northward, to see what I might learn. Pushing on through rain and mud and sludgy snow, crossing many brown, boulder-choked torrents, wading, jumping, and wallowing in snow up to my shoulders was mountaineering of the most trying kind. After crouching cramped and benumbed in the canoe, poulticed in wet or damp clothing night and day, my limbs had been asleep. This day they were awakened and in the hour of trial proved that they had not lost the cunning learned on many a mountain peak of the High Sierra. I reached a height of fifteen hundred feet, on the ridge that bounds the second of the great glaciers. All the landscape was smothered in clouds and I began to fear that as far as wide views were concerned I had climbed in vain. But at length the clouds lifted a little, and beneath their gray fringes I saw the berg-filled expanse of the bay, and the feet of the mountains that stand about it, and the imposing fronts of five huge glaciers, the nearest being immediately beneath me. This was my first general view of Glacier Bay, a solitude of ice and snow and newborn rocks, dim, dreary, mysterious. I held the ground I had so dearly won for an hour or two, sheltering myself from the blast as best I could, while with benumbed fingers I sketched what I could see of the landscape, and wrote a few lines in my note-book. Then, breasting the snow again, crossing the shifting avalanche slopes and torrents, I reached camp about dark, wet and weary and glad.

While I was getting some coffee and hardtack, Mr. Young told me that the Indians were discouraged, and had been talking about turning back, fearing that I would be lost, the canoe broken, or in some other mysterious way the expedition would come to grief if I persisted in going farther. They had been asking him what possible motive I could have in climbing mountains when storms were blowing; and when he replied that I was only seeking knowledge, Toyatte said, "Muir must be a witch to seek knowledge in such a place as this and in such miserable weather."

After supper, crouching about a dull fire of fossil wood, they became still more doleful, and talked in tones that accorded well with the wind and water and growling torrents about us, telling sad old stories of crushed canoes, drowned Indians, and hunters frozen in snowstorms. Even brave old Toyatte, dreading the treeless, forlorn appearance of the region, said that his heart was not strong, and that he feared his canoe, on the safety of which our lives depended, might be entering a skookum-house (jail) of ice, from which there might be no escape; while the Hoona guide said bluntly that if I was so fond of danger, and meant to go close up to the noses of the ice-mountains, he would not consent to go any farther; for we should all be lost, as many of his tribe had been, by the sudden rising of bergs from the bottom. They seemed to be losing heart with every howl of the wind, and, fearing that they might fail me now that I was in the midst of so grand a congregation of glaciers, I made haste to reassure them, telling them that for ten years I had wandered alone among mountains and storms, and good luck always followed me; that with me, therefore, they need fear nothing. The storm would soon cease and the sun would shine to show us the way we should go, for God cares for us and guides us as long as we are trustful and brave, therefore all childish fear must be put away. This little speech did good. Kadachan, with some show of enthusiasm, said he liked to travel with good-luck people; and dignified old Toyatte declared that now his heart was strong again, and he would venture on with me as far as I liked for my "wawa" was "delait" (my talk was very good). The old warrior even became a little sentimental, and said that even if the canoe was broken he would not greatly care, because on the way to the other world he would have good companions.

Next morning it was still raining and snowing, but the south wind swept us bravely forward and swept the bergs from our course. In about an hour we reached the second of the big glaciers, which I afterwards named for Hugh Miller. We rowed up its fiord and landed to make a slight examination of its grand frontal wall. The berg-producing portion we found to be about a mile and a half wide, and broken into an imposing array of jagged spires and pyramids, and flat-topped towers and battlements, of many shades of blue, from pale, shimmering, limpid tones in the crevasses and hollows, to the most startling, chilling, almost shrieking vitriol blue on the plain mural spaces from which bergs had just been discharged. Back from the front for a few miles the glacier rises in a series of wide steps, as if this portion of the glacier had sunk in successive sections as it reached deep water, and the sea had found its way beneath it. Beyond this it extends indefinitely in a gently rising prairie-like expanse, and branches along the slopes and cañons of the Fairweather Range.

From here a run of two hours brought us to the head of the bay, and to the mouth of the northwest fiord, at the head of which lie the Hoona sealing-grounds, and the great glacier now called the Pacific, and another called the Hoona. The fiord is about five miles long, and two miles wide at the mouth. Here our Hoona guide had a store of dry wood, which we took aboard. Then, setting sail, we were driven wildly up the fiord, as if the storm-wind were saying, "Go, then, if you will, into my icy chamber; but you shall stay in until I am ready to let you out." All this time sleety rain was falling on the bay, and snow on the mountains; but soon after we landed the sky began to open. The camp was made on a rocky bench near the front of the Pacific Glacier, and the canoe was carried beyond the reach of the bergs and berg-waves. The bergs were now crowded in a dense pack against the discharging front, as if the storm-wind had determined to make the glacier take back her crystal offspring and keep them at home.

While camp affairs were being attended to, I set out to climb a mountain for comprehensive views; and before I had reached a height of a thousand feet the rain ceased, and the clouds began to rise from the lower altitudes, slowly lifting their white skirts, and lingering in majestic, wing-shaped masses about the mountains that rise out of the broad, icy sea, the highest of all the white mountains, and the greatest of all the glaciers I had yet seen. Climbing higher for a still broader outlook, I made notes and sketched, improving the precious time while sunshine streamed through the luminous fringes of the clouds and fell on the green waters of the fiord, the glittering bergs, the crystal bluffs of the vast glacier, the intensely white, far-spreading fields of ice, and the ineffably chaste and spiritual heights of the Fairweather Range, which were now hidden, now partly revealed, the whole making a picture of icy wildness unspeakably pure and sublime.

Looking southward, a broad ice-sheet was seen extending in a gently undulating plain from the Pacific Fiord in the foreground to the horizon, dotted and ridged here and there with mountains which were as white as the snow-covered ice in which they were half, or more than half, submerged. Several of the great glaciers of the bay flow from this one grand fountain. It is an instructive example of a general glacier covering the hills and dales of a country that is not yet ready to be brought to the light of day — not only covering but creating a landscape with the features it is destined to have when, in the fullness of time, the fashioning ice-sheet shall be lifted by the sun, and the land become warm and fruitful. The view to the westward is bounded and almost filled by the glorious Fairweather Mountains, the highest among them springing aloft in sublime beauty to a height of nearly sixteen thousand feet, while from base to summit every peak and spire and dividing ridge of all the mighty host was spotless white, as if painted. It would seem that snow could never be made to lie on the steepest slopes and precipices unless plastered on when wet, and then frozen. But this snow could not have been wet. It must have been fixed by being driven and set in small particles like the storm-dust of drifts, which, when in this condition, is fixed not only on sheer cliffs, but in massive, overcurling cornices. Along the base of this majestic range sweeps the Pacific Glacier, fed by innumerable cascading tributaries, and discharging into the head of its fiord by two mouths only partly separated by the brow of an island rock about one thousand feet high, each nearly a mile wide.

Dancing down the mountain to camp, my mind glowing like the sun-beaten glaciers, I found the Indians seated around a good fire, entirely happy now that the farthest point of the journey was safely reached and the long, dark storm was cleared away. How hopefully, peacefully bright that night were the stars in the frosty sky, and how impressive was the thunder of the icebergs, rolling, swelling, reverberating through the solemn stillness! I was too happy to sleep.

(Travels in Alaska)

Glaciers by Starlight

ONE OF THE astonishing things about Muir's life and writings is the combination of strenousness and delicacy, of unyielding exterior and sensitive inner feeling. The harsh life of his youth toughened his body to rawhide but, miraculously, it neither calloused nor hardened his spirit. Wherever he went he saw nature with a poet's delight. This glimpse of the beauty of a world of ice and stars is a memory of Muir's first trip to Alaska.

W E GATHERED a lot of fossil wood and after supper made a big fire, and as we sat around it the brightness of the sky brought on a long talk with the Indians about the stars; and their eager, childlike attention was refreshing to see as compared with the deathlike apathy of weary town-dwellers, in whom natural curiosity has been quenched in toil and care and poor shallow comfort.

After sleeping a few hours, I stole quietly out of the camp, and climbed the mountain that stands between the two glaciers. The ground was frozen, making the climbing difficult in the steepest places; but the views over the icy bay, sparkling beneath the stars, were enchanting. It seemed then a sad thing that any part of so precious a night had been lost in sleep. The starlight was so full that I distinctly saw not only the berg-filled bay, but most of the lower portions of the glaciers, lying pale and spirit-like amid the mountains. The nearest glacier in particular was so distinct that it seemed to be glowing with light that came from within itself. Not even in dark nights have I ever found any difficulty in seeing large glaciers; but on this mountain-top, amid so much ice, in the heart of so clear and frosty a night, everything was more or less luminous, and I seemed to be poised in a vast hollow between two skies of almost equal brightness. This exhilarating scramble made me glad and strong and I rejoiced that my studies called me before the glorious night succeeding so glorious a morning had been spent!

(Travels in Alaska)

Fire in the Rain

THE SCENE of this adventure is Wrangell Island, the time the latter part of July 1879. In Muir's writings there are many vivid descriptions of campfires. "One can make a day of any size and regulate the rising and setting of his own sun and the brightness of its shining," he noted in his Sierra journal in August 1875. "You gaze around at the illumined trees as if you never saw trees before. The bossy boles and branches ascend in fire to heaven, the light slowly gathered from the suns of centuries going again to the sun, in clear eddying sparks and flames of ever changing motion. Sparks stream off like comets or in round starlike worlds from a sun. They fly into space in milky ways of lavishness, then fall in white flakes feathery and pure as snow." But of all the fires that warmed and lighted his solitary nights among the forests and the mountains none produced more adventurous excitement or elemental beauty than this fire in the night and the rain in Alaska.

ONE NIGHT when a heavy rainstorm was blowing I unwittingly caused a lot of wondering excitement among the whites as well as the superstitious Indians. Being anxious to see how the Alaska trees behave in storms and hear the songs they sing, I stole quietly away through the gray drenching blast to the hill back of the town, without being observed. Night was falling when I set out and it was pitch dark when I reached the top. The glad, rejoicing storm in glorious voice was singing through the woods, noble compensation for mere body discomfort. But I wanted a fire, a big one, to see as well as hear how the storm and trees were behaving. After long, patient groping I found a little dry punk in a hollow trunk and carefully stored it beside my matchbox and an inch or two of candle in an inside pocket that the rain had not yet reached; then, wiping some dead twigs and whittling them into thin shavings, stored them with the punk. I then made a little conical bark hut about a foot high, and, carefully leaning over it and sheltering it as much as possible from the driving rain, I wiped and stored a lot of dead twigs, lighted the candle, and set it in the hut, carefully added pinches of punk and shavings, and at length got a little blaze, by the light of which I gradually added larger shavings, then twigs all set on end astride the inner flame, making the little hut higher and wider. Soon I had light enough to enable me to select the best dead branches and large sections of bark, which were set on end, gradually increasing the height and corresponding light of the hut fire. A considerable area was thus well lighted, from which I gathered abundance of wood, and kept adding to the fire until it had a strong, hot heart and sent up a pillar of flame thirty or forty feet high, illuminating a wide circle in spite of the rain, and casting a red glare into the flying clouds. Of all the thousands of camp-fires I have elsewhere built none was just like this one, rejoicing in triumphant strength and beauty in the heart of the rain-laden gale. It was wonderful — the illumined rain and clouds mingled together and the trees glowing against the jet background, the colors of the mossy, lichened trunks with sparkling streams pouring down the furrows of the bark, and the gray-bearded old patriarchs bowing low and chanting in passionate worship!

My fire was in all its glory about midnight, and, having made a bark shed to shelter me from the rain and partially dry my clothing, I had nothing to do but look and listen and join the trees in their hymns and prayers.

Neither the great white heart of the fire nor the quivering enthusiastic flames shooting aloft like auroral lances could be seen from the village on account of the trees in front of it and its being back a little way over the brow of the hill; but the light in the clouds made a great show, a portentous sign in the stormy heavens unlike anything ever before seen or heard of in Wrangell.

Some wakeful Indians, happening to see it about midnight, in great alarm aroused the Collecter of Customs and begged him to go to the missionaries and get them to pray away the frightful omen, and inquired anxiously whether white men had ever seen anything like that sky-fire, which instead of being quenched by the rain was burning brighter and brighter. The Collector said he had heard of such strange fires, and this one he thought might perhaps be what the white man called a "volcano, or an *ignis fatuus.*" When Mr. Young was called from his bed to pray, he, too, confoundedly astonished and at a loss for any sort of explanation, confessed that he had never seen anything like it in the sky or anywhere else in such cold wet weather, but that it was probably some sort of spontaneous combustion "that the white man called St. Elmo's fire, or Will-of-the-Wisp." These explanations, though not convincingly clear, perhaps served to veil their own astonishment and in some measure to diminish the superstitious fears of the natives; but from what I heard, the few whites who happened to see the strange light wondered about as wildly as the Indians.

I have enjoyed thousands of camp-fires in all sort of weather and places, warm-hearted, short-flamed, friendly little beauties glowing in the dark on open spots in high Sierra gardens, daisies and lilies circled about them, gazing like enchanted children; and large fires in Silver Fir forests, with spires of flame towering like the trees about them, and sending up multitudes of starry sparks to enrich the sky; and still greater fires on the mountains in winter, changing camp climate to summer, and making the frosty snow look like beds of white flowers, and oftentimes mingling their swarms of swift-flying sparks with falling snow-crystals when the clouds were in bloom. But this Wrangell camp-fire, my first in Alaska, I shall always remember for its triumphant storm-defying grandeur, and the wondrous beauty of the psalm-singing, lichen-painted trees which it brought to light.

(Travels in Alaska)

Stickeen

IT WAS JANUARY 1880, before Muir returned to California from his first Alaskan voyage. On April 14, when nearly 42, he married Louie Wanda Strenzel and settled down at Martinez to raise fruit. From July to October each year, while the grapes were ripening, there was a lull in the ranch work. This period, he and his wife had agreed, should be his for wilderness wandering. So on the last day of July Muir was sailing north again on his second trip to Alaska. This time, with his missionary friend, he traveled north to Sum Dum Bay and, indirectly was responsible for the founding of the city of Juneau. Although he was never interested in what he called "$ geology," he mentioned to two prospectors a likely-looking spot for gold in a gravelly creek bed. Their discovery of the precious metal at this place started the historic stampede that resulted in the founding of Juneau. But more important to Muir was his adventure, with his missionary friend's little black dog, Stickeen, on Taylor Glacier, August 30, 1880. Wherever he went in his later years he was called on to tell "the story of the minister's dog." Nothing Muir wrote reached a wider or more responsive audience than this account of a brave little dog on an Alaskan glacier. It has been ranked among dog stories with "Rab and His Friends" and Bob, Son of Battle. *Nineteen years after the events recorded in the story, Muir sailed past Taylor Glacier with the Harriman Expedition aboard the* George W. Elder. *In the night, Muir stood alone by the rail in silent tribute to the little dog that had taken so lasting a place in his affections.*

IN THE SUMMER of 1880 I set out from Fort Wrangell in a canoe to continue the exploration of the icy region of southeastern Alaska, begun in the fall of 1879. After the necessary provisions, blankets, etc., had been collected and stowed away, and my Indian crew were in their places ready to start, while a crowd of their relatives and friends on the wharf were bidding them good-by and good-luck, my companion, the Rev. S. H. Young, for whom we were waiting, at last came aboard, followed by a little black dog, that immediately made himself at home by curling up in a hollow among the baggage. I like dogs, but this one seemed so small and worthless that I objected to his going, and asked the missionary why he was taking him.

"Such a little helpless creature will only be in the way," I said; "you had better pass him up to the Indian boys on the wharf, to be taken home to play with the children. This trip is not likely to be good for toy-dogs. The poor silly thing will be in rain and snow for weeks or months, and will require care like a baby."

But his master assured me that he would be no trouble at all; that he was a perfect wonder of a dog, could endure cold and hunger like a bear, swim like a seal, and was wondrous wise and cunning, etc., making out a list of virtues to show he might be the most interesting member of the party.

Nobody could hope to unravel the lines of his ancestry. In all the wonderfully mixed and varied dog-tribe I never saw any creature very much like him, though in some of his sly, soft, gliding motions and gestures he brought the fox to mind. He was short-legged and bunchy-bodied, and his hair, though smooth, was long and silky and slightly waved, so that when the wind was at his back it ruffled, making him look shaggy. At first sight his only noticeable feature was his fine tail, which was about as airy and shady as a squirrel's, and was carried curling forward almost to his nose. On closer inspection you might notice his thin sensitive ears, and sharp eyes with cunning tan-spots above them. Mr. Young told me that when the little fellow was a pup about the

size of a woodrat he was presented to his wife by an Irish pros-
pector at Sitka, and that on his arrival at Fort Wrangell he was
adopted with enthusiasm by the Stickeen Indians as a sort of new
good-luck totem, was named "Stickeen" for the tribe, and became
a universal favorite; petted, protected, and admired wherever he
went, and regarded as a mysterious fountain of wisdom.

On our trip he soon proved himself a queer character — odd,
concealed, independent, keeping invincibly quiet, and doing many
little puzzling things that piqued my curiosity. As we sailed
week after week through the long intricate channels and inlets
among the innumerable islands and mountains of the coast, he
spent most of the dull days in sluggish ease, motionless, and apparently as unobserving as if in deep sleep. But I discovered that
somehow he always knew what was going on. When the Indians
were about to shoot at ducks or seals, or when anything along the
shore was exciting our attention, he would rest his chin on the
edge of the canoe and calmly look out like a dreamy-eyed tourist.
And when he heard us talking about making a landing, he immediately roused himself to see what sort of a place we were coming
to, and made ready to jump overboard and swim ashore as soon
as the canoe neared the beach. Then, with a vigorous shake to get
rid of the brine in his hair, he ran into the woods to hunt small
game. But though always the first out of the canoe, he was always the last to get into it. When we were ready to start he
could never be found, and refused to come to our call. We soon
found out, however, that though we could not see him at such
times, he saw us, and from the cover of the briers and huckleberry bushes in the fringe of the woods was watching the canoe
with wary eye. For as soon as we were fairly off he came trotting
down the beach, plunged into the surf, and swam after us, knowing well that we would cease rowing and take him in. When
the contrary little vagabond came alongside, he was lifted by
the neck, held at arm's length a moment to drip, and dropped
aboard. We tried to cure him of this trick by compelling him to
swim a long way, as if we had a mind to abandon him; but this
did no good: the longer the swim the better he seemed to like it.

Though capable of great idleness, he never failed to be ready for all sorts of adventures and excursions. One pitch-dark rainy night we landed about ten o'clock at the mouth of a salmon stream when the water was phosphorescent. The salmon were running, and the myriad fins of the onrushing multitude were churning all the stream into a silvery glow, wonderfully beautiful and impressive in the ebon darkness. To get a good view of the show I set out with one of the Indians and sailed up through the midst of it to the foot of a rapid about half a mile from camp, where the swift current dashing over rocks made the luminous glow most glorious. Happening to look back down the stream, while the Indian was catching a few of the struggling fish, I saw a long spreading fan of light like the tail of a comet, which we thought must be made by some big strange animal that was pursuing us. On it came with its magnificent train, until we imagined we could see the monster's head and eyes; but it was only Stickeen, who, finding I had left the camp, came swimming after me to see what was up.

When we camped early, the best hunter of the crew usually went to the woods for a deer, and Stickeen was sure to be at his heels, provided I had not gone out. For, strange to say, though I never carried a gun, he always followed me, forsaking the hunter and even his master to share my wanderings. The days that were too stormy for sailing I spent in the woods, or on the adjacent mountains, wherever my studies called me; and Stickeen always insisted on going with me, however wild the weather, gliding like a fox through dripping huckleberry bushes and thorny tangles of panax and rubus, scarce stirring their rain-laden leaves; wading and wallowing through snow, swimming icy streams, skipping over logs and rocks and the crevasses of glaciers with the patience and endurance of a determined mountaineer, never tiring or getting discouraged. Once he followed me over a glacier the surface of which was so crusty and rough that it cut his feet until every step was marked with blood; but he trotted on with Indian fortitude until I noticed his red track, and, taking pity on him, made him a set of moccasins out of a handkerchief. However great his troubles he never asked help or made any complaint, as if, like a philosopher, he had learned that without hard work and suffering there could be no pleasure worth having.

Yet none of us was able to make out what Stickeen was really good for. He seemed to meet danger and hardships without anything like reason, insisted on having his own way, never obeyed an order, and the hunter could never set him on anything, or make him fetch the birds he shot. His equanimity was so steady it seemed due to want of feeling; ordinary storms were pleasures to him, and as for mere rain, he flourished in it like a vegetable. No matter what advances you might make, scarce a glance or a tail-wag would you get for your pains. But though he was apparently as cold as a glacier and about as impervious to fun, I tried hard to make his acquaintance, guessing there must be something worth while hidden beneath so much courage, endurance, and love of wild-weathery adventure. No superannuated mastiff or bulldog grown old in office surpassed this fluffy midget in stoic dignity. He sometimes reminded me of a small, squat, unshakable desert cactus. For he never displayed a single trace of the merry, tricksy, elfish fun of the terriers and collies that we all know, nor of their touching affection and devotion. Like children, most small dogs beg to be loved and allowed to love; but Stickeen seemed a very Diogenes, asking only to be let alone: a true child of the wilderness, holding the even tenor of his hidden life with the silence and serenity of nature. His strength of character lay in his eyes. They looked as old as the hills, and as young, and as wild. I never tired of looking into them: it was like looking into a landscape; but they were small and rather deep-set, and had no explaining lines around them to give out particulars. I was accustomed to look into the faces of plants and animals, and I watched the little sphinx more and more keenly as an interesting study. But there is no estimating the wit and wisdom concealed and latent in our lower fellow mortals until made manifest by profound experiences; for it is through suffering that dogs as well as saints are developed and made perfect.

After exploring the Sum Dum and Tahkoo fiords and their glaciers, we sailed through Stephen's Passage into Lynn Canal and thence through Icy Strait into Cross Sound, searching for unexplored inlets leading toward the great fountain ice-fields of the

Fairweather Range. Here, while the tide was in our favor, we were accompanied by a fleet of icebergs drifting out to the ocean from Glacier Bay. Slowly we paddled around Vancouver's Point, Wimbledon, our frail canoe tossed like a feather on the massive heaving swells coming in past Cape Spenser. For miles the sound is bounded by precipitous mural cliffs, which, lashed with wave-spray and their heads hidden in clouds, looked terribly threatening and stern. Had our canoe been crushed or upset we could have made no landing here, for the cliffs, as high as those of Yosemite, sink sheer into deep water. Eagerly we scanned the wall on the north side for the first sign of an opening fiord or harbor, all of us anxious except Stickeen, who dozed in peace or gazed dreamily at the tremendous precipices when he heard us talking about them. At length we made the joyful discovery of the mouth of thé inlet now called "Taylor Bay," and about five o'clock reached the head of it and encamped in a Spruce grove near the front of a large glacier.

While camp was being made, Joe the hunter climbed the mountain wall on the east side of the fiord in pursuit of wild goats, while Mr. Young and I went to the glacier. We found that it is separated from the waters of the inlet by a tide-washed moraine, and extends, an abrupt barrier, all the way across from wall to wall of the inlet, a distance of about three miles. But our most interesting discovery was that it had recently advanced, though again slightly receding. A portion of the terminal moraine had been plowed up and shoved forward, uprooting and overwhelming the woods on the east side. Many of the trees were down and buried, or nearly so, others were leaning away from the ice-cliffs, ready to fall, and some stood erect, with the bottom of the ice plow still beneath their roots and its lofty crystal spires towering high above their tops. The spectacle presented by these century-old trees standing close beside a spiry wall of ice, with their branches almost touching it, was most novel and striking. And when I climbed around the front, and a little way up the west side of the glacier, I found that it had swelled and increased in height and width in accordance with its advance, and carried away the outer ranks of trees on its bank.

On our way back to camp after these first observations I planned a far-and-wide excursion for the morrow. I awoke early, called not only by the glacier, which had been on my mind all night, but by a grand flood-storm. The wind was blowing a gale from the north and the rain was flying with the clouds in a wide passionate horizontal flood, as if it were all passing over the country instead of falling on it. The main perennial streams were booming high above their banks, and hundreds of new ones, roaring like the sea, almost covered the lofty gray walls of the inlet with white cascades and falls. I had intended making a cup of coffee and getting something like a breakfast before starting, but when I heard the storm and looked out I made haste to join it; for many of Nature's finest lessons are to be found in her storms, and if careful to keep in right relations with them, we may go safely abroad with them, rejoicing in the grandeur and beauty of their works and ways, and chanting with the old Norsemen, "The blast of the tempest aids our oars, the hurricane is our servant and drives us whither we wish to go." So, omitting breakfast, I put a piece of bread in my pocket and hurried away.

Mr. Young and the Indians were asleep, and so, I hoped, was Stickeen; but I had not gone a dozen rods before he left his bed in the tent and came boring through the blast after me. That a man should welcome storms for their exhilarating music and motion, and go forth to see God making landscapes, is reasonable enough; but what fascination could there be in such tremendous weather for a dog? Surely nothing akin to human enthusiasm for scenery or geology. Anyhow, on he came, breakfastless, through the choking blast. I stopped and did my best to turn him back. "Now don't," I said, shouting to make myself heard in the storm, "now don't, Stickeen. What has got into your queer noddle now? You must be daft. This wild day has nothing for you. There is no game abroad, nothing but weather. Go back to camp and keep warm, get a good breakfast with your master, and be sensible for once. I can't carry you all day or feed you, and this storm will kill you."

But Nature, it seems, was at the bottom of the affair, and she gains her ends with dogs as well as with men, making us do as she likes, shoving and pulling us along her ways, however rough, all but killing us at times in getting her lessons driven hard home. After I had stopped again and again, shouting good warning advice, I saw that he was not to be shaken off; as well might the earth try to shake off the moon. I had once led his master into trouble, when he fell on one of the topmost jags of a mountain and dislocated his arm; now the turn of his humble companion was coming. The pitiful wanderer just stood there in the wind, drenched and blinking, saying doggedly, "Where thou goest I will go." So at last I told him to come on if he must, and gave him a piece of the bread I had in my pocket; then we struggled on together, and thus began the most memorable of all my wild days.

The level flood, driving hard in our faces, thrashed and washed us wildly until we got into the shelter of a grove on the east side of the glacier near the front, where we stopped awhile for breath and to listen and look out. The exploration of the glacier was my main object, but the wind was too high to allow excursions over its open surface, where one might be dangerously shoved while balancing for a jump on the brink of a crevasse. In the mean time the storm was a fine study. Here the end of the glacier, descending an abrupt swell of resisting rock about five hundred feet high, leans forward and falls in ice-cascades. And as the storm came down the glacier from the north, Stickeen and I were beneath the main current of the blast, while favorably located to see and hear it. What a psalm the storm was singing, and how fresh the smell of the washed earth and leaves, and how sweet the still small voices of the storm! Detached wafts and swirls were coming through the woods, with music from the leaves and branches and furrowed boles, and even from the splintered rocks and ice-crags overhead, many of the tones soft and low and flute-like, as if each leaf and tree, crag and spire were a tuned reed. A broad torrent, draining the side of the glacier, now swollen by scores of new streams from the mountains, was rolling boulders along its rocky channel, with thudding, bumping, muffled sounds, rushing toward the bay with tremendous energy, as if in haste to get out of the mountains; the waters above and beneath calling to each other, and all to the ocean, their home.

Looking southward from our shelter, we had this great torrent and the forested mountain wall above it on our left, the spiry ice-crags on our right, and smooth gray gloom ahead. I tried to draw the marvelous scene in my note-book, but the rain blurred the page in spite of all my pains to shelter it, and the sketch was almost worthless. When the wind began to abate, I traced the east side of the glacier. All the trees standing on the edge of the woods were barked and bruised, showing high-ice mark in a very telling way, while tens of thousands of those that had stood for centuries on the bank of the glacier farther out lay crushed and being crushed. In many places I could see down fifty feet or so beneath the margin of the glacier-mill, where trunks from one to two feet in diameter were being ground to pulp against outstanding rock-ribs and bosses of the bank.

About three miles above the front of the glacier I climbed to the surface of it by means of axe-steps made easy for Stickeen. As far as the eye could reach, the level, or nearly level, glacier stretched away indefinitely beneath the gray sky, a seemingly boundless prairie of ice. The rain continued, and grew colder, which I did not mind, but a dim snowy look in the drooping clouds made me hesitate about venturing far from land. No trace of the west shore was visible, and in case the clouds should settle and give snow, or the wind again become violent, I feared getting caught in a tangle of crevasses. Snow-crystals, the flowers of the mountain clouds, are frail, beautiful things, but terrible when flying on storm-winds in darkening, benumbing swarms or when welded together into glaciers full of deadly crevasses. Watching the weather, I sauntered about on the crystal sea. For a mile or two out I found the ice remarkably safe. The marginal crevasses were mostly narrow, while the few wider ones were easily avoided by passing around them, and the clouds began to open here and there.

Thus encouraged, I at last pushed out for the other side; for Nature can make us do anything she likes. At first we made rapid progress, and the sky was not very threatening, while I took bearings occasionally with a pocket compass to enable me to find my way back more surely in case the storm should become blinding; but the structure lines of the glacier were my main guide. Toward the west side we came to a closely crevassed section in which we had to make long, narrow tacks and doublings, tracing the edges of tremendous transverse and longitudinal crevasses, many of which were from twenty to thirty feet wide, and perhaps a thousand feet deep — beautiful and awful. In working a way through them I was severely cautious, but Stickeen came on as unhesitating as the flying clouds. The widest crevasse that I could jump he would leap without so much as halting to take a look at it. The weather was now making quick changes, scattering bits of dazzling brightness through the wintry gloom; at rare intervals, when the sun broke forth wholly free, the glacier was seen from shore to shore with a bright array of encompassing mountains partly revealed, wearing the clouds as garments, while the prairie bloomed and sparkled with irised light from myriads of washed crystals. Then suddenly all the glorious show would be darkened and blotted out.

Stickeen seemed to care for none of these things, bright or dark, nor for the crevasses, wells, moulins, or swift flashing streams into which he might fall. The little adventurer was only about two years old, yet nothing seemed novel to him, nothing daunted him. He showed neither caution nor curiosity, wonder nor fear, but bravely trotted on as if glaciers were playgrounds. His stout, muffled body seemed all one skipping muscle, and it was truly wonderful to see how swiftly and to all appearance heedlessly he flashed across nerve-trying chasms six or eight feet wide. His courage was so unwavering that it seemed to be due to dullness of perception, as if he were only blindly bold; and I kept warning him to be careful. For we had been close companions on so many wilderness trips that I had formed the habit of talking to him as if he were a boy and understood every word.

We gained the west shore in about three hours; the width of the glacier here being about seven miles. Then I pushed northward in order to see as far back as possible into the fountains of the Fairweather Mountains, in case the clouds should rise. The walking was easy along the margin of the forest, which, of course, like that on the other side, had been invaded and crushed by the swollen, overflowing glacier. In an hour or so, after passing a massive headland, we came suddenly on a branch of the glacier, which, in the form of a magnificent ice-cascade two miles wide, was pouring over the rim of the main basin in a westerly direction, its surface broken into wave-shaped blades and shattered blocks, suggesting the wildest updashing, heaving, plunging motion of a great river cataract. Tracing it down three or four miles, I found that it discharged into a lake, filling it with icebergs.

I would gladly have followed the lake outlet to tide-water, but the day was already far spent, and the threatening sky called for haste on the return trip to get off the ice before dark. I decided therefore to go no farther and, after taking a general view of the wonderful region, turned back, hoping to see it again under more favorable auspices. We made good speed up the cañon of the great ice-torrent, and out on the main glacier until we had left the west shore about two miles behind us. Here we got into a difficult network of crevasses, the gathering clouds began to drop misty fringes, and soon the dreaded snow came flying thick and fast. I now began to feel anxious about finding a way in the blurring storm. Stickeen showed no trace of fear. He was still the same silent, able little hero. I noticed, however, that after the storm-darkness came on he kept close up behind me. The snow urged us to make still greater haste, but at the same time hid our way. I pushed on as best I could, jumping innumerable crevasses, and for every hundred rods or so of direct advance traveling a mile in doubling up and down in the turmoil of chasms and dislocated ice-blocks. After an hour or two of this work we came to a series of longitudinal crevasses of appalling width, and almost straight and regular in trend, like immense furrows. These I traced with firm nerve, excited and strengthened by the danger, making wide jumps, poising cautiously on their dizzy edges after cutting hollows for my feet before making the spring, to avoid possible slipping or any uncertainty on the farther sides, where only one trial is granted — exercise at once frightful and inspiring. Stickeen followed seemingly without effort.

Many a mile we thus traveled, mostly up and down, making but little real headway in crossing, running instead of walking most of the time as the danger of being compelled to spend the night on the glacier became threatening. Stickeen seemed able for anything. Doubtless we could have weathered the storm for one night, dancing on a flat spot to keep from freezing, and I faced the threat without feeling anything like despair; but we were hungry and wet, and the wind from the mountains was still thick with snow and bitterly cold, so of course that night would have seemed a very long one. I could not see far enough through the blurring snow to judge in which general direction the least dangerous route lay, while the few dim, momentary glimpses I caught of mountains through rifts in the flying clouds were far from encouraging either as weather signs or as guides. I had simply to grope my way from crevasse to crevasse, holding a general direction by the ice-structure, which was not to be seen everywhere, and partly by the wind. Again and again I was put to my mettle, but Stickeen followed easily, his nerve apparently growing more unflinching as the danger increased. So it always is with mountaineers when hard beset. Running hard and jumping, holding every minute of the remaining daylight, poor as it was, precious, we doggedly persevered and tried to hope that every difficult crevasse we overcame would prove to be the last of its kind. But on the contrary, as we advanced they became more deadly trying.

At length our way was barred by a very wide and straight crevasse, which I traced rapidly northward a mile or so without finding a crossing or hope of one; then down the glacier about as far, to where it united with another uncrossable crevasse. In all this distance of perhaps two miles there was only one place where I could possibly jump it, but the width of this jump was the utmost I dared attempt, while the danger of slipping on the farther side was so great that I was loath to try it. Furthermore, the side I was on was about a foot higher than the other, and even with this advantage the crevasse seemed dangerously wide. One is liable to underestimate the width of crevasses where the magnitudes in general are great. I therefore stared at this one mighty keenly, estimating its width and the shape of the edge on the farther side, until I thought that I could jump it if necessary, but that in case I should be compelled to jump back from the lower side I might fail. Now, a cautious mountaineer seldom takes a step on unknown ground which seems at all dangerous that he cannot retrace in case he should be stopped by unseen obstacles ahead. This is the rule of mountaineers who live long, and, though in haste, I compelled myself to sit down and calmly deliberate before I broke it.

Retracing my devious path in imagination as if it were drawn on a chart, I saw that I was recrossing the glacier a mile or two farther up stream than the course pursued in the morning, and that I was now entangled in a section I had not before seen. Should I risk this dangerous jump, or try to regain the woods on the west shore, make a fire, and have only hunger to endure while waiting for a new day? I had already crossed so broad a stretch of dangerous ice that I saw it would be difficult to get back to the woods through the storm, before dark, and the attempt would most likely result in a dismal night-dance on the glacier; while just beyond the present barrier the surface seemed more promising, and the east shore was now perhaps about as near as the west. I was therefore eager to go on. But this wide jump was a dreadful obstacle.

At length, because of the dangers already behind me, I determined to venture against those that might be ahead, jumped and landed well, but with so little to spare that I more than ever dreaded being compelled to take that jump back from the lower side. Stickeen followed, making nothing of it, and we ran eagerly forward, hoping we were leaving all our troubles behind. But within the distance of a few hundred yards we were stopped by the widest crevasse yet encountered. Of course I made haste to explore it, hoping all might yet be remedied by finding a bridge or a way around either end. About three fourths of a mile upstream I found that it united with the one we had just crossed, as I feared it would. Then, tracing it down, I found it joined the same crevasse at the lower end also, maintaining throughout its whole course a width of forty to fifty feet. Thus to my dismay I discovered that we were on a narrow island about two miles long, with two barely possible ways to escape: one back by the way we came, the other ahead by an almost inaccessible sliver-bridge that crossed the great crevasse from near the middle of it!

After this nerve-trying discovery I ran back to the sliver-bridge and cautiously examined it. Crevasses, caused by strains from variations in the rate of motion of different parts of the glacier and convexities in the channel, are mere cracks when they first open, so narrow as hardly to admit the blade of a pocket-knife, and gradually widen according to the extent of the strain and the depth of the glacier. Now some of these cracks are interrupted, like the cracks in wood, and in opening, the strip of ice between overlapping ends is dragged out, and may maintain a continuous connection between the side, just as the two sides of a slivered crack in wood that is being split are connected. Some crevasses remain open for months or even years, and by the melting of their sides continue to increase in width long after the opening strain has ceased; while the sliver-bridges, level on top at first and perfectly safe, are at length melted to thin, vertical, knife-edged blades, the upper portion being most exposed to the weather; and since the exposure is greatest in the middle, they at length curve downward like the cables of suspension bridges. This one was evidently very old, for it had been weathered and wasted until it was the most dangerous and inaccessible that ever lay in my way. The width of the crevasse was here about fifty feet, and the sliver crossing diagonally was about seventy feet long; its thin knife-edge near the middle was depressed twenty-five or thirty feet below the level of the glacier, and the up-curving ends were attached to the sides eight or ten feet below the brink. Getting down the nearly vertical wall to the end of the sliver and up the other side were the main difficulties, and they seemed all but insurmountable. Of the many perils encountered in my years of wandering on mountains and glaciers none seemed so plain and stern and merciless as this. And it was presented when we were wet to the skin and hungry, the sky dark with quick driving snow, and the night near. But we were forced to face it. It was a tremendous necessity.

Beginning, not immediately above the sunken end of the bridge, but a little to one side, I cut a deep hollow on the brink for my knees to rest in. Then, leaning over, with my short-handled axe I cut a step sixteen or eighteen inches below, which on account of the sheerness of the wall was necessarily shallow. That step, however, was well made; its floor sloped slightly inward and formed a good hold for my heels. Then, slipping cautiously upon it, and crouching as low as possible, with my left side toward the wall, I steadied myself against the wind with my left hand in a slight notch, while with the right I cut other similar steps and notches in succession, guarding against losing balance by glinting of the axe, or by wind-gusts, for life and death were in every stroke and in the niceness of finish of every foothold.

After the end of the bridge was reached I chipped it down until I had made a level platform six or eight inches wide, and it was a trying thing to poise on this little slippery platform while bending over to get safely astride of the sliver. Crossing was then comparatively easy by chipping off the sharp edge with short, careful strokes, and hitching forward an inch or two at a time, keeping my balance with my knees pressed against the sides. The tremendous abyss on either hand I studiously ignored. To me the edge of that blue sliver was then all the world. But the most trying part of the adventure, after working my way across inch by inch and chipping another small platform, was to rise from the safe postion astride and to cut a step-ladder in the nearly vertical face of the wall — chipping, climbing, holding on with feet and fingers in mere notches. At such times one's whole body is eye, and common skill and fortitude are replaced by power beyond our call or knowledge. Never before had I been so long under deadly strain. How I got up that cliff I never could tell. The thing seemed to have been done by somebody else. I never have held death in contempt, though in the course of my explorations I have oftentimes felt that to meet one's fate on a noble mountain, or in the heart of a glacier, would be blessed as compared with death from disease, or from some shabby lowland accident. But the best death, quick and crystal-pure, set so glaringly open before us, is hard enough to face, even though we feel gratefully sure that we have already had happiness enough for a dozen lives.

But poor Stickeen, the wee, hairy, sleekit beastie, think of him!

When I had decided to dare the bridge, and while I was on my knees chipping a hollow on the rounded brow above it, he came behind me, pushed his head past my shoulder, looked down and across, scanned the sliver and its approaches with his mysterious eyes, then looked me in the face with a startled air of surprise and concern, and began to mutter and whine; saying as plainly as if speaking with words, "Surely, you are not going into that awful place." This was the first time I had seen him gaze deliberately into a crevasse, or into my face with an eager, speaking, troubled look. That he should have recognized and appreciated the danger at the first glance showed wonderful sagacity. Never before had the daring midget seemed to know that ice was slippery or that there was any such thing as danger anywhere. His looks and tones of voice when he began to complain and speak his fears were so human that I unconsciously talked to him in sympathy as I would to a frightened boy, and in trying to calm his fears perhaps in some measure moderated my own. "Hush your fears, my boy," I said, "we will get across safe, though it is not going to be easy. No right way is easy in this rough world. We must risk our lives to save them. At the worst we can only slip, and then how grand a grave we will have, and by and by our nice bones will do good in the terminal moraine."

But my sermon was far from reassuring him: he began to cry, and after taking another piercing look at the tremendous gulf, ran away in desperate excitement, seeking some other crossing. By the time he got back, baffled of course, I had made a step or two. I dared not look back, but he made himself heard; and when he saw that I was certainly bent on crossing he cried aloud in despair. The danger was enough to daunt anybody, but it seems wonderful that he should have been able to weigh and appreciate it so justly. No mountaineer could have seen it more quickly or judged it more wisely, discriminating between real and apparent peril.

When I gained the other side, he screamed louder than ever, and after running back and forth in vain search for a way of escape, he would return to the brink of the crevasse above the bridge, moaning and wailing as if in the bitterness of death. Could this be the silent, philosophic Stickeen? I shouted encouragement, telling him the bridge was not so bad as it looked, that I had left it flat and safe for his feet, and he could walk it easily. But he was afraid to try. Strange so small an animal should be capable of such big, wise fears. I called again and again in a reassuring tone to come on and fear nothing; that he could come if he would only try. He would hush for a moment, look down again at the bridge, and shout his unshakable conviction that he could never, never come that way; then lie back in despair, as if howling, "O-o-oh! what a place! No-o-o, I can never go-o-o down there!" His natural composure and courage had vanished utterly in a tumultuous storm of fear. Had the danger been less, his distress would have seemed ridiculous. But in this dismal, merciless abyss lay the shadow of death, and his heart-rending cries might well have called Heaven to his help. Perhaps they did. So hidden before, he was now transparent, and one could see the workings of his heart and mind like the movements of a clock out of its case. His voice and gestures, hopes and fears, were so perfectly human that none could mistake them; while he seemed to understand every word of mine. I was troubled at the thought of having to leave him out all night, and of the danger of not finding him in the morning. It seemed impossible to get him to venture. To compel him to try through fear of being abandoned, I started off as if leaving him to his fate, and disappeared back of a hummock; but this did no good; he only lay down and moaned in utter hopeless misery. So, after hiding a few minutes, I went back to the brink of the crevasse and in a severe tone of voice shouted across to him that now I must certainly leave him, I could wait no longer, and that, if he would not come, all I could promise was that I would return to seek him next day. I warned him that if he went back to the woods the wolves would kill him, and finished by urging him once more by words and gestures to come on, come on.

He knew very well what I meant, and at last, with the courage of despair, hushed and breathless, he crouched down on the brink in the hollow I had made for my knees, pressed his body against the ice as if trying to get the advantage of the friction of every hair, gazed into the first step, put his little feet together and slid them slowly, slowly over the edge and down into it, bunching all four in it and almost standing on his head. Then, without lifting his feet, as well as I could see through the snow, he slowly worked them over the edge of the step and down into the next and the next in succession in the same way, and gained the end of the bridge. Then, lifting his feet with the regularity and slowness of the vibrations of a seconds pendulum, as if counting and measuring *one-two-three*, holding himself steady against the gusty wind, and giving separate attention to each little step, he gained the foot of the cliff, while I was on my knees leaning over to give him a lift should he succeed in getting within reach of my arm. Here he halted in dead silence, and it was here I feared he might fail, for dogs are poor climbers. I had no cord. If I had had one, I would have dropped a noose over his head and hauled him up. But while I was thinking whether an available cord might be made out of clothing, he was looking keenly into the series of notched steps and finger-holds I had made, as if counting them, and fixing the position of each one of them in his mind. Then suddenly up he came in a springy rush, hooking his paws into the steps and notches so quickly that I could not see how it was done, and whizzed past my head, safe at last!

And now came a scene! "Well done, well done, little boy! Brave boy!" I cried, trying to catch and caress him; but he would not be caught. Never before or since have I seen anything like so passionate a revulsion from the depths of despair to exultant, triumphant, uncontrollable joy. He flashed and darted hither and thither as if fairly demented, screaming and shouting, swirling round and round in giddy loops and circles like a leaf in a whirl-wind, lying down, and rolling over and over, sidewise and heels over head, and pouring forth a tumultuous flood of hysterical cries and sobs and gasping mutterings. When I ran up to him to shake him, fearing he might die of joy, he flashed off two or three hundred yards, his feet in a mist of motion; then, turning sud-denly, came back in a wild rush and launched himself at my face, almost knocking me down, all the time screeching and screaming and shouting as if saying, "Saved! saved! saved!" Then away again, dropping suddenly at times with his feet in the air, trem-bling and fairly sobbing. Such passionate emotion was enough to kill him. Moses' stately song of triumph after escaping the Egyptians and the Red Sea was nothing to it. Who could have guessed the capacity of the dull, enduring little fellow for all that most stirs this mortal frame? Nobody could have helped crying with him!

But there is nothing like work for toning down excessive fear or joy. So I ran ahead, calling him in as gruff a voice as I could command to come on and stop his nonsense, for we had far to go and it would soon be dark. Neither of us feared another trial like this. Heaven would surely count one enough for a lifetime. The ice ahead was gashed by thousands of crevasses, but they were common ones. The joy of deliverance burned in us like fire, and we ran without fatigue, every muscle with immense rebound glorying in its strength. Stickeen flew across everything in his way, and not till dark did he settle into his normal fox-like trot. At last the cloudy mountains came in sight, and we soon felt the solid rock beneath our feet, and were safe. Then came weakness. Danger had vanished, and so had our strength. We tottered down the lateral moraine in the dark, over boulders and tree trunks, through the bushes and devil-club thickets of the grove where we had sheltered ourselves in the morning, and across the level mud-slope of the terminal moraine. We reached camp about ten o'clock, and found a big fire and a big supper. A party of Hoona Indians had visited Mr. Young, bringing a gift of porpoise meat and wild strawberries, and Hunter Joe had brought in a wild goat. But we lay down, too tired to eat much, and soon fell into a troubled sleep. The man who said, "The harder the toil, the sweeter the rest," never was profoundly tired. Stickeen kept springing up and muttering in his sleep, no doubt dreaming that he was still on the brink of the crevasse; and so did I, that night and many others long afterward, when I was over-tired.

Thereafter Stickeen was a changed dog. During the rest of the trip, instead of holding aloof, he always lay by my side, tried to keep me constantly in sight, and would hardly accept a morsel of food, however tempting, from any hand but mine. At night, when all was quiet about the camp-fire, he would come to me and rest his head on my knee with a look of devotion as if I were his god. And often as he caught my eye he seemed to be trying to say, "Wasn't that an awful time we had together on the glacier?"

Nothing in after years has dimmed that Alaska storm-day. As I write it all comes rushing and roaring to mind as if I were again in the heart of it. Again I see the gray flying clouds with their rain-floods and snow, the ice-cliffs towering above the shrinking forest, the majestic ice-cascade, the vast glacier outspread before its white mountain-fountains, and in the heart of it the tremendous crevasse — emblem of the valley of the shadow of death — low clouds trailing over it, the snow falling into it; and on its brink I see little Stickeen, and I hear his cries for help and his shouts of joy. I have known many dogs, and many a story I could tell of their wisdom and devotion; but to none do I owe so much as to Stickeen. At first the least promising and least known of my dog-friends, he suddenly became the best known of them all. Our storm-battle for life brought him to light, and through him as through a window I have ever since been looking with deeper sympathy into all my fellow mortals.

None of Stickeen's friends knows what finally became of him. After my work for the season was done I departed for California, and I never saw the dear little fellow again. In reply to anxious inquiries his master wrote me that in the summer of 1883 he was stolen by a tourist at Fort Wrangell and taken away on a steamer. His fate is wrapped in mystery. Doubtless he has left this world — crossed the last crevasse — and gone to another. But he will not be forgotten. To me Stickeen is immortal.

(*Stickeen*)

Villages of the Dead

THE SUMMER of 1881 saw Muir back in the Arctic again. He had been invited to go north on the revenue cutter Thomas Corwin *in search of the lost* Jeannette, *the ship on which George Washington De Long's polar expedition disappeared in 1879. From May to October the unsuccessful hunt continued. At one point the cutter maneuvered close to mysterious Wrangel Land and Muir and the captain of the* Corwin, *C. L. Hooper, landed — the first white men to set foot on this desolate shore. Opposite the mouth of the Yukon in the Bering Sea, Muir visited silent villages of the dead on Lawrence Island. During the winter of 1878–79 fully 1000 of the 1500 natives on this island had died of starvation. Among those who visited the island with Muir was E. W. Nelson, a scientist making a collection for the Smithsonian Institution in Washington.*

ST. LAWRENCE ISLAND, the largest in Bering Sea, is situated at a distance of about one hundred and twenty miles off the mouths of the Yukon, and forty-five miles from the nearest point on the coast of Siberia. It is about a hundred miles in length from east to west and fifteen miles in average width; a dreary, cheerless-looking mass of black lava, dotted with volcanoes, covered with snow, without a single tree, and rigidly bound in ocean ice for more than half the year.

Inasmuch as it lies broadwise to the way pursued by the great ice-sheet that once filled Bering Sea, it is traversed by numerous valleys and ridges and low gaps, some of which have been worn down nearly to the sea-level. Had the glaciation to which it has been subjected been carried on much longer, then, instead of this one large island, we should have had several smaller ones. Nearly all of the volcanic cones with which the central portion of the island is in great part covered, are post-glacial in age and present well-formed craters but little weathered as yet.

All the surface of the low grounds, in the glacial gaps, as well as the flat table-lands, is covered with wet, spongy tundra of mosses and lichens, with patches of blooming heathworts and dwarf willows, and grasses and sedges, diversified here and there by drier spots, planted with larkspurs, saxifrages, daisies, primulas, anemones, ferns, etc. These form gardens with a luxuriance and brightness of color little to be hoped for in so cold and dreary-looking a region.

Three years ago there were about fifteen hundred inhabitants on the island, chiefly Eskimos, living in ten villages located around the shores, and subsisting on the seals, walruses, whales, and waterbirds that abound here. Now there are only about five hundred people, most of them in one village on the northwest end of the island, nearly two thirds of the population having died of starvation during the winter of 1878–79. In seven of the villages not a single soul was left alive. In the largest village at the northwest end of the island, which suffered least, two hundred out of six hundred died. In the one at the southwest end only fifteen out of about two hundred survived. There are a few survivors also at one of the villages on the east end of the island.

After landing our interpreter at Marcus Bay we steered for St. Michael, and in passing along the north side of this island we stopped an hour or so this morning at one of the smallest of the dead villages. Mr. Nelson went ashore and obtained a lot of skulls and specimens of one sort and another for the Smithsonian Institution. Twenty-five skeletons were seen.

A few miles farther on we anchored before a larger village, situated about halfway between the east and west ends of the island, which I visited in company with Mr. Nelson, the Captain, and the Surgeon. We found twelve desolate huts close to the beach with about two hundred skeletons in them or strewn about on the rocks and rubbish heaps within a few yards of the doors.

The scene was indescribably ghastly and desolate, though laid in a country purified by frost as by fire. Gulls, plovers, and ducks were swimming and flying about in happy life, the pure salt sea was dashing white against the shore, the blooming tundra swept back to the snow-clad volcanoes, and the wide azure sky bent kindly over all — nature intensely fresh and sweet, the village lying in the foulest and most glaring death. The shrunken bodies, with rotting furs on them, or white, bleaching skeletons, picked bare by the crows, were lying mixed with kitchen-midden rubbish where they had been cast out by surviving relatives while they yet had strength to carry them.

In the huts those who had been the last to perish were found in bed, lying evenly side by side, beneath their rotting deerskins. A grinning skull might be seen looking out here and there, and a pile of skeletons in a corner, laid there no doubt when no one was left strong enough to carry them through the narrow underground passage to the door. Thirty were found in one house, about half of them piled like firewood in a corner, the other half in bed, seeming as if they had met their fate with tranquil apathy. Evidently these people did not suffer from cold, however rigorous the winter may have been, as some of the huts had in them piles of deerskins that had not been in use. Nor, although their survivors and neighbors all say that hunger was the sole cause of their death, could they have battled with famine to the bitter end, because a considerable amount of walrus rawhide and skins of other animals was found in the huts. These would have sustained life at least a week or two longer.

The facts all tend to show that the winter of 1878–79 was, from whatever cause, one of great scarcity, and as these people never lay up any considerable supply of food from one season to another, they began to perish. The first to succumb were carried out of the huts to the ordinary ground for the dead, about half a mile from the village. Then, as the survivors became weaker, they carried the dead a shorter distance, and made no effort to mark their positions or to lay their effects beside them, as they customarily do. At length the bodies were only dragged to the doors of the huts, or laid in a corner, and the last survivors lay down in despair without making any struggle to prolong their wretched lives by eating the last scraps of skin.

Mr. Nelson went into this Golgotha with hearty enthusiasm, gathering the fine white harvest of skulls spread before him, and throwing them in heaps like a boy gathering pumpkins. He brought nearly a hundred on board, which will be shipped with specimens of bone armor, weapons, utensils, etc., on the Alaska Commercial Company's steamer *St. Paul.*

We also landed at the village on the southwest corner of the island and interviewed the fifteen survivors. When we inquired where the other people of the village were, one of the group, who speaks a few words of English, answered with a happy, heedless smile, "All mucky." "All gone!" "Dead?" "Yes, dead, all dead!" Then he led us a few yards back of his hut and pointed to twelve or fourteen skeletons lying on the brown grass, repeating in almost a merry tone of voice, "Dead, yes, all dead, all mucky, all gone!"

About two hundred perished here, and unless some aid be extended by our government which claims these people, in a few years at most every soul of them will have vanished from the face of the earth; for, even where alcohol is left out of the count, the few articles of food, clothing, guns, etc., furnished by the traders, exert a degrading influence, making them less self-reliant, and less skillful as hunters. They seem easily susceptible of civilization, and well deserve the attention of our government.

(The Cruise of the Corwin)

Slaughter of the Walruses

A GLIMPSE of the ruthless slaughter that went on year after year in the Arctic during the last decades of the nineteenth century is afforded by the following entry in Muir's Corwin *journal. As always he was on the side of the hunted. In 1899, when other members of the Harriman Expedition were rejoicing at the success of a hunting party that returned with a bear and cub from Kodiak Island, Muir noted in his journal: "Harriman returned last evening after killing two bears — mother and child."*

A LOVELY EVENING, bracing, cool, with a light breeze blowing over the polar pack. The ice is marvelously distorted and miraged; thousands of blocks seem suspended in the air; some even poised on slender black poles and pinnacles; a bridge of ice with innumerable piers, the ice and water wavering with quick, glancing motion. At midnight the sun is still above the horizon about two diameters; purple to west and east, gradually fading to dark slate color in the south with a few banks of cloud. A bar of gold in the path of the sun lay on the water and across the pack, the large blocks in the line [of vision] burning like huge coals of fire.

A little schooner has a boat out in the edge of the pack killing walruses, while she is lying a little to east of the sun. A puff of smoke now and then, a dull report, and a huge animal rears and falls — another, and another, as they lie on the ice without showing any alarm, waiting to be killed, like cattle lying in a barnyard! Nearer, we hear the roar, lion-like, mixed with hoarse grunts, from hundreds like black bundles on the white ice. A small red flag is planted near the pile of slain. Then the three men puff off to their schooner, as it is now midnight, and time for the other watch to go to work.

These magnificent animals are killed oftentimes for their tusks alone, like buffaloes for their tongues, ostriches for their feathers, or for mere sport and exercise. In nothing does man, with his grand notions of heaven and charity, show forth his innate, low-bred, wild animalism more clearly than in his treatment of his brother beasts. From the shepherd with his lambs to the red-handed hunter, it is the same; no recognition of rights — only murder in one form or another.

(The Cruise of the Corwin)

Alaskan Auroras

JOHN MUIR'S last days were spent in the square gray house of the Martinez ranch revising his Alaskan journals for publication. Marion Randall Parsons, who helped him with the work, recalls that as each chapter was finished it was tied up with a red ribbon and stored in an orange crate. Fog is rather common in the Alhambra Valley; two of the three times I visited Martinez, Muir's home was veiled in heavy mist. The fall of 1914, Muir wrote to a friend, was the stormiest and foggiest he had ever experienced. He came down with colds and the grippe. In December, with the Alaskan manuscript in his suitcase, he traveled to Daggett, eight miles from Barstow on the Mojave Desert, to spend the holidays with his daughter, Helen. She had been living in the desert after recovering from tuberculosis contracted in 1905, the year Mrs. Muir died. It was 2.30 A.M. on a cold, windy night when he reached Daggett. Chilled severely, he fell ill. Pneumonia set in and he was taken to a Los Angeles hospital where, on Christmas Eve, 1914, he died. Scattered over his hospital bed when the end came were the manuscript sheets of his Alaska book. Appropriately enough for one whose life was so largely devoted to the natural beauty of the world, the final pages deal with the serene, almost spiritual radiance of the Alaskan auroras. The displays described occurred in 1880. At the time, Professor Harry Fielding Reid of Cleveland, Ohio, and a party of students were camped near Muir.

❀

AFTER A HARD, anxious struggle, I reached the mouth of
the Hugh Miller fiord about sundown, and tried to find a camp-
spot on its steep, boulder-bound shore. But no landing-place
where it seemed possible to drag the canoe above high-tide mark
was discovered after examining a mile or more of this dreary,
forbidding barrier, and as night was closing down, I decided to
try to grope my way across the mouth of the fiord in the starlight
to an open sandy spot on which I had camped in October, 1879,
a distance of about three or four miles.

With the utmost caution I picked my way through the sparkling
bergs, and after an hour or two of this nerve-trying work, when I
was perhaps less than halfway across and dreading the loss of the
frail canoe which would include the loss of myself, I came to a
pack of very large bergs which loomed threateningly, offering no
visible thoroughfare. Paddling and pushing to right and left, I at
last discovered a sheer-walled opening about four feet wide and
perhaps two hundred feet long, formed apparently by the splitting
of a huge iceberg. I hesitated to enter this passage, fearing that
the slightest change in the tide-current might close it, but ventured nevertheless, judging that the dangers ahead might not be
greater than those I had already passed. When I had got about a
third of the way in, I suddenly discovered that the smooth-walled
ice-lane was growing narrower, and with desperate haste backed
out. Just as the bow of the canoe cleared the sheer walls they
came together with a growling crunch. Terror-stricken, I turned
back, and in an anxious hour or two gladly reached the rock-
bound shore that had at first repelled me, determined to stay on
guard all night in the canoe or find some place where with the
strength that comes in a fight for life I could drag it up the boulder
wall beyond ice danger. This at last was happily done about midnight, and with no thought of sleep I went to bed rejoicing.

My bed was two boulders, and as I lay wedged and bent on
their up-bulging sides, beguiling the hard, cold time in gazing
into the starry sky and across the sparkling bay, magnificent upright bars of light in bright prismatic colors suddenly appeared,

marching swiftly in close succession along the northern horizon from west to east as if in diligent haste, an auroral display very different from any I had ever before beheld. Once long ago in Wisconsin I saw the heavens draped in rich purple auroral clouds fringed and folded in most magnificent forms; but in this glory of light, so pure, so bright, so enthusiastic in motion, there was nothing in the least cloud-like. The short color-bars, apparently about two degrees in height, though blending, seemed to be as well defined as those of the solar spectrum.

How long these glad, eager soldiers of light held on their way I cannot tell; for sense of time was charmed out of mind and the blessed night circled away in measureless rejoicing enthusiasm.

In the early morning after so inspiring a night I launched my canoe feeling able for anything, crossed the mouth of the Hugh Miller fiord, and forced a way three or four miles along the shore of the bay, hoping to reach the Grand Pacific Glacier in front of Mount Fairweather. But the farther I went, the ice-pack, instead of showing inviting little open streaks here and there, became so much harder jammed that on some parts of the shore the bergs, drifting south with the tide, were shoving one another out of the water beyond high-tide line. Farther progress to northward was thus rigidly stopped, and now I had to fight for a way back to my cabin, hoping that by good tide luck I might reach it before dark. But at sundown I was less than halfway home, and though very hungry was glad to land on a little rock island with a smooth beach for the canoe and a thicket of alder bushes for fire and bed and a little sleep. But shortly after sundown, while these arrangements were being made, lo and behold another aurora enriching the heavens! and though it proved to be one of the ordinary almost colorless kind, thrusting long, quivering lances toward the zenith from a dark, cloud-like base, after last night's wonderful display one's expectations might well be extravagant and I lay wide awake watching.

On the third night I reached my cabin and food. Professor Reid and his party came in to talk over the results of our excursions, and just as the last one of the visitors opened the door after bidding good-night, he shouted, "Muir, come look here. Here's something fine."

I ran out in auroral excitement, and sure enough here was another aurora, as novel and wonderful as the marching rainbow-colored columns — a glowing silver bow spanning the Muir Inlet in a magnificent arch right under the zenith, or a little to the south of it, the ends resting on the top of the mountain-walls. And though colorless and steadfast, its intense, solid white splendor, noble proportions, and fineness of finish excited boundless admiration. In form and proportion it was like a rainbow, a bridge of one span five miles wide; and so brilliant, so fine and solid and homogeneous in every part, I fancy that if all the stars were raked together into one windrow, fused and welded and run through some celestial rolling-mill, all would be required to make this one glowing white colossal bridge.

After my last visitor went to bed, I lay down on the moraine in front of the cabin and gazed and watched. Hour after hour the wonderful arch stood perfectly motionless, sharply defined and substantial-looking as if it were a permanent addition to the furniture of the sky. At length while it yet spanned the inlet in serene, unchanging splendor, a band of fluffy, pale-gray, quivering ringlets came suddenly all in a row over the eastern mountain-top, glided in nervous haste up and down the under side of the bow and over the western mountain-wall. They were about one and a half times the apparent diameter of the bow in length, maintained a vertical posture all the way across, and slipped swiftly along as if they were suspended like a curtain on rings. Had these lively auroral fairies marched across the fiord on the top of the bow instead of shuffling along the under side of it, one might have fancied they were a happy band of spirit people on a journey making use of the splendid bow for a bridge. There must have been hundreds of miles of them; for the time required for each to cross from one end of the bridge to the other seemed only a minute or less, while nearly an hour elapsed from their first appearance until the last of the rushing throng vanished behind the western mountain, leaving the bridge as bright and solid and steadfast as before they arrived. But later, half an hour or so, it began to fade. Fissures or cracks crossed it diagonally through which a few stars were seen, and gradually it became thin and nebulous until it looked like the Milky Way, and at last vanished, leaving no visible monument of any sort to mark its place.

I now returned to my cabin, replenished the fire, warmed myself, and prepared to go to bed, though too aurorally rich and happy to go to sleep. But just as I was about to retire, I thought I had better take another look at the sky, to make sure that the glorious show was over; and, contrary to all reasonable expectations, I found that the pale foundation for another bow was being laid right overhead like the first. Then losing all thought of sleep, I ran back to my cabin, carried out blankets and lay down on the moraine to keep watch until daybreak, that none of the sky wonders of the glorious night within reach of my eyes might be lost.

I had seen the first bow when it stood complete in full splendor, and its gradual fading decay. Now I was to see the building of a new one from the beginning. Perhaps in less than half an hour the silvery material was gathered, condensed, and welded into a glowing, evenly proportioned arc like the first and in the same part of the sky. Then in due time over the eastern mountain-wall came another throng of restless electric auroral fairies, the infinitely fine pale-gray garments of each lightly touching those of their neighbors as they swept swiftly along the under side of the bridge and down over the western mountain like the merry band that had gone the same way before them, all keeping quivery step and time to music too fine for mortal ears.

While the gay throng was gliding swiftly along, I watched the bridge for any change they might make upon it, but not the slightest could I detect. They left no visible track, and after all had passed the glowing arc stood firm and apparently immutable, but at last faded slowly away like its glorious predecessor.

Excepting only the vast purple aurora mentioned above, said to have been visible over nearly all the continent, these two silver bows in supreme, serene, supernal beauty surpassed everything auroral I ever beheld.

(Travels in Alaska)

VII

THE PHILOSOPHY OF JOHN MUIR

The Philosophy of John Muir

BENEATH a eucalyptus tree on the Martinez ranch, in a spot he chose, Muir is buried beside his wife. In his journal he once noted concerning his lifelong devotion to nature: "I only went out for a walk and finally concluded to stay out till sundown, for going out, I found, was really going in." Throughout his books Muir's philosophy of life is an important feature of his writings. It is reflected in the following random thoughts set down at various times and in various places — a philosophy distilled from his wilderness world, a philosophy of outdoor sanity and health.

I USED TO ENVY the father of our race, dwelling as he did in contact with the new-made fields and plants of Eden; but I do so no more, because I have discovered that I also live in "creation's dawn." The morning stars still sing together, and the world, not yet half made, becomes more beautiful every day.

Climb the mountains and get their good tidings. Nature's peace will flow into you as sunshine flows into trees. The winds will blow their own freshness into you, and the storms their energy, while cares will drop off like autumn leaves.

There is a love of wild nature in everybody, an ancient mother-love ever showing itself whether recognized or no, and however covered by cares and duties.

After I had lived many years in the mountains, I spent my first winter in San Francisco, writing up notes. I used to run out on short excursions to Mount Tamalpais, or the hills across the bay, for rest and exercise, and I always brought back a lot of flowers — as many as I could carry — and it was most touching to see the quick natural enthusiasm in the hearts of the ragged, neglected, defrauded, dirty little wretches of the Tar Flat water-front of the city I used to pass through on my way home. As soon as they caught sight of my wild bouquet, they quit their pitiful attempts at amusement in the miserable dirty streets and ran after me begging a flower. "Please, Mister, give me a flower — give me a flower, Mister," in a humble begging tone as if expecting to be refused. And when I stopped and distributed the treasures, giving each a lily or daisy or calachortus, anemone, gilia, flowering Dogwood, spray of Ceanothus, Manzanita, or a branch of Redwood, the dirty faces fairly glowed with enthusiasm while they gazed at them and fondled them reverently as if looking into the faces of angels from heaven. It was a hopeful sign, and made me say: "No matter into what depths of degradation humanity may sink, I will never despair while the lowest love the pure and the beautiful and know it when they see it."

This grand show is eternal. It is always sunrise somewhere; the dew is never all dried at once; a shower is forever falling; vapor is ever rising. Eternal sunrise, eternal sunset, eternal dawn and gloaming, on sea and continents and islands, each in its turn, as the round earth rolls.

How hard to realize that every camp of men or beast has this glorious starry firmament for a roof! In such places standing alone on the mountain-top it is easy to realize that whatever special nests we make — leaves and moss like the marmots and birds, or tents or piled stone — we all dwell in a house of one room — the world with the firmament for its roof — and are sailing the celestial spaces without leaving any track.

The clearest way into the Universe is through a forest wilderness.

Thoughts on Finding a Dead Yosemite Bear. Toiling in the treadmills of life we hide from the lessons of Nature. We gaze morbidly through civilized fog upon our beautiful world clad with seamless beauty, and see ferocious beasts and wastes and deserts. But savage deserts and beasts and storms are expressions of God's power inseparably companioned by love. Civilized man chokes his soul as the heathen Chinese their feet. We depreciate bears.

But grandly they blend with their native mountains. They roam the sandy slopes on lily meads, through polished glacier canyons, among the solemn Firs and brown Sequoia, Manzanita, and chaparral, living upon redberries and gooseberries, little caring for rain or snow. Magnificent bears of the Sierra are worthy of their magnificent homes. They are not companions of men, but children of God, and His charity is broad enough for bears.

There are no square-edged inflexible lines in Nature. We seek to establish a narrow line between ourselves and the feathery zeros we dare to call angels, but ask a partition barrier of infinite width to show the rest of creation its proper place.

Bears are made of the same dust as we, and breathe the same winds and drink of the same waters. A bear's days are warmed by the same sun, his dwellings are overdomed by the same blue sky, and his life turns and ebbs with heart-pulsings like ours, and was poured from the same First Fountain. And whether he at last goes to our stingy heaven or no, he has terrestrial immortality. His life not long, not short, knows no beginning, no ending. To him life unstinted, unplanned, is above the accidents of time, and his years, markless and boundless, equal Eternity.

God bless Yosemite bears!

Most people are *on* the world, not in it — have no conscious sympathy or relationship to anything about them — undiffused, separate, and rigidly alone like marbles of polished stone, touching but separate.

When one is alone at night in the depths of these woods, the stillness is at once awful and sublime. Every leaf seems to speak.

One gets close to Nature, and the love of beauty grows as it cannot in the distractions of a camp. The sense of utter loneliness is heightened by the invisibility of bird or beast that dwells here. But it is not in the deeps of the woods that people are soothed into perfect rest, nor in mountain valleys, however beautifully bounded by lofty walls. One feels submerged and ever seeks the free expanse. Nor yet on lofty summits, islands of the sky, but on the tranquil uplands where exhilarating air and a free far outlook are combined with the loveliest of the flora. In that zone below the ice and snow and above the darkling woods, where the sunshine sleeps on alpine gardens and the young rivers flow rejoicing from the glacial caves, and the groves of eriogonums are open to the light — perfect quietude is there, and freedom from every curable care.

Only by going alone in silence, without baggage, can one truly get into the heart of the wilderness. All other travel is mere dust and hotels and baggage and chatter.

Come to the woods, for here is rest. There is no repose like that of the green deep woods. Here grow the wallflower and the violet. The squirrel will come and sit upon your knee, the logcock will wake you in the morning. Sleep in forgetfulness of all ill. Of all the upness accessible to mortals, there is no upness comparable to the mountains.

Hunting. Making some bird or beast go lame the rest of its life is a sore thing on one's conscience, at least nothing to boast of, and it has no religion in it.

The murder business and sport by saint and sinner alike has been pushed ruthlessly, merrily on, until at last protective measures are being called for, partly, I suppose, because the pleasure of killing is in danger of being lost from there being little or nothing left to kill, and partly, let us hope, from a dim glimmering recognition of the rights of animals and their kinship to ourselves.

The astronomer looks high, the geologist low. Who looks between on the surface of the earth? The farmer, I suppose, but too often he sees only grain, and of that only the mere bread-bushel-and-price side of it.

It has been said that trees are imperfect men, and seem to bemoan their imprisonment rooted in the ground. But they never seem so to me. I never saw a discontented tree. They grip the ground as though they liked it, and though fast rooted they travel about as far as we do. They go wandering forth in all directions with every wind, going and coming like ourselves, traveling with us around the sun two million miles a day, and through space heaven knows how fast and far!

If my soul could get away from this so-called prison, be granted all the list of attributes generally bestowed on spirits, my first ramble on spirit-wings would not be among the volcanoes of the moon. Nor should I follow the sunbeams to their sources in the sun. I should hover about the beauty of our own good star. I should not go moping among the tombs, nor around the artificial desolation of men. I should study Nature's laws in all their crossings and unions; I should follow magnetic streams to their source and follow the shores of our magnetic oceans. I should go among the rays of the aurora, and follow them to their beginnings, and study their dealings and communions with other powers and expressions of matter. And I should go to the very center of our globe and read the whole splendid page from the beginning.

But my first journeys would be into the inner substance of flowers, and among the folds and mazes of Yosemite's falls. How grand to move about in the very tissue of falling columns, and in the very birthplace of their heavenly harmonies, looking outward as from windows of ever-varying transparency and staining!

In God's wildness lies the hope of the world — the great fresh, unblighted, unredeemed wilderness. The galling harness of civilization drops off, and the wounds heal ere we are aware.

The world, we are told, was made especially for man — a presumption not supported by all the facts. A numerous class of men are painfully astonished whenever they find anything, living or dead, in all God's universe, which they cannot eat or render in some way what they call useful to themselves. They have precise dogmatic insight into the intentions of the Creator, and it is hardly possible to be guilty of irreverence in speaking of *their* God any more than of heathen idols. He is regarded as a civilized, law-abiding gentleman in favor either of a republican form of government or of a limited monarchy; believes in the literature and language of England; is a warm supporter of the English constitution and Sunday schools and missionary societies; and is as purely a manufactured article as any puppet at a half-penny theater.

With such views of the Creator it is, of course, not surprising that erroneous views should be entertained of the creation. To such properly trimmed people, the sheep, for example, is an easy problem — food and clothing "for us," eating grass and daisies white by divine appointment for this predestined purpose, on perceiving the demand for wool that would be occasioned by the eating of the apple in the Garden of Eden.

In the same pleasant plan, whales are storehouses of oil for us, to help out the stars in lighting our dark ways until the discovery of the Pennsylvania oil wells. Among plants, hemp, to say nothing of the cereals, is a case of evident destination for ships' rigging, wrapping packages, and hanging the wicked. Cotton is another plain case of clothing. Iron was made for hammers and ploughs, and lead for bullets; all intended for us. And so of other small handfuls of insignificant things.

But if we should ask these profound expositors of God's intentions, How about those man-eating animals — lions, tigers, alligators — which smack their lips over raw man? Or about those myriads of noxious insects that destroy labor and drink his blood? Doubtless man was intended for food and drink for all these? Oh, no! Not at all! These are unresolvable difficulties connected with Eden's apple and the Devil. Why does water drown its lord? Why do so many minerals poison him? Why are so many plants and fishes deadly enemies? Why is the lord of creation subjected to the same laws of life as his subjects? Oh, all these things are satanic, or in some way connected with the first garden.

Now, it never seems to occur to these far-seeing teachers that Nature's object in making animals and plants might possibly be first of all the happiness of each one of them, not the creation of all for the happiness of one. Why should man value himself as more than a small part of the one great unit of creation? And what creature of all that the Lord has taken the pains to make is not essential to the completeness of that unit — the cosmos? The universe would be incomplete without man; but it would also be incomplete without the smallest transmicroscopic creature that dwells beyond our conceitful eyes and knowledge.

From the dust of the earth, from the common elementary fund, the Creator has made *Homo sapiens*. From the same material he has made every other creature, however noxious and insignificant to us. They are earth-born companions and our fellow mortals. The fearfully good, the orthodox, of this laborious patch-work of modern civilization cry "Heresy" on every one whose sympathies reach a single hair's breadth beyond the boundary epidermis of our own species. Not content with taking all of earth, they also claim the celestial country as the only ones who possess the kind of souls for which that imponderable empire was planned.

This star, our own good earth, made many a successful journey around the heavens ere man was made, and whole kingdoms of creatures enjoyed existence and returned to dust ere man appeared to claim them. After human beings have also played their part in Creation's plan, they too may disappear without any general burning or extraordinary commotion whatever.

Plants are credited with but dim and uncertain sensation, and minerals with positively none at all. But why may not even a mineral arrangement of matter be endowed with sensation of a kind that we in our blind exclusive perfection can have no manner of communication with?

But I have wandered from my subject. I stated a page or two back that man claimed the earth was made for him, and I was going to say that venomous beasts, thorny plants, and deadly diseases of certain parts of the earth prove that the whole world was not made for him. When an animal from a tropical climate is taken to high latitudes, it may perish of cold, and we say that such an animal was never intended for so severe a climate. But when man betakes himself to sickly parts of the tropics and perishes, he cannot see that he was never intended for such deadly climates. No, he will rather accuse the first mother of the cause of the difficulty, though she may never have seen a fever district; or will consider it a providential chastisement for some self-invented form of sin.

Furthermore, all uneatable and uncivilized animals, and all plants which carry prickles, are deplorable evils which, according to closest researches of clergy, require the cleansing chemistry of universal planetary combustion. But more than aught else mankind requires burning, as being in great part wicked, and if that transmundane furnace can be so applied and regulated as to smelt and purify us into conformity with the rest of the terrestrial creation, then the tophetization of the erratic genius *Homo* were a consummation devoutly to be prayed for. But, glad to leave these ecclesiastical fires and blunders, I joyfully return to the immortal truth and immortal beauty of Nature.

I have a low opinion of books; they are but piles of stones set up to show coming travelers where other minds have been, or at best signal smokes to call attention. Cadmus and all the other inventors of letters receive a thousand-fold more credit than they deserve. No amount of word-making will ever make a single soul to *know* these mountains. As well seek to warm the naked and frost-bitten by lectures on caloric and pictures of flame. One day's exposure to mountains is better than cartloads of books. See how willingly Nature poses herself upon photographer's plates. No earthly chemicals are so sensitive as those of the human soul. All that is required is exposure, and purity of material. "The pure in heart shall see God!"

No synonym for God is so perfect as Beauty. Whether as seen carving the lines of the mountains with glaciers, or gathering matter into stars, or planning the movements of water, or gardening — still all is Beauty!

Tell me what you will of the benefactions of city civilization, of the sweet security of streets — all as part of the natural upgrowth of man toward the high destiny we hear so much of. I know that our bodies were made to thrive only in pure air, and the scenes in which pure air is found. If the death exhalations that brood the broad towns in which we so fondly compact ourselves were made visible, we should flee as from a plague. All are more or less sick; there is not a perfectly sane man in San Francisco.

Go now and then for fresh life — if most of humanity must go through this town stage of development — just as divers hold their breath and come ever and anon to the surface to breathe. Go whether or not you have faith. Form parties, if you must be social, to go to the snow-flowers in winter, to the sun-flowers in summer. Anyway, go up and away for life; be fleet!

I know some will heed the warning. Most will not, so full of pagan slavery is the boasted freedom of the town, and those who need rest and clean snow and sky the most will be the last to move.

Once I was let down into a deep well into which chokedamp had settled, and nearly lost my life. The deeper I was immersed in the invisible poison, the less capable I became of willing measures of escape from it. And in just this condition are those who toil or dawdle or dissipate in crowded towns, in the sinks of commerce or pleasure.

When I first came down to the city from my mountain home, I began to wither, and wish instinctively for the vital woods and high sky. Yet I lingered month after month, plodding at "duty." At length I chanced to see a lovely goldenrod in bloom in a weedy spot alongside one of the less frequented sidewalks there. Suddenly I was aware of the ending of summer and fled. Then, once away, I saw how shrunken and lean I was, and how glad I was I had gone.

Our crude civilization engenders a multitude of wants, and lawgivers are ever at their wit's end devising. The hall and the theater and the church have been invented, and compulsory education. Why not add compulsory recreation? Our forefathers forged chains of duty and habit, which bind us notwithstanding our boasted freedom, and we ourselves in desperation add link to link, groaning and making medicinal laws for relief. Yet few think of pure rest or of the healing power of Nature. How hard to pull or shake people out of town! Earthquakes cannot do it, nor even plagues. These only cause the civilized to pray and ring bells and cower in corners of bedrooms and churches.

One is constantly reminded of the infinite lavishness and fertility of Nature — inexhaustible abundance amid what seems enormous waste. And yet when we look into any of her operations that lie within reach of our minds, we learn that no particle of her material is wasted or worn out. It is eternally flowing from use to use, beauty to yet higher beauty; and we soon cease to lament waste and death, and rather rejoice and exult in the imperishable, unspendable wealth of the universe, and faithfully watch and wait the reappearance of everything that melts and fades and dies about us, feeling sure that its next appearance will be better and more beautiful than the last.

These temple-destroyers, devotees of ravaging commercialism, seem to have a perfect contempt for Nature, and, instead of lifting their eyes to the God of the mountains, lift them to the Almighty Dollar. Dam Hetch Hetchy! As well dam for water-tanks the people's cathedrals and churches, for no holier temple has ever been consecrated by the heart of man.

Most civilized folks cry morbidness, lunacy upon all that will not weigh on Fairbanks's scales or measure to that seconds rod of English brass. But we know that much that is most real will not counterpoise cast-iron, or dent our human flesh.

How infinitely superior to our physical senses are those of the mind! The spiritual eye sees not only rivers of water but of air. It sees the crystals of the rock in rapid sympathetic motion, giving enthusiastic obedience to the sun's rays, then sinking back to rest in the night. The whole world is in motion to the center. So also sounds. We hear only woodpeckers and squirrels and the rush of turbulent streams. But imagination gives us the sweet music of tiniest insect wings, enables us to hear, all around the world, the vibration of every needle, the waving of every bole and branch, the sound of stars in circulation like particles in the blood. The Sierra canyons are full of avalanche débris — we hear them boom again, and we read the past sounds from present conditions. Again we hear the earthquake rock-falls. Imagination is usually regarded as a synonym for the unreal. Yet is true imagination healthful and real, no more likely to mislead than the coarse senses. Indeed, the power of imagination makes us infinite.

The mountains are fountains of men as well as of rivers, of glaciers, of fertile soil. The great poets, philosophers, prophets, able men whose thoughts and deeds have moved the world, have come down from the mountains — mountain-dwellers who have grown strong there with the forest trees in Nature's work-shops.

Yosemite Park is a place of rest, a refuge from the roar and dust and weary, nervous, wasting work of the lowlands, in which one gains the advantages of both solitude and society. Nowhere will you find more company of a soothing peace-be-still kind. Your animal fellow-beings, so seldom regarded in civilization, and every rock-brow and mountain, stream, and lake, and every plant soon come to be regarded as brothers; even one learns to like the storms and clouds and tireless winds. This one noble park is big enough and rich enough for a whole life of study and aesthetic enjoyment. It is good for everybody, no matter how benumbed with care, encrusted with a mail of business habits like a tree with bark. None can escape its charms. Its natural beauty cleanses and warms like fire, and you will be willing to stay forever in one place like a tree.

Government protection should be thrown around every wild grove and forest on the mountains, as it is around every private orchard, and the trees in public parks. To say nothing of their value as fountains of timber, they are worth infinitely more than all the gardens and parks of towns.

How little note is taken of the deeds of Nature! What paper publishes her reports? If one Pine were placed in a town square, what admiration it would excite! Yet who is conscious of the Pine-tree multitudes in the free woods, though open to everybody? Who publishes the sheet-music of winds or the written music of water written in river-lines? Who reports the works and ways of the clouds, those wondrous creations coming into being every day like freshly upheaved mountains? And what record is kept of Nature's colors — the clothes she wears — of her birds, her beasts — her livestock?

Contemplating the lace-like fabric of streams outspread over the mountains, we are reminded that everything is flowing — going somewhere, animals and so-called lifeless rocks as well as water. Thus the snow flows fast or slow in grand beauty-making glaciers and avalanches; the air in majestic floods carrying minerals, plant leaves, seeds, spores, with streams of music and fragrance; water streams carrying rocks both in solution and in the form of mud particles, sand, pebbles, and boulders. Rocks flow from volcanoes like water from springs, and animals flock together and flow in currents modified by stepping, leaping, gliding, flying, swimming, etc. While the stars go streaming through space pulsed on and on forever like blood globules in Nature's warm heart.

The rugged old Norsemen spoke of death as *Heimgang* — home-going. So the snow-flowers go home when they melt and flow to the sea, and the rock-ferns, after unrolling their fronds to the light and beautifying the rocks, roll them up close again in the autumn and blend with the soil. Myriads of rejoicing living creatures, daily, hourly, perhaps every moment sink into death's arms, dust to dust, spirit to spirit — waited on, watched over, noticed only by their Maker, each arriving at its own Heavendealt destiny. All the merry dwellers of the trees and streams, and the myriad swarms of the air, called into life by the sunbeam of a summer morning, go home through death, wings folded perhaps in the last red rays of sunset of the day they were first tried. Trees towering in the sky, braving storms of centuries, flowers turning faces to the light for a single day or hour, having enjoyed their share of life's feast — all alike pass on and away under the law of death and love. Yet all are our brothers and they enjoy life as we do, share Heaven's blessings with us, die and are buried in hallowed ground, come with us out of eternity and return into eternity. "Our lives are rounded with a sleep."

Index